TABLE OF CONTENTS

Above: Paddlers on the Wacissa River.

While we sleep, dream, eat, work, love, or play, Florida's rivers are running 24 hours a day, 365 days a year. Before we came, they flowed downhill to the sea, as they will after we are gone. There are over 1,700 Florida rivers, some too shallow to paddle. Some river journeys can be done as day trips, while other rivers require overnight trips or several day trips to complete.

Florida rivers are usually the domain of canoeists, while kayakers generally prefer Florida's plentiful bays and other estuaries, although this rule of thumb is often broken. Some sea kayakers take on the open Florida seas, exploring the coasts. Others "play" in Florida's surf.

Florida is blessed with over 1,000 miles of coastline. Like the rivers, the seas are in constant motion, peaceful or tempest, with the sea constantly attacking and changing the land.

With all this room to paddle, Florida is now considered something of a paddling capital. The Sunshine State has temperate climate compared to most of the US which experiences severe cold. Such temperatures allow year-round paddling, with a few unusual and bitter-cold exceptions, and a few too stormy days.

Given so many paddling opportunities, a challenge for the design of this book was not what to include, but what to leave out. The decision was made to include all 38 state-designated paddling trails and any trails previously described in print that, upon investigation, were thought to be of interest to paddlers. Paddles recommended by local enthusiasts and canoe clubs are included. In a few cases, county and state officials requested a trail be included in the book because paddling attracts people interested in protecting these resources.

These are exciting times for paddlers. Trails are springing up everywhere. Inspired by grassroots movements and assisted at times by experienced National Park Service personnel, many Florida counties are creating "Blueways," or water trails, often combining freshwater rivers and estuaries into very lengthy potential trips.

People paddle for a variety of reasons. Some do it for exercise, others for comradeship. Many do it for solitude, enjoying the sounds of paddles dipping in the water and the slice of the cutting hull. Nature enthusiasts paddle for the wild splendor they will witness and the wildlife. Many paddle for all these reasons.

Natural Florida is nowhere more glorious than where water touches the shore or bank. Inland, water paints the land a rich green, and along the coasts water contributes to the beauty of seaside vistas. On a personal boat, one can travel to remote areas where driving or hiking might be impossible.

There are many ecological issues that become evident with paddling. Hopefully, new paddlers will become acquainted with Florida's problems and help find solutions. Water is life, but some people do not treat it that way. This is unfortunate, but an informed citizenry is one guard against officials turning their heads for special interests.

ORGANIZATION

This book is organized into four geographic regions with three appendices. The regions are: Northwest, North, Central, and South Florida, which includes the Keys. These regions are arbitrary. Within the regions, paddling trips are presented in alphabetical order. Tributaries of rivers may have separate accounts.

If a river has more than one trip, landings given are presented in order of flow. Florida's rivers flow to all points of the compass.

Directions for all trips and most river landings are included. When possible, reference is made to an interstate. A direction may well be the apparent direction. For example, driving on a north bound road, north is presumed to be ahead and east is presumed to be to the right. However, our roads frequently do not travel in straight lines.

Mileage is given for most long trips. This mileage is a difficult thing to determine. Not only do rivers wind, and bays lack straight lines, but distances given by government agencies differ, maps differ, guides and guidebooks differ. Mileage used in this book have been provided by people who paddle and are all approximations.

PADDLING INFORMATION

Experienced paddlers know that you often do not get far, especially on rivers, without the help of outfitters who provide rentals and livery. Outfitters also know conditions on the river and can be very helpful.

Three appendices include information on: (A) outfitters, guides, and livery services; (B) management for public land units along waterways, some with camping or canoe rentals, and; (C) private paddling clubs and organizations. The information in Appendix A is alphabetical by paddling location. The other two appendices are in alphabetical order. Included are addresses, phone numbers, fax numbers, and in some cases email addresses and web sites. Rapid growth in Florida may change some of this information, such as area codes, and businesses do come and go. Each new edition will be updated.

Many books rate the difficulty of paddling river segments from landing to landing. When water is high, rivers are always dangerous, and when water is low, rivers usually present physical challenges because submerged logs and limestone create obstacles, drag-overs, and in some cases drag-arounds. Degree of difficulty also depends on individual skills. Such generalized ratings were considered, and rejected as largely meaningless, thus no rating system is included. Appropriate cautions are given.

The practice of rating natural scenery along the way, common in some paddling guides, has also been chucked. It is all glorious, and all worthy of our love and devotion.

Maps from the Florida Office of Greenways and Trails are included for state-designated trails. Landings have been modified by reference number presented in the text. Maps are often unnecessary for Florida rivers, most of which have clear runs and little chance for a paddler to become lost. There are those who like a map showing ever detail on the river so they know exactly where they are at all times and paddlers who like to be surprised. This book has been written by someone who likes surprises. As many maps as possible have been included, but fortunately, surprises remain.

AMAZING FLORIDA

There is nothing boring about the Sunshine State. Paddles can range from idyllic to downright challenging. The diversity is mind-boggling.

Florida rivers are not at all what one would think without going there. They include spectacular whitewater areas and waterfalls. Many have turbulent limestone runs to pass over and around. Wildlife shows up often in unexpected places, and sometimes really unexpected wildlife shows up. Giant Gulf sturgeon, monkeys, and manatees are just some of the unusual creatures. Some rivers disappear underground, and others have caves, above or underwater. First-magnitude springs pour forth from a number of river headwaters. Rivers can be murky or sparkling clear, sand or muck-bottomed, shallow or deep, twisty or gently bending.

Florida's coastlines show wide variety too. In the Northwest, sand dunes may approach 200 feet. The North has sand dunes too, not as tall, and sometimes composed of dark sand. In the Central Region, mangroves appear and (where not cleared for development) provide rich estuaries and convoluted paddling in a tidal environment. Saltmarsh, coastal scrub, and coastal hammocks are found around the state, including tropical hardwood hammocks in the southerly reaches. South Florida paddles include those in Everglades National Park and Big Cypress National Preserve, unique Florida vistas. The chain of islands known as the Keys provides sea kayaking challenges.

It is a pleasant thought that this book may present to the beginning paddler a series of adventures leading to lifelong memories. There are some paddles in Florida so wonderful they linger in memory long after they are over.

THE FLORIDA CIRCUMNAVIGATIONAL TRAIL

When the first edition of this book was published in 2003, the so-called "Florida Blueway," or paddling trail along the Florida coast, was a concept and not a reality. Through-paddlers faced difficulties finding camping sites and often practiced "guerilla camping" wherever they could find dry space. The trail itself was not clearly defined, although portions of it, like the Big Bend Saltwater Trail, did exist.

All this changed in 2007 and 2008. A finalized Florida Circumnavigational Paddling Trail has been clearly organized so that one can paddle from Big Lagoon State Park near Pensacola and the Alabama border to Fort Clinch State Park north of Jacksonville below the St. Marys River and Georgia. Further information can be found

at www.floridagreenwaysandtrails.com.

Making this trail a reality was a task that would try anyone's patience. Campsite creation required the cooperation of a number of government agencies—local, county, state, and federal. To maintain the trail required voluntary efforts by hundreds of folks. Florida's Office of Greenways and Trails is to be commended for making what had been a mad paddler's dream into a substantial, vibrant trail.

Why would someone want to paddle this trail? Because it would be the adventure of a lifetime. It would challenge the paddler with fickle weather, shifting tides, storms, and finding one's way, but it would also provide sights that would be treasured for a lifetime.

Portions of the trail can be deceptively easy. Others are clearly more challenging. Paddlers attempting this trail should take all safely precautions and properly provision for the trip.

Fortunately, the trail has been organized. It has been broken into 26 segments, each with a supporting team of volunteers who maintain the campsites. The volunteer organization formed in 2007 and named itself The Florida Paddling Trail Association. Further information is in Appendix A.

Above: Paddling the mighty Apalachicola River.

APALACHICOLA RIVER
(Calhoun, Franklin, Gadsden, Gulf, Jackson, and Liberty counties)

While the Suwannee River has often been described as Florida's Mississippi, the Apalachicola River has more similarities to "old man river." Like the Mississippi, its waters are alluvial, carrying rich soil deposits. It is Florida's most powerful river in terms of water flow. And, it is river-fed like the Mississippi.

Two rivers in Georgia feed the Apalachicola - the Chattahoochee and Flint. The Flint is more than 280 miles long, and the Chattahoochee is even longer.

The Apalachicola has 105 miles within Florida, flowing from the Jim Woodruff Dam on Lake Seminole. The dam, completed in 1957, has been both a curse and a blessing. It has protected Florida's Apalachicola from pollution coming from the two northern rivers. On the other hand, it has allowed silt to build-up and damaged fish spawning grounds, particularly for Gulf sturgeon.

The Corps of Engineers has dredged the river for years in order to keep it navigable,

piling up small mountains of silt in the process. The dredging is very uneconomical, because there is little significant commercial traffic. Although the dredging is opposed by most Floridians, it still continues for now.

Paddling this river is for the experienced and self-reliant. The "Apalach" is powerful and often wide. At its mouth between the cities of Eastpoint and Apalachicola it may be 5 miles wide. When traveling on such a swift a river, hitting an obstacle could cause a quick spill. Paddlers report moving at a pace of around 4-6 miles per hour without any paddling. With even moderate paddling, the speed may reach 7 mph.

The Apalachicola is part of the life list of many fervent Florida paddlers. These enthusiasts often start on one of the Georgia rivers and travel the river in its entirety.

There are also many backwaters and some riverine swamps. These are quite visually stunning and worthy of exploration. Some boaters who travel this river carry a canoe or kayak, launching out whenever the view is most beckoning.

From north of I-10, and running a

considerable distance south, cliffs approach 200 feet in height. The antebellum, white building on the eastern bluff is the Gregory House at Torreya State Park. Some of the most gorgeous bluffs are found in the Apalachicola Bluffs and Ravines, Nature Conservancy land also on the east bank. Below Blountstown, much of the east bank is in Apalachicola National Forest.

POSSIBLE TRIPS

1. From Victory Bridge on US-90 to Torreya State Park, 12 miles. Exit I-10 west of Quincy and go north on SR-270A. This quickly becomes SR-269. Near Chattahoochee, turn west on US-90. The landing is on the southeast side before crossing the bridge.

2. From Torreya State Park to SR-20 at Bristol/Blountstown, 13 miles. Torreya State Park is on the east bank. There is no true landing as there are slopes 200 feet in height. But it is certainly possible to stop, pull ashore, climb-up to the ranger office, and camp overnight.

3. From SR-20 to the City of Apalachicola, 80 miles. SR-20 crosses the Apalachicola

between Blountstown to the west and Bristol to the east. There is a boat ramp on the Bristol side. This long stretch is bordered to the east by Apalachicola National Forest.

4. The city of Apalachicola is located on US-98 about 1.5 hours west of US-19 at Perry. There are two marinas.

CAMPING

Favored camping sites are on the numerous sand deposits all along the river. Torreya State Park and Apalachicola National Forest offer camping options.

PC

Above: Lost Creek in Apalachicola National Forest.

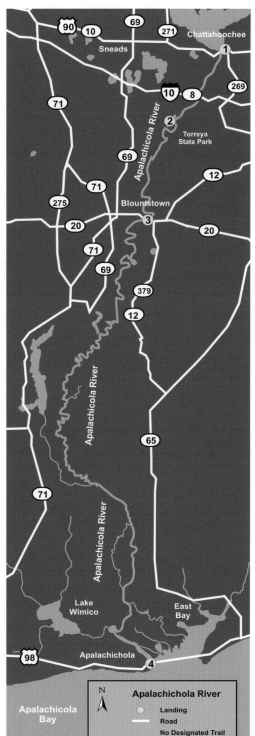

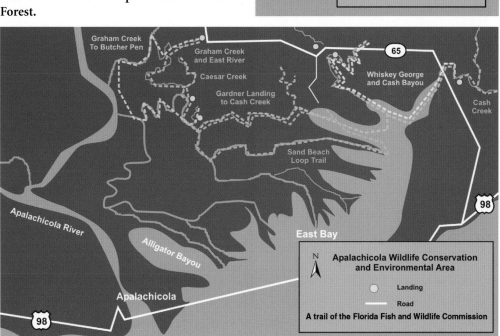

APALACHICOLA RIVER WILDLIFE AND ENVIRONMENTAL AREA
(Franklin County)

This 55,000-plus acre land managed by the Florida Fish and Wildlife Conservation Commission, has ten newly established trails. All but one lie along the east bank near the mouth of the Apalachicola River. There is a single but worthwhile West Bay trail.

These trails lie in beautiful bayous, sawgrass, saltmarsh, and pass around tree islands and through rich estuary. Directional markers were only included where it was felt the way could be lost in order to leave the trails as natural in appearance as possible.

One paddle is along Cash, also known as Cashie Bayou. This is listed in the Gazetteer as Cash Creek, as well as by USGS. The sign on the bridges at times has read Cashie Bayou. Locals often call it Cashie Bayou too.

You may paddle two ways: west from SR-65 just north of US-98 to the east of Eastpoint, or east entering perhaps the most attractive section of Tate's Hell State Forest. Farther north on SR-65 it is possible to put in also at West Bayou. Both run into the Apalachicola River's East Bay

From US-98, SR-65 is a north turn east of Apalachicola. There are five landings and three entrances into the conservation lands on the west side of SR-65. There are prominent signs announcing the wildlife and environmental and launch signs for the put-ins area.

There are a number of house boats docked along these waters. Prudent paddlers will avoid these house boats as they are private property.

AUCILLA RIVER
(Jefferson, Madison, and Taylor counties)

The 69-mile Aucilla River has its headwaters in a swamp in Thomas County, Georgia. A blackwater river, so colored from tannin and detritus, the Aucilla is also spring-fed. The river is magnificent and primitive, its beauty perhaps unparalleled in the state. It has a number of small tributaries, including Beasley, Cow, Gum, Jones Mill, Raysor, and Woof creeks, and the Wacissa merges with it near Nuttal Rise. It is the border between Jefferson and Taylor counties, and in times past was a border between neighboring Native Americans.

Traveling the Aucilla is not a task for those with few skills. Upper reaches of the Aucilla can be so shallow at times they are a chore to travel. Below US-19/27, there are remnant fords and whitewater runs. Below CR-257, the whitewater becomes challenging with Little Rapid, one run that is S-shaped, and finally Big Rapid.

Big Rapid is serious, although short, whitewater. Limestone boulders appear to block the path and inspire caution in the intrepid. For many years, the sole path through the fury has been to the left as you face it, but a submerged rock sits hidden in the middle of this chute, providing heart-stopping bumps.

The river goes underground near Goose Pasture in Aucilla Wildlife Management Area and reappears at Nuttall Rise. The river disappears after the state-designated canoe trail ends at CR-257.

The journey on the Aucilla usually resumes on the Wacissa River at Goose Pasture, passing through a cut known as the Slave Canal, because it was allegedly widened by slaves. Another legend says the canal was a Seminole secret short-cut, and that its existence was tortured out of a captive. The Aucilla continues on under US-98 to the Gulf.

The Slave Canal (connecting the Aucilla and Wacissa) is not easy to find. It is hidden from view by a large area of wild rice. The path is to the right, through the rice, and within a few feet, the Slave Canal is revealed. At times, there have also been a number of downed trees making crossing through more difficult.

Although a few homes and hunting lodges impinge on the river in spots, the Aucilla travels through rugged natural terrain with few dwellings. Limestone outcrops on the lower portion earn the Aucilla the nickname "Little Suwannee."

Alligators, bears, bobcats, deer, and tricolor herons are among the plenitude of wildlife. Large brown water snakes are seen along the shoreline.

Top: Canoeists paddle through Big Rapid on the Aucilla River. Turbulent water on the Aucilla, particularly around the rapids, produces a sort of froth on the surface. This happens on many other rivers and is sometimes mistaken for pollution.

POSSIBLE TRIPS AND LANDINGS

1. From Sneads Smokehouse to US-19/27, 21 miles. Sneads Landing is located at Sneads Lake. On US-90 east of Monticello, go east/northeast on SR-146. The landing is marked by Suwannee River Water Management District signs, as are several of the following landings. The district does not feel that most of this section is canoeable as it is mostly swamp. It is exceptionally beautiful.

2. From US-19/27 to Lanier Grade, 4 miles. One landing is on the apparent northwest side of the road at the bridge. This landing is a little rugged. Just to the south of the bridge, there is a launch sign indicating an east turn to a gentler launch site. The bridge is substantially north of Perry on US-19/27 just before the town of Lamont.

3. From Lanier Grade to Eridu Grade, 4 miles. In Lamont, turn south (apparent west) on CR-257. A sign indicates the launch from Lanier Road, a turn to the east.

4. From Eridu Grade to CR-257, 5 miles.

In Lamont, turn south (apparent west) on CR-257 and proceed to the second canoe launch sign and turn east at the road. When visited, this road had no identifying sign.

5. From CR-257 to Aucilla Wildlife Management Area, 9.5 miles. The bridge on CR-257 is south of the town of Lamont. The landing is on the southeast side of the road.

6. The take-out in Aucilla Wildlife Management Area is reached from US-98 by turning north on Powell Hammock Road (this is abbreviated in spots and known as Pal Hammock Road). Continue off the pavement and make a turn west on Goose Pasture Road. Just before the Florida Trail crosses the road, there is a hard-to-find, north turn into the woods that will bring you within a few hundred yards of the river. To complete the journey, it is now necessary to take-out and move to the Wacissa landing at Goose Pasture.

7. From Goose Pasture to US-98, 5 miles. From US-98, proceed west across the bridge on the Aucilla. Take the first graded road north. There is a canoe launch sign. The launch is at the Wacissa side of Goose Pasture.

8. From US-98 to Aucilla Boat Ramp, 2 miles. The landing is on the northeast side of US-98 at the Aucilla River.

9. Aucilla Boat Ramp. The boat ramp is at the end of the river south of US-98, and the turn from that road is east of the bridge and clearly marked. This ramp is actually located in St. Marks National Wildlife Refuge.

CAMPING.

Nearby Econfina River State Park has a private campground. Camping at Goose Pasture is controlled through the Suwannee River Water Management District.

Map. Aucilla River Canoe Trail, Office of Greenways and Trails. The 19 miles of state-designated trail runs from US-19/27 south of Lamont to just above Goose Pasture.

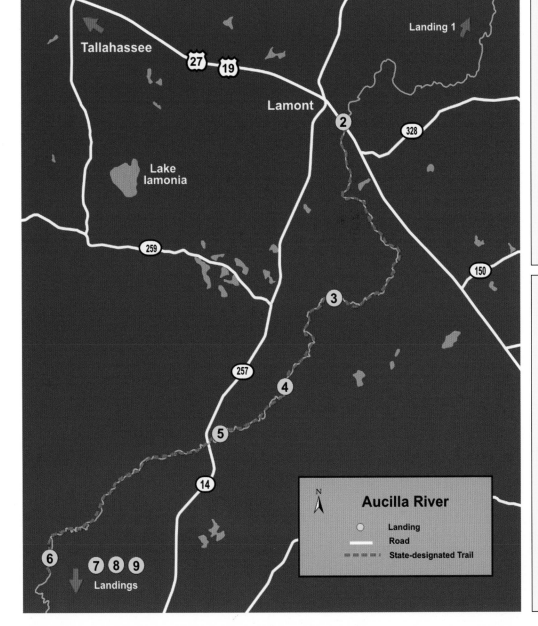

TO CANOE OR TO KAYAK?

The current trend is toward kayaks. Comparing sales, more kayaks are sold than canoes, although the sales of both are up.

There are two broad categories of kayaks: sit-on-tops or those where you sit in compartments. Other types are flatwater, recreational, surf, sea, and whitewater kayaks.

Surprisingly, women now buy more kayaks then men. With the proper equipment and sufficient stamina, a 90 pound woman can keep up with (or maybe beat) a 170 pound man. Janet Reno loves to kayak in Florida waters.

Those who have never paddled might do well to start with a canoe. A wide beam canoe is a steady craft and perhaps best for gaining one's confidence.

Beginning kayakers would do best to start with a little instruction and a stable, wide sit-on-top or the type of sea kayak called "recreational." Kayaks are amazingly stable, more so than a canoe, but a little knowledge is needed to know how to use the paddle, get in and out, and recover from a spill.

It is easy to get caught up in the joys of paddling and want to buy a personal boat. Probably the wise will not purchase a canoe or kayak until trying out various craft through outfitters.

Many enthusiasts end up with both canoes and kayaks. Canoes are often better on rivers, with logs, rocks, stumps, and limestone rapids. Sea kayaks are the safer of the two for exploring bays, estuaries, and open waters of Florida's seas.

Although it is assumed kayaks are the more expensive of the two, some canoes cost just as much.

UNEXPECTED GUEST

Paddlers have had snakes drop down from branches into the boat. Although a rare event, this adds a new dimension to the word thrill. What do you do? Stay calm? "Easy for you to say." The snake does not want to be there any more than you want the snake there, and usually it will slither rapidly out of the boat and over the side. If not, the best action is to rapidly take-out and motivate the snake to leave the boat.

Some experienced paddlers think that reports of snakes falling from trees into boats are mostly tall tales. However, snakes do get into boats, sometimes climbing aboard if not falling in. Boats should be turned over at night and carefully checked in the morning too.

BASIN CREEK CANOE TRAIL
(Walton County)

This Eglin Air Force Base canoe trail is approximately 3 miles long. It begins at Range Road (RR) 218 and ends at Choctawhatchee Bay. Much of the way is shaded by red maple. Use of Eglin requires an annual permit from Natural Resources at Jackson Guard on SR-85 in Niceville. A map helping you to navigate Eglin is available there also. Eglin offers camping options.

Below: Paddling on Eglin Air Force Base.

EGLIN AIR FORCE BASE PADDLES

In addition to the Yellow and Shoal rivers passing by Eglin, there are many excellent small streams that provide remote paddling in glorious nature. Eglin is very large, over 460,000 acres, roughly equivalent to Ocala and Osceola national forests combined.

Eglin has rules and regulations to protect both its visitors and natural resources. These are available when the annual pass is obtained from Natural Resources at the Jackson Guard on SR-85 at Niceville. Using Eglin without an annual pass will likely result in a fine, and the pass costs a pittance.

Eglin has won wide-spread recognition for its friendliness to recreational users and the environment. Thus, there are many sights on Eglin to delight. Camping is allowed at designated campsites.

Above: Boiling Creek on Eglin Air Force Base.

Above: A portion of the coastal area near Steinhatchee.

BIG BEND TRAIL
(Dixie, Franklin, Lafayette, Levy, Taylor, and Wakulla counties)

This 105-mile trail is segment 6 of the Florida Circumnavigational Trail and now managed by The Florida Fish and Wildlife Commission through the Office of Recreation Services. It can be reached on the web at www.myfwc.com/recreation/big_bend/paddling_trail.asp.

A fine and detailed guide to paddling this trail has been written by David Gluckman, who helped establish the trail. This account is found in Sea Kayaking in Florida (Pineapple Press, 1995). David Gluckman's account would be very helpful to those who intend to take on this long saltwater trail. In addition to David's excellent book, paddlers can use the Fish and Wildlife website for detailed maps and up-to-date camping information.

It is certainly possible to take-out at many areas along the way and make this a series of day trips. Bad weather can cut trips short. Good preparation is essential for venturing forth on Florida's seas. Even brief thunderstorms on the Gulf can at times produce six foot seas. Wind is definitely a factor in successfully navigating this trail in its entirety. A good 20 mph headwind on the open sea can produce more resistance training than most paddlers would like.

Watch out for the tide going out in many of the shallow areas. Carrying a kayak across mud flats should be only a brief interlude while kayaking Florida.

Flat fishing in this area is very popular and produces abundant catches of spotted trout and red drum. Bay scallops are also very plentiful in late summer.

Flowing from Perry into the Gulf is the infamously polluted Fenholloway River. Sadly, effluents from this river are notoriously darker than surrounding waters and contain high levels of dioxin.

Map. Historic Big Bend Saltwater Paddling Trail, Office of Greenways and Trails.

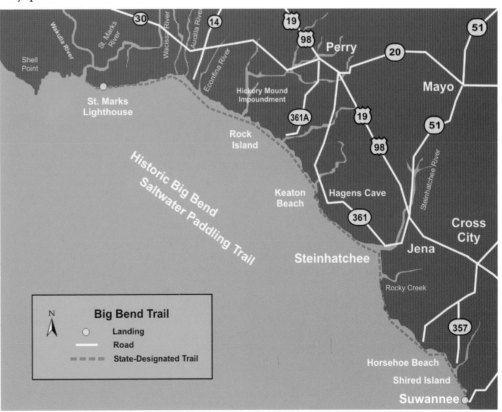

Above: Equestrian rider crossing a shallow portion of Blackwater River.

CANOE CAPITAL

The state legislature has declared Milton the "Canoe Capital of Florida," and with good reason. Around Milton lies the Blackwater River System which includes over 60 miles of premier paddles, mostly through wilderness or forest. Much of the nearby paddling lies within Blackwater River State Forest, which also includes some of the most wonderful hiking trails in Northwest Florida.

BLACKWATER RIVER
(Okaloosa and Santa Rosa counties)

Paddling trails in the Blackwater System lie north of the city of Milton, proclaimed by the state legislature "Canoe Capitol of Florida." Premier journeys are along Blackwater River and its tributaries, Coldwater, Juniper, and Sweetwater creeks. All are state-designated canoe trails, and Blackwater is the longest at 31 miles. Small seeps feed the system.

These rivers have exceptionally pure and clear water. The bottoms are sand with gravel. The Blackwater System at normal water levels is nifty and easy paddling. Lots of turns around submerged logs will please those who love technical work, but in general it is just a matter of paddling. Those looking for beautiful landscapes and wild animals will not be disappointed. One of the very nice things about the system is that it is mostly off in the woods, quiet, secluded, and studded with wildlife.

A fifth stream, West Coldwater Creek, is generally not traveled, except by those looking for a workout. It is said to be too shallow and tangled, although some local enthusiasts force their way down it. It is best to check with local outfitters on current conditions on this and other parts of the rivers.

Plentiful, excellent sandbars enable the long-distance, primitive camper to take uninterrupted journeys. A Blackwater River State Forest map will be helpful in finding the forest roads.

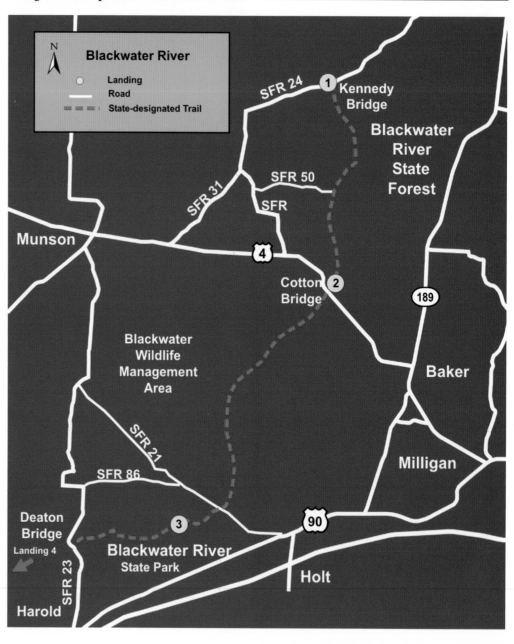

POSSIBLE TRIPS AND LANDINGS

Closed Sections. Other guides report paddling above Alligator Branch Bridge into dense marsh. They also report paddling from Alligator Branch Bridge to Kennedy Bridge, a 5-mile trip. In fact, the author traveled those sections. However, Blackwater River State Forest, management for the adjacent lands and river, at last report says that the river is open only from Kennedy Bridge south to Deaton Bridge. There are said to be substantial logjams, and indeed there were a lot of hang-ups when this section was traveled. These are the directions for Alligator Branch Bridge in case the section is opened. Going west from Crestview via US-90, take SR-189 north. At the intersection of SR-189 and SR-180, go west 5 miles to Alligator Branch Bridge. This area is north of the small town of Baker.

1. From Kennedy Bridge to SR-4 (Cotton Bridge), 10 miles. Go west from Crestview via US-90, and take SR-189 north. At the intersection of SR-189 and SR-4, go west across the river to Beaver Creek Road (the first paved road), turn north, and proceed to FR-24 (Kennedy Bridge Road). This is the start of the state-designated canoe trail.

2. From SR-4 (Cotton Bridge) to Bryant Bridge, 12 miles. Go west from Crestview via US-90 and take SR-189 north. Go west on SR-4 to Cotton Bridge.

3. From Bryant Bridge to Deaton Bridge (Blackwater River State Park), 8 miles. From SR-90 west of Crestview, proceed west of Holt to John Road. Turn north on John Road which turns into Bryant Bridge Road. The forest roads to the north lead to FR-21. Bryant Bridge is the first bridge encountered when proceeding west on FR-21.

4. From Deaton Bridge into marsh. Go west on US-90 from Holt and follow the signs to Blackwater River State Park. Deaton Bridge is within the park and is the end of the state-designated canoe trail. Going downstream from the state park, the paddler encounters a 0.5-mile portage after the Juniper joins up and before the Coldwater. Traveling into the marsh is discouraged by local outfitters and paddlers.

CAMPING

Numerous sandbars exist in Blackwater River State Forest. There are camping options at Blackwater River State Forest and Blackwater River State Park.

Opposite page: Map. Blackwater River Canoe Trail, Office of Greenways and Trails. The 31-mile, state-designated trail runs from Kennedy Bridge to Deaton Bridge (Blackwater River State Park).

SANDBARS

A sandbar builds-up due to the slower, inside current as a river goes around a bend. Deeper channels are usually along the other bank. On the next curve in the river, the sandbar and the deep channel will normally be on reverse banks from the previous one. This is useful information to keep in mind when navigating a river. A lightly loaded craft can take a direct route across shallows and deeper waters, while a heavily loaded one might need to stay in the deeper channel.

Banks which are covered with sand and sand islands in the middle of rivers usually make excellent camping spots. There is little danger that camp fires built on these places can spread. Also, the soft sand acts as an excellent cushion under the body of the sleeping camper. The Blackwater River System is particularly rich in banks covered with sand which was deposited at times when water levels were high.

STATE-DESIGNATED CANOE TRAILS

At present, there are 40 state-designated canoe trails. Hopefully more will be added in time. A designated canoe trail does not always go from the beginning of the river to the end. Sometimes the trail is just a portion of the river length. The 40 trails have over 1,000 miles of paddling. Maps of each of these trails are available from Department of Environmental Protection, Office of Greenways and Trails. At present, there is a limit on the number of maps given to a paddler at one time.

Trail	Counties
Alafia River	Hillsborough
Aucilla River	Jefferson, Madison, Taylor
Big Bend Saltwater Trail	Dixie, Jefferson, Taylor, Wakulla
Blackwater River	Okaloosa, Santa Rosa
Blackwater River/Royal Palm Hammock	Collier
Bulow Creek	Flagler, Volusia
Chipola River	Calhoun, Jackson
Coldwater Creek	Santa Rosa
Econfina Creek	Bay, Washington
Econlockhatchee River	Seminole
Estero River	Lee
Florida Circumnavigational Trail	All coastal counties
Hickey's Creek	Lee
Hillsborough River	Hillsborough, Pasco
Holmes Creek	Washington
Little Manatee River	Hillsborough
Loxahatchee River	Martin, Palm Beach
Ochlockonee River (Lower)	Franklin, Leon, Liberty, Wakulla
Ochlockonee River (Upper)	Gadsden, Leon
Peace River	Charlotte, DeSoto, Hardee, Polk
Perdido River	Escambia
Pellicer Creek	Flagler, St. Johns
Pithlachascotee River	Pasco
Sante Fe River	Alachua, Columbia, Gilchrist, Suwannee
Shoal River	Okaloosa, Walton
Sopchoppy River	Wakulla
Spruce Creek	Volusia
St. Marys River	Baker, Nassau
Suwannee River (Lower)	Hamilton, Lafayette, Madison, Suwannee
Suwannee River (Upper)	Columbia, Hamilton, Suwannee
Sweetwater/Juniper Creek	Santa Rosa
Tomoka River	Volusia
Upper Manatee River	Manatee
Wacissa River	Jefferson
Wakulla River	Wakulla
Wekiva River/Rock Springs Run	Lake, Orange, Seminole
Withlacoochee River South	Citrus, Hernando, Pasco, Sumter
Withlacoochee River North	Hamilton, Madison
Yellow River	Okaloosa, Santa Rosa

BOILING CREEK
(Santa Rosa County)

Five absolutely gorgeous miles of Boiling Creek spill into the Yellow River near an area often active with large Gulf sturgeon. The creek is lined with white-top pitcher plants, and in May and early June, the plants have gorgeous flowers.

Since the Creek is on Eglin Air Force Base, it is necessary to have an annual permit from Natural Resources at Jackson Guard on the east side SR-85 in Niceville. A map is available to help you navigate Eglin. The trail begins on RR-211 and ends on the Yellow River at the SR-87 bridge. Paddling on the Yellow River is work there because it is wide, thus subject to wind. Camping is available on Eglin.

Above: A narrow pathway off Boiling Creek. Here, the bottom boils with springs.

Above: A spring off the Chipola River.

FINDING ONE'S WAY

Traveling along rivers is usually very straight-forward. One goes from landing to landing. Traveling along the coasts, usually in sea kayaks, is another matter. Often there are no good reference points, and in South and Central Florida, there are similar appearing mangroves, without any noticeable landmark.

GPS systems are most useful when combined with other navigational aids. Charts are available from the National Oceanic and Atmospheric Administration. Topographical maps are available from the US Geological Survey. Both have web sites. Local marinas usually supply charts and tidal information and warn of dangerous conditions.

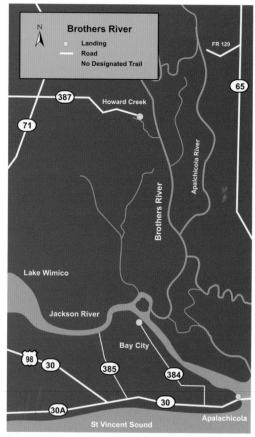

BROTHERS RIVER
(Franklin, Gulf, and Liberty counties)

The Brothers is a parallel off-shoot of the Apalachicola River. It is wild and includes swampy floodplain and marsh.

A 21-mile circular loop has been described as going north on the Brothers at Howard's Creek Fish Camp, onto the Apalachicola, and south to Fort Gadsden, then back up the Brothers to Howard's Creek. This paddle is for the experienced and confident, and paddling upstream might not be a joy.

Some explore this river by having a charter drop them and their canoes or kayaks north of Apalachicola and travel south back to the city.

Howard's Creek Fish Camp and Howard Creek are located at the end of CR-387. This is an east turn from SR-71 north of Port St. Joe. SR-71 joins US-98 in Port St. Joe.

BRADFORD BROOK
(Leon County)

Bradford Brook one of many paddles located within Apalachicola National Forest. The stream lies west of Tallahassee.

Perhaps the best way to approach it is to locate a convenient put-in and paddle up and down it. There is virtually no flow.

Bradford Brook is accessed from FR-370 in the northeast extreme of the forest. Forest maps can be obtained in advance from either ranger district office, or they can be picked up during business hours.

The national forest has many camping opportunities. Camping is also available at nearby Lake Talquin.

CHIPOLA RIVER
(Calhoun, Gulf, and Jackson counties)

Its waters usually a soft emerald green, the Chipola River flows from Cowarts Creek and Marshalls Creek some 80 miles into the Dead Lakes and the Apalachicola River. Much of the trip is in isolation. Fifty-two of the miles are a state-designated canoe trail. A number of springs flow in along its path, as well as some creeks.

Above Florida Caverns and CR-162, one of Florida's Blue Springs pours in from the east. In Florida Caverns State Park, the Chipola goes underground for 0.5 miles. Although a lumbering cut was made years ago to connect the river above the sink and below the rise, this cut is jammed with logs. Thus the prudent take-out before the park and put-in below it.

There are a number of limestone runs on the Chipola, and depending on the water level, some can become whitewater rapids. In fact, there is so much stone in the river that motoring is not wise during low water level (particularly in more northern sections). While the limestone usually creates no more than a scrape on a canoe, or a jarring stop, it has ripped more than one motor from a boat.

With the exception of the runs, paddling is fairly easy on the Chipola. The runs generally require merely aiming at the inverted V in the current and going through at that point, sometimes with a bump or a scrape. "Look and Tremble" Rapids above SR-20 can be more challenging, especially in low water.

A navigational cut from the 1800s allows the more powerful Apalachicola to cutoff a portion of the Chipola, creating the Dead Lakes. They are a backwater with dead cypress that have essentially been drowned. The dead trees look sufficiently weird in the morning fogs to inspire a few ghost tales. Paddling within the Dead Lakes, while

Above: A kayaker pauses, nudging the bow of his boat into a limestone nook. Large limestone boulders are plentiful on the Chipola River.

very visually interesting, can be confusing, and there are sizable stumps to run-up on. During low water, it is largely impassable.

While Dead Lakes State Park is at the end of the river, Florida Caverns State Park is closer to its beginning. Florida Caverns has an extensive underground cave system. About 1 mile is open for the public in ranger-guided tours lasting perhaps 45 minutes.

One of the interesting features of the river are the caves. Below the state park, The Oven is a long cave leading away from the river, dry except in very high water. Other caves are north of the state park in high embankments. The caves in the park shelter bats, including the endangered gray bat, and the smallest flying mammal in eastern North America, the eastern pipistrelle.

POSSIBLE TRIPS AND LANDINGS

This is largely a remote area. For orientation, the relatively large and well-known city of Marianna is used for reference for all landings. Marianna has two exits on I-10 west of Tallahassee.

1. From SR-162 to Florida Caverns State Park, 5 miles. From Marianna, go north on SR-71. Go west on SR-162 from the small town of Greenwood to the Chipola Bridge. Florida Caverns State Park is located off I-10 in the city of Marianna, and there are prominent directional signs from the interstate and US-90, which passes through Marianna.

2. From SR-166 to SR-280A (Magnolia Bridge), 10 miles. From Marianna below the state park, go north on SR-166 to the bridge. This road was once designated SR-167 and is still listed in other guides as the SR-167 Bridge. Actually, SR-166 merges with SR-167 north of the bridge.

3. From SR-280/280A (Magnolia Bridge) to SR-278, 10 miles. In Marianna, go south on SR-71 and west on SR-280/280A to the bridge. The two roads play "piggy back" with each other.

4. From SR-278 to SR-274, 8 miles. From Marianna, go south on SR-71 and west on SR-278 to the bridge.

5. From SR-274 to SR-20, 10 miles. In Marianna, go south on SR-71 to Altha and west on SR-274 to the bridge. "Look and Tremble" rapid is below SR-274, a small whitewater area that is most severe at low water.

6. From SR-20 to SR-71 (Scotts Ferry), 13 miles. From Marianna, go south on SR-73 and east on SR-20 to the bridge.

7. From SR-71 into the Dead Lakes is a short trip, however the Dead Lakes continue for miles. There are at least eight landings in the Dead Lakes, include one at Dead Lakes State Park. From Marianna, go south on SR-73. At the junction with SR-71, continue south to the bridge across the Chipola. There is an outfitter near this bridge.

8. Dead Lakes State Park. The state park is a few miles farther south on SR-71.

CAMPING

Florida Caverns State Park is located in Mariana. There is much private land adjoining portions of the river and some negative feelings toward paddlers because trash in the river is wrongly blamed on canoeists. It would be wise to check with local outfitters concerning camping options. With the state park, it is best to check in advance.

Map. Chipola River Canoe Trail, Office of Greenways and Trails. The official trail starts north of Florida Caverns State Park and ends at Scotts Ferry, 52 miles later.

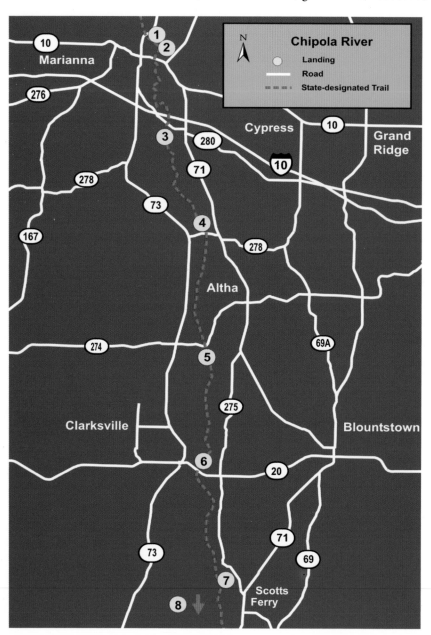

CHOCTAWHATCHEE
(Bay, Holmes, Walton, and Washington counties).

Like the Apalachicola, the Choctawhatchee is an alluvial river, rich in sediments, usually muddy brown or dirty yellow, with a swift southerly flow. Also, like the Apalachicola, much of it lies in another state, Alabama - approximately 70 miles. Both rivers are considered major rivers by those who define our streams.

Most of the river is in wild and primitive condition, with red clay banks coloring vistas. There are a number of runs, and one rapid, Big Gum, between US-90 and Hinson Cross Roads.

Approximately 100 miles of the Choctawhatchee flow through Florida to exit into the Gulf at Choctawhatchee Bay. One Florida tributary, Holmes Creek, is a first-class, scenic canoe trail. A tributary, the Pea River, flows into the Choctawhatchee just below Geneva, Alabama.

From SR-20 to Choctawhatchee Bay the river is wide and subject to motor boat traffic. Many paddlers stop at Boynton Cutoff.

POSSIBLE TRIPS AND LANDINGS

With the exception of SR-20, most of these landings are difficult to find.

1. From Geneva, Alabama, to SR-2, 8 miles. Alabama SR-52 passes through Geneva. To the east of town, turn north on CR-41. Turn west at the junction with CR-34 and proceed to the landing at the dead-end.

2. From SR-2 to US-90, 10 miles. (Locally, this is known as the "Old Warehouse" Landing.) On US-90 west of Bonifay, turn north on SR-177A, then west on SR-2. The landing was not at the bridge when visited because of construction. Instead, the put-in was down a gravel and clay road on the southeast side of the bridge.

3. From US-90 to Hinsons Crossroads, 12 miles. On US-90 west of Bonifay, go through Caryville to the river and the ramp.

4. From Hinsons Crossroads to Boynton Cutoff Boat Ramp, 15 miles. From Bonifay on US-90, go south on SR-79 to Douglas Ferry Road (CR-280). Turn west on CR-280 and proceed approximately 12 miles. When you come to the stop sign, go directly across the road and travel about 1 mile to the landing.

5. From Boynton Cutoff Boat Ramp to SR-20, 7 miles. Boynton Cutoff is on a dirt road off CR-284A south of CR-284 between New Hope and Hinsons Crossroads. To reach it, take SR-79 south from Bonifay to SR-280. Go west on SR-280 to SR-170. Continue on SR-280/170 to CR-284. Go south on CR-284 to CR-284A. It is about 3 miles to the dirt road.

6. From SR-20 to Choctawhatchee Bay, 20 miles. From I-10 near Ponce de Leon, take SR-81 south to SR-20. Turn east and proceed to the river. Most paddlers do not make this trip. The river spreads out and is sometimes difficult to follow to the bay. There are apparently no convenient landings after reaching the bay.

CAMPING

At normal to low water levels, the river has many areas along clay banks for camping. The Northwest Florida Water Management District has public lands on the banks almost the entire length of the river.

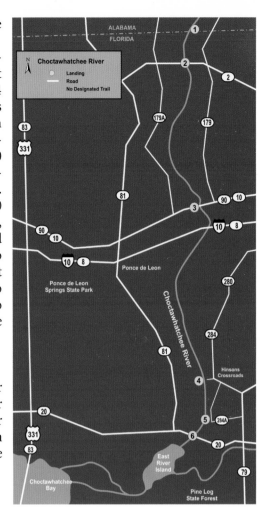

Below: Gazing at the Aucilla River from an unusually flat limestone rock.

CLEAR CREEK
(Santa Rosa County)

Clear Creek can be paddled from Whiting Field north of Milton to Pat Brown Road on the east side of Milton. It is a 5-mile paddle recommended by local paddling clubs who describe it as a very narrow creek for the experienced paddler. For the put-in, go north on SR-87 from Milton and east on Whiting Field Entrance Road. For the take-out, from SR-87 in Milton, turn east on SR-191 (Munson Highway) and proceed to Pat Brown Road.

COLD WEATHER DANGER

Sadly, two friends attempting to recreate a childhood trip tried to cross Choctawhatchee Bay in winter, capsized, and died of hypothermia.

Cold water paddlers on rivers may wish to carry extra clothing in dry storage in case of a spill. Those who venture onto large waters in tiny boats during the cold months might consider special thermal clothing.

Clear Creek
● Landing
— Road
— No Designated Trail

Whiting Field US Naval Station

Clear Creek

Munson

Pat Brown Road

Cooper Basin

Wright Basin

Milton

Below: Canoeist crossing over an old rock ford on the Aucilla river. This challenging section is followed by Little Rapid, an S-shaped section, and Big Rapid, a brief, but turbulent area of whitewater.

Above: Young kayakers on Coldwater Creek near a small sandbar island.

COLDWATER CREEK
(Santa Rosa County)

Like Sweetwater and Juniper creeks, Coldwater is a tributary of the Blackwater System. It is seep-fed along the way, and like the Escambia and several other rivers in the area, has its source in Conecuh National Forest.

At normal water levels, paddling is generally easy going. Generally swift and deeper than its sister rivers, Coldwater offers more than 20 miles of isolated splendor along its approximate 28 miles. Eighteen miles of the creek are a state-designated canoe trail.

About midway, Coldwater is joined by West Coldwater Creek, where it becomes noticeably wider. Members of local canoe clubs have traveled West Coldwater. However, it has shallows and many fallen trees.

All the Blackwater System has excellent sandbars for those who prefer primitive camping with their river journey. Coldwater's sandbars are plentiful and often large. Adventures Unlimited, a local and large outfitter, is located on Coldwater

Map. Coldwater Creek Canoe Trail, Office of Greenways and Trails. The 18-mile, state-designated trail runs from SR-4 to SR-191 Bridge.

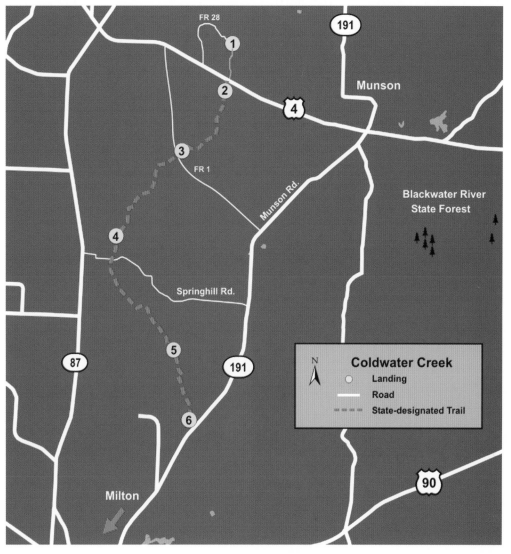

Coldwater Creek

○ Landing
— Road
- - - State-designated Trail

Above: Paddling over the sandy shallows of Coldwater Creek.

Creek and offers a variety of camping options.

Locals refer to the most northern section of the Coldwater as Buck's Creek. The outfitters are not convinced that it is the same river, a tributary, or passable. Some report they have plowed through Buck Creek to emerge at the gorgeous sand dunes south of Calloway Swamp. Most, however, make a short, 2-mile trip, and return.

SR-191 is the end of the journey for most. Shallow sections can turn paddling into carrying. A Blackwater River State Forest map is helpful for finding the forest roads.

POSSIBLE TRIPS AND LANDINGS

1. From Camp Lowry to Calloway Swamp, 2 miles (or 4 miles round trip). Exit I-10 on SR-87 north, then turn west on US-90 into the substantial town of Milton. Go north on SR-87 again, turn northeast on SR-191, and proceed to Munson. From Munson, travel west on SR-4 to FR-13 and turn north. Turn west on FR-28 and go to the bridge.
2. From SR-4 to Jernigan Bridge, 4 miles. From Munson, go 5 miles west on SR-4 to the bridge at Coldwater Creek.
3. From Jernigan Bridge to Berrydale Bridge, 5 miles. From Munson, go west

on SR-4 across Coldwater Creek, and south on FR-1. It is a little over 3 miles to the bridge.
4. From Berrydale Bridge to Tomahawk Landing, 4 miles. From Milton, go north on SR-87 to the Adventures Unlimited Sign. At the "T," go right to the bridge.
5. From Tomahawk Landing to SR-191, 5 miles. From Berrydale Bridge, go east on Spring Hill Road for about 2.5 miles. Turn south at the Tomahawk Landing sign.
6. SR-191. The Coldwater Creek Bridge is on SR-191 north of Milton.
   It is possible to continue paddling into Milton by continuing to the confluence with the Blackwater River. Check the depth first with local outfitters.

CAMPING

Numerous sandbars. Other options include Adventures Unlimited, the properties of other outfitters, Blackwater River State Forest, and Blackwater River State Park.

Right: Rounding a sandy bend on Coldwater Creek.

CROOKED RIVER
(Franklin County)

This river was suggested for paddling by a member of the Apalachee Canoe and Kayak Club. Crooked River connects to the Ochlockonee River to the west of Ochlockonee Bay and flows west through Tate's Hell State Forest. Paddlers usually put-in from the Ochlockonee River.

Both the Crooked and Ochlockonee rivers are wide, subject to wind, and have motorboats, but they also have some fine natural beauty. There are also side creeks, often somewhat parallel to the larger rivers.

Crooked River makes its way to the Carrabelle River after a meandering path of 10 miles or so. The New River also flows into the Carabelle River.

It is possible to reach Crooked River from other rivers along SR-67 in the national forest. There are designated campsites on the river in Tates Hell State Forest.

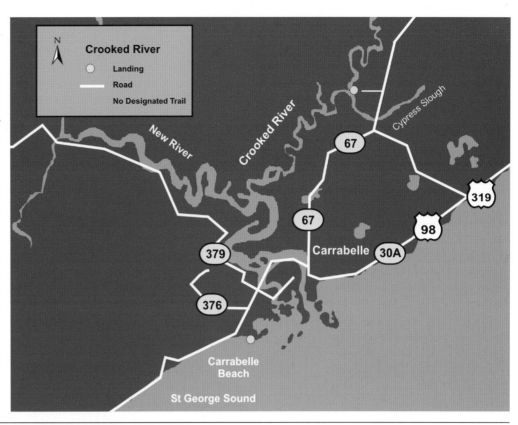

OUTFITTERS AND GUIDES

Even those who own their own small boats will at times need the services of outfitters for transportation or pickup. There are many private businesses providing such services.

One outfitter for Blackwater, Coldwater, Juniper, and Sweetwater, for example, is Adventures Unlimited. They are a very large, long-established company. In addition to a large fleet of canoes and kayaks, they offer primitive camping, group camping, and comparatively luxurious cabins, some with fireplaces. Adventures Unlimited's campground is family oriented and no alcoholic beverages or rowdy behavior are tolerated.

EAST BAY RIVER CANOE TRAIL
(Okaloosa and Santa Rosa counties)

This Eglin Air Force Base trail begins at RR-259 on the East Bay River and runs slightly more than 6 miles to the SR-87 bridge. The final 3 miles of the trail pass by private property.

Use of Eglin Air Force Base requires an annual permit. This can be obtained at a modest fee from Natural Resources at Jackson Guard on SR-85 in Niceville. A map is also available which shows all the range roads. Eglin has camping options.

Right: Canoeists stand at the entrance of a cave called The Oven which is located along the Chipola River.

ECONFINA CREEK
(Bay and Washington counties)

This 22-mile, state-designated trail can be one of the most difficult and strenuous water journeys in the Sunshine State. Despite its difficulty (or perhaps because of it, for many paddlers love a challenge) it is one of the favorite Florida canoe trails for its natural beauty. The ruggedness is enhanced by eroded channels that act like small canyons. Traveling between these walls, some 15 feet high, it feels like going down a chute at rapid speed.

A water gauge is located at Scotts Bridge. If the gauge is under 2.5 feet or over 6 feet, paddling should be avoided. Actually, 4 feet would be a good level.

The most popular paddling is between Scotts Bridge to Walsingham Park and from the Econfina Canoe Livery to SR-20. This is a difficult section, not for the unskilled paddler. Also watch the area below Walsingham Park which can have significant log jams; it is difficult in low water.

There are three large springs and many smaller ones. Below SR-20 lies Emerald Spring. At SR-20 is Pitt Spring and above SR-20 is Blue Spring.

Below SR-388 lies a lake and dam. Econfina Creek is the water supply for Panama City to the south. On the weekends, there is boating activity below SR-388, so paddlers should be cautious.

Magnolias are more noticeable along Econfina Creek than many other rivers. This includes not only southern magnolia, but pyramid magnolia and others. Tupelo, maple and large cypress also abound.

Econfina Creek is quite far from Econfina River. The two are sometimes confused. Some people pronounce them differently even though they are spelled identically: E-con-fine-a Creek and E-con-feen-a River.

POSSIBLE TRIPS AND LANDINGS

1. From Scotts Bridge to Walsingham Bridge, 10 miles. The small community of Fountain is along US-231 between I-10 to the north and SR-20 to the south. From Fountain, go north 4 miles on US-231 past the junction with SR-167. Shortly thereafter, turn west on Scott Road and go to the bridge.
2. From Walsingham Bridge to SR-20, 6 miles. From US-231, turn west on SR-20 and go north on Strickland Road. Follow Porter Pond Road to Hampshire Boulevard and then Walsingham Road to Walsingham Park. Four-wheel drive is very helpful in this section.
3. From SR-20 to SR-388 (Bennett Bridge), 6 miles. From US-231, go west on SR-

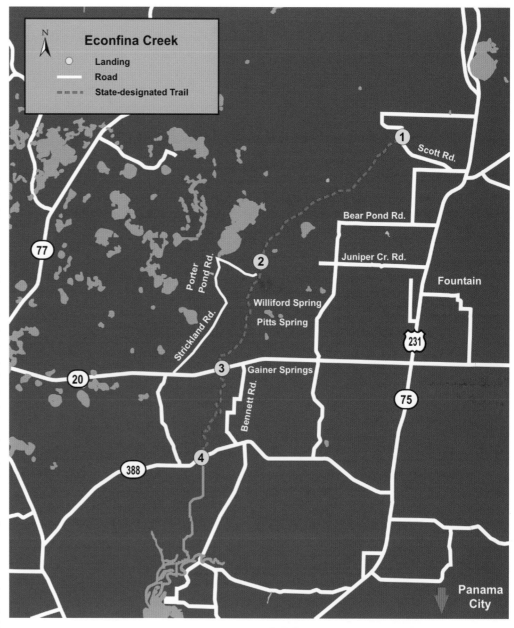

Map. Econfina Creek Canoe Trail, Office of Greenways and Trails.

20. A parking area has been established just to the east of Pitt Spring Recreation Area. The water management district has built a canoe launch and take-out just below Pitt Spring. It is not permissible to launch or take-out at Blue or Pitt springs.
4. Bennett Bridge. From SR-20 to the east of Pitt Spring Recreation Area, turn south on Blue Springs Road. Turn west on SR-388 and proceed to the bridge. On Blue Springs Road there is a one lane bridge, so use caution.

CAMPING

Camping is possible at Walsingham Bridge Park by permission. Contact the Northwest Florida Water Management District.

ECONFINA RIVER
(Madison and Taylor counties)

The Econfina is a blackwater river with its origin in swamps of Madison and Taylor counties. It is narrow, shallow, and twisty, and the farther inland, the more difficult to paddle, especially during periods of low water. Most of the river is remote and gorgeous, with some surprising limestone runs. Although it is 35 miles long, most of the upper portions are usually too shallow for paddling

Near the Gulf at Econfina River State Park, the river opens up into wide vistas of saltmarsh and tree islands. There are razor-sharp oyster beds during low tide at the river mouth to avoid which might scrape up a kayak or cut unprotected feet. It is possible to paddle considerable distance within the saltmarsh and tree hammocks.

In Taylor County, the lower portion from US-98 should only be attempted with high tide in mind. Otherwise there are some wicked limestone shoals and many portages.

This river should not be confused with the creek of the same name as the two are

Above: Canoes passing through the chute on Econfina Creek.

Below: Exploring a cave along the Suwannee River.

POLIS

not connected and are quite far apart.

POSSIBLE TRIPS AND LANDINGS

1. Problematical. The Suwannee River Water Management District Recreational Guide shows a landing to the northeast of US-27. To reach this landing when traveling north, turn east on the first road after the Econfina Bridge on US-19/27. There are also various other landings from roads of the Foley Timber Company running down to Cabbage Grove Road. The water levels in this area make this a problematic journey. A copy of the Recreation Guide can be requested from Suwannee River Water Management District.

2. From Cabbage Grove Road to US-98, 4 miles. Cabbage Grove Road is an often unmarked road heading northwest from US-98 some distance west of Perry. Thus, for certainty of finding it, turn north from US-98 onto CR-14. (South on CR-14 leads to Econfina River State Park.) At the intersection of CR-14 and Cabbage Grove Road, turn southeast and proceed to the bridge.

3. From US-98 to Econfina River State Park, 8 miles. About 18 miles to the west of Perry, the landing is at the US-98 Bridge.

4. Econfina River State Park is a south turn from US-98 to the west of Perry. It is possible to paddle beyond the park into saltmarsh.

CAMPING

Options include Goose Pasture, managed by Suwannee River Water Management District, and Econfina River State Park, where camping is managed by private concession.

Above: Negotiating a narrow passage on the Econfina River north of US-98 and west of Perry, Florida.

Opposite page: The Big Rapid on the Aucilla river.

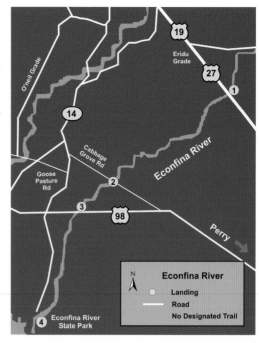

ESCAMBIA RIVER
(Escambia and Santa Rosa counties)

Like the Apalachicola, the Escambia is a major alluvial (soil-bearing) river. Its Florida length has been given variously at between 54 and 60 miles, and it is easy to see why sources might be uncertain. The river twists and turns, forms many oxbows along the way, then flows widely out into Escambia Bay. There is another problem in computing distance since the river forks in many places. There are shorter forks and longer paths. Thus, someone familiar with the river might find it to be considerably shorter than someone new to it. However, getting lost is not an issue, because despite all the forks, after the river splits, it comes back together. The Escambia changes names at the state line; in Alabama, it is known as the Conecuh River.

When asked about the Escambia, one experienced paddler and outfitter located only a few miles from it said, "Why would you want to paddle the Escambia? People can paddle at sea too." However, upper Florida reaches of the Escambia are not wide and are far from sea-like. Rather, the upper reaches are narrow and twisty, with great camping sandbars. The river is something like the Shoal or Yellow rivers, but deeper.

Below McDavid, the lower two-thirds of the river does widen, but it is not terrifically wide (unless flooded) until it reaches Escambia Bay. At the bay, of course, it is tidal with plenty of water at all times, but upper stretches run low during dry spells.

Above: Sandy Landing on the Escambia River is northwest of Chumuckla, a small community north of Pensacola.

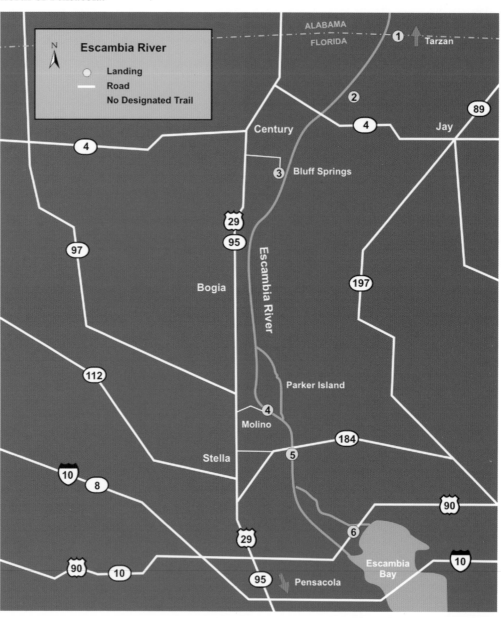

Perhaps there are several reasons why local paddlers are less interested in the Escambia. The Blackwater River System is nearby, an extensive area of state-designated canoe trails located in what the state legislature has proclaimed the Canoe Capital of Florida. There are also other state-designated trails in the area, including the Perdido, Shoal, and Yellow rivers, and there are many streams on Eglin Air Force Base to paddle.

The Escambia is a little mysterious, access not so easy to find, and the number of paddlers who have traveled it, smaller by far. Then, too, most Floridians and tourists experience the Escambia either crossing its bay on US-90 or I-10. The bay is perhaps 3 miles wide then, wider farther south. This reinforces the impression that the river is wide, subject to wind, and not fine paddling.

If you feel like becoming an explorer, the Northwest Florida Water Management District has a map of the Escambia River Water Management Area. On it, you will find mysteries like Brosnaham Island, Brown Lake, Spanish Mill Creek, Horseshoe Lake, and Salters Lake. The most scenic areas of the river are in the oxbow lakes and many creeks feeding the river, making for great side trips. The water management area begins at SR-4 and runs out before US-90.

The Escambia is a gorgeous, remote river: more than enough challenge to interest many of the serious paddlers out there. There are no outfitters for the Escambia, but local fish camps should be able to help with current conditions and directions.

There are at times some significant logjams.

POSSIBLE TRIPS AND LANDINGS

Mileage given is a very rough estimate. Distance will vary depending upon how the river is paddled.

1. Alabama Highway 41 to above SR-4, Florida, 20 miles. From I-10, exit north on US-29 to SR-4. Go east across the bridge to Jay. Turn north at SR-89 in the direction of Mt. Carmel. At the fork, continue on CR-55 until reaching Alabama Highway 41. Turn left or north. The landing is at the river.
2. Above SR-4 to Bluff Springs, 6 miles. The landing at SR-4 is currently closed. There is access, however. From I-10 north of Pensacola, turn north on US-29, turn east on SR-4, then cross over the bridge. Upon reaching Jay, turn north on the road to the refinery. At the gate, turn left and follow the fence. When the fence ends, take the dirt road until reaching the boat ramp. (Untested

instructions also advise going east from US-29 north of Pensacola on SR-4, then north on Campbell Road, then left on Boat Ramp Road to Oyster Lodge.) The landing, of course, may someday reopen at SR-4.
3. Bluff Springs to Molino Landing, 15 miles. From I-10, go north on US-29. Two miles south of Century (30 miles north of I-10), turn east on Bluff Springs Road. Go 0.7 miles, cross the railroad track, and take an immediate right. Proceed about 0.5 miles to the end of the road. This landing does not have a paved ramp.
4. Molino Landing to Quintette Bridge (CR-184), 5 miles. Exit I-10 north on US-29. Go 16 miles to CR-182 (Molino Road) and turn east. Go 1.7 miles to Brickyard Road which is located a mile beyond SR-95A. Turn right on Brickyard Road following it to its end at Fairgrounds Road. Turn left on Fairgrounds Road, cross the railroad track, and proceed to the well-maintained landing.

5. Quintette Bridge (CR-184) to US-90, 10 miles. From I-10, exit north on US-29, and turn east on CR-184. The access is across the bridge.
6. US-90. From Quintette Bridge south, the river is wide with saltmarsh, and with much boating. For fishing kayakers, however, the fishing is fine, including trout.

CAMPING

Consult the Northwest Florida Water Management District.

FISHER CREEK
(Leon County)

Fisher Creek stretches 5 miles roughly north-to-south in Apalachicola National Forest about 7 miles southwest of Tallahassee. It is crossed by SR-373. Various forest roads approach it. In drought, Fisher Creek may be impassable. With sufficient water, it will be difficult and strenuous. It is for the able with good technical skills, and not for the casual paddler. Before proceeding check with the national forest. A map is essential to finding one's way around the forest and can be obtained for either ranger district.

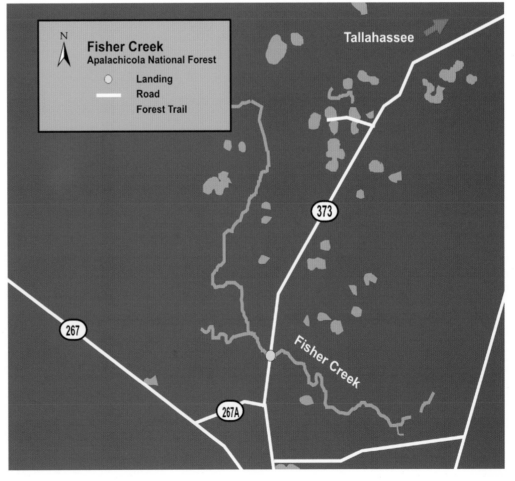

FLORIDA RIVER
(Liberty County)

Short and shaded, the Florida River runs into the Apalachicola River on the west border of Apalachicola National Forest. When visited in winter, fog rose from the river adding mystery to a usually remote nature paddle. There is a forest bridge at the end of FR-188 for a put-in. Paddle up or down river. There is usually little flow. From Bristol, go south on SR-12 and west on CR-379 to FR-188.

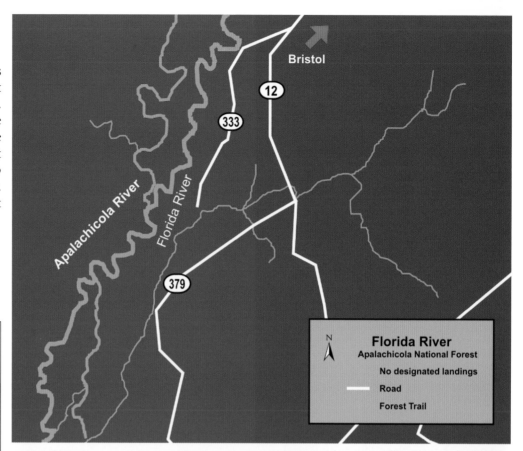

Florida River
Apalachicola National Forest
No designated landings
—— Road
Forest Trail

EMERGENCIES

On any long river journey, it is a wise idea to have alternative take-outs in case of emergency. Local outfitters can be counted on to supply this information. On a river like the Escambia, where there are no outfitters, fish camps or marinas may be the best source for the location of alternative take-outs.

Through-out most of the state help is available by dialing 911 on a cellular phone. However, cellular phones often do not work on the remote rivers and streams of Florida. Cellular phones do usually work in near coastal situations. Some cellular companies have better reception in certain areas than others. So, if paddlers subscribe to different cellphone providers, then everyone should bring their cellphones along, hopefully stored in watertight bags.

It is always a good idea to advise family, friends and local outfitters of travel and camping plans. If there is an emergency on the river, or a paddling group fails to show up on time, rescuers will have a good idea where to search.

PADDLING SHOES

While footwear may seem more important for hiking, it is equally important for paddling. Many paddlers wear water sandals, sometimes with socks. Water sandals, special shoes for rivers and bays, are often sold by outfitters and in sporting good stores. They are convenient, keep shoes from getting wet, and in case of a spill, make swimming easy. Other paddlers, particularly in shallow rivers, wear recreational shoes, like sneakers, because they may have to walk the boat. In cold weather, waders are a great investment because wet feet on a chilly morning can be miserable.

Above: Putting-in a kayak on the Sopchoppy River.

HOLMES CREEK
(Washington County)

The creek is a tributary of the Choctaw-hatchee River. Even experienced paddlers are sometimes awed by this beautiful creek and its ancient cypress. A 16-mile, state-designated canoe trail begins at Vernon Wayside Park and ends at Live Oak Landing.

Two middle-size but lovely springs lie above the park: Cypress and Magnolia springs. It is also possible to start above the Wayside Park at Cypress Springs, the more productive of the two springs, adding 3 miles to the trip.

There is an outfitter for the Cypress Springs to Vernon Wayside Park trip, but they do not outfit for the state-designated trail.

LANDINGS

1. From Crystal Springs to Vernon Wayside Park, 3 miles. Crystal Springs is north of Vernon to the east of SR-79 at the red canoe sign.

2. From Vernon Wayside Park to Hightower Springs Landing, 6 miles. Wayside Park is on the east side of the road 0.5 miles north of Vernon on SR-79.

3. From Hightower Springs Landing to Spurling Landing, 4 miles. The landing is prominently announced by a launch sign on SR-79 southwest of Vernon.

4. From Spurling Landing to Reedy Branch, 1 mile. The landing is prominently announced by a launch sign on SR-79 south of Vernon.

5. From Reedy Branch to Millers Ferry Bridge (CR-284), 8 miles. Take SR-79 southwest from Vernon for 6 miles and turn right at the canoe launch sign, proceeding until reaching the creek.

6. From Millers Ferry Bridge to Live Oak/Shell Landing, 6 miles. Take SR-79 southwest from Vernon and turn west on CR-284 and proceed to the bridge.

7. Live Oak/Shell Landing. To reach Shell Landing, take SR-79 southwest from Vernon 7 miles to CR-284. Go west for about 4 miles to SR-284A. Turn south on SR-284A and go 3 miles to the landing. It is possible to proceed from Shell Landing to the Choctawhatchee River.

CAMPING

A permit is required from the Northwest Florida Water Management District for camping at Hightower Springs, Millers Ferry Bridge, and Spurling landings. An annual permit is $11.00 and is good for 190,000 acres of water management lands. Call the district to find out where there is a convenient place to purchase the permit.

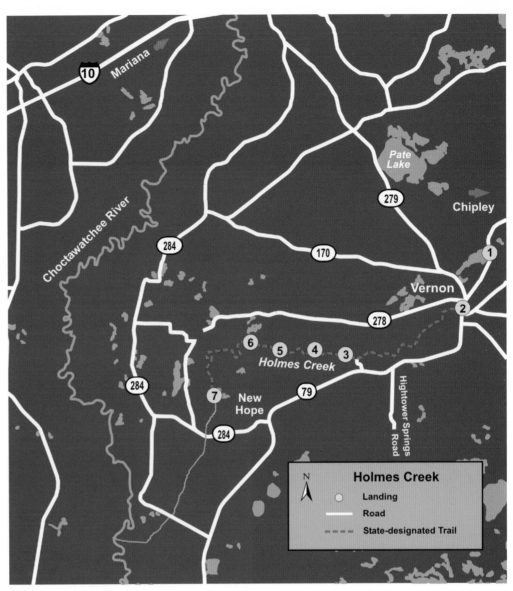

No permit is needed for those under 16 or 65 and over.

Map. Holmes Creek Canoe Trail, Office of Greenways and Trails.

Below: The Blackwater River.

JUNIPER CREEK
(Santa Rosa County)

Juniper Creek is a tributary of the Blackwater River. Once on Juniper the paddling is pretty easy and the scenery gorgeous. The 11-mile, state-designated canoe trail, however, begins with Sweetwater Creek where paddling is no picnic. Rather it is a rugged, claustrophobic trip, left and right around fallen logs, with climbs over and sometimes through openings hacked and sawed into trees.

Just clearing and keeping Sweetwater open is a task in itself, and thanks should be given to dedicated members of local paddling clubs, who (with a few chain saws and good muscles) have done us all a favor. Many paddlers will want to start with SR-191 and skip the Rambo portion of Sweetwater.

However, struggling through Sweetwater is rewarded at the confluence with Juniper. It is like rebirth. Stop at the sandbar. Wade in the shallow water. Jump in the air to celebrate.

Later, Juniper is exceptionally scenic with high bluffs, including Red Rock Bluffs, overlooking the river from a height of perhaps 100 feet. These bluffs are arguably the most attractive section of the entire Blackwater River System. On its slopes grow longleaf pine, some hanging tenuously to washed-out ravines. The ground is red from clay, hence the name Red Rock Bluffs.

Deer are frequently seen, sometimes running across the river or straight down the shallow center. Deer hoof prints will be found stamped all over the sandbars within the entire Blackwater System.

A map of Blackwater River State Forest will be very helpful in finding the forest roads.

POSSIBLE TRIPS AND LANDINGS
1. (Sweetwater) SR-4 to Munson School Bridge. When last visited, this section was closed. The bridge on SR-4 is about 1 mile east of Munson. Munson is north of Milton, Exit I-10 on SR-87 north and take US-90 west. Rejoin SR-87 north, turn on SR-191 north, and proceed to SR-4.
2. (Sweetwater) Munson School Bridge to Red Rock Bridge, 5 miles. From SR-191 south of Munson and north of Milton, turn east on FR-21 (Sandy Landing Road) at Munson Elementary School. Proceed 2 miles to the Munson School Bridge. Just before the bridge, there is a sign on the dirt road going to the put-in.
3. (Juniper) From SR-191 to Red Rock, 5 miles. SR-191 Bridge crosses Juniper Creek considerably north of Milton and

Above: Juniper Creek as seen from Red Rock Bluffs.

south of Munson.

4. (Juniper) From Red Rock to Indian Ford Bridge, 6 miles. From SR-191, 12 miles north of Milton, turn east on Red Rock Road. Go east 6 miles to the bridge.
5. (Juniper) From Indian Ford Bridge to the confluence with Blackwater River, 3-4 miles. The canoe journey normally ends at Indian Ford Bridge. Local outfitters and paddlers do not recommend going beyond there. Portions beyond this bridge are considered too shallow in spots and

there is a substantial portage. From Milton, take SR-191 north to Indian Ford Road and go east 2.5 miles to the bridge.

CAMPING
Numerous sandbars. Other options include Blackwater River State Forest and Blackwater River State Park.

Map. Sweetwater/Juniper Creeks Canoe Trail, Office of Greenways and Trails.

Above: The bluffs along Juniper Creek.

THE GREATEST MAP OF ALL

National forests have their own maps, free or at a small fee, revealing the intricate maze of forest roads, made mostly for lumbering and big trucks. DeLorme publishes FLORIDA ATLAS AND GAZETTEER. This atlas is essential for adventuresome outdoor people. The atlas is revised annually and shows almost all federal, state, or county highways, including many (but not all) forest roads.

Below: Another view of Juniper Creek.

TH

Above: Kennedy Creek.

KENNEDY CREEK
(Liberty County)

Kennedy Creek is a tributary of the Apalachicola River located in Apalachicola National Forest. This is generally an easy trip back-and-forth to the Apalachicola, and there is usually no great water level fluctuation. Kennedy Creek is 75-100 feet wide in places.

This gorgeous 4-mile trip begins at Cotton Landing. To reach Cotton Landing, go north from Sumatra on SR-379, then go west 3 miles on FR-123, and farther west on FR-123B. A forest map is available from either ranger district in Apalachicola National Forest and is highly recommended. There are numerous camping options in this national forest and on Northwest Florida Water Management District property.

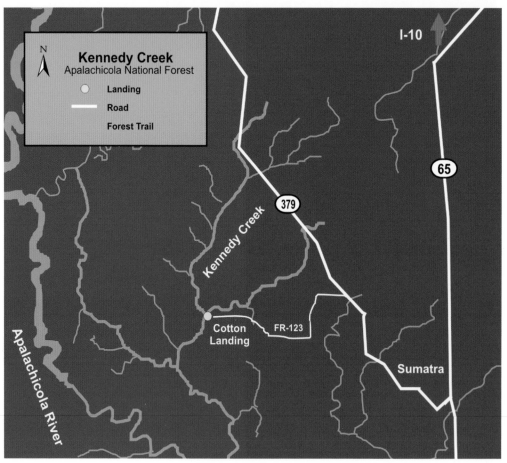

LITTLE RIVER
(Gadsden and Leon counties)

Little River flows into Lake Talquin and thus is a tributary of Ochlockonee River. It is a short journey, but it can be shallow with obstructions. The closer to Lake Talquin, the wider and deeper the river becomes.

POSSIBLE TRIPS AND LANDINGS

1. US-90 to SR-268, 4 miles. Take US-90 west from Tallahassee 15-16 miles to the Little River.
2. SR-268 to Lake Talquin, 5 miles. Take US-90 west from Tallahassee 11-12 miles, turn south on SR-268, and continue to the Little River.
3. Lake Talquin. There are many landings on Lake Talquin. Since there is no livery service, it would be wise to scout the landing in advance and park an adequate number of vehicles there.

CAMPING

Lake Talquin State Forest.

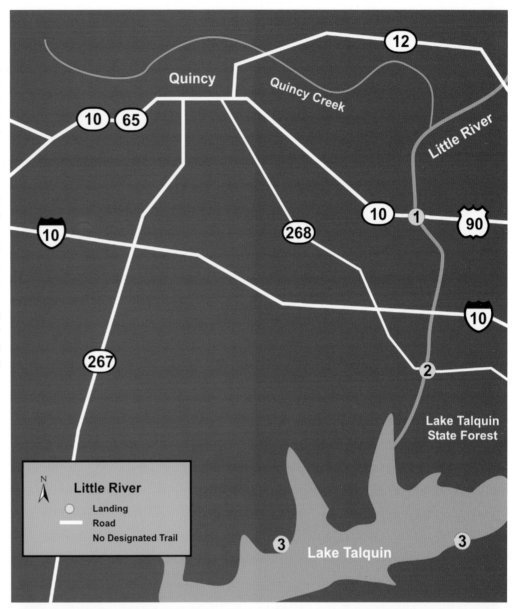

LOST CREEK
(Wakulla County)

Lost Creek is located in Apalachicola National Forest. The creek is narrow, with sharp bends, and (depending on water level) log lift-overs. This river is 10 miles long and ends at a sink where the river goes underground. It passes through two areas which may give the paddler an idea of the terrain: Cow Swamp and Mosquito Bay.

A full trip on the creek would run from FR-360 southeast to FR-368. However, there may not be that much water, so at times one might just put-in where accessible and travel as far as possible and return. All the effort to travel the creek will be worth it for those who like rugged wilderness. It is some of the most remote canoeing in Florida.

A forest map is available from either ranger district and highly recommended. From US-319 in Crawfordville, turn west on Arran Road. Turn north on FR-350 and proceed to the creek.

There are numerous camping options in this national forest.

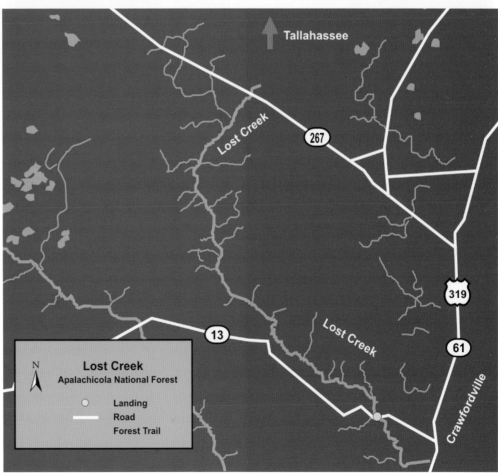

NEW RIVER
(Liberty County)

Tough and remote, this river passes through titi and cypress swamps and is best traveled at high water. Mileage depends upon the amount of water. Although the river extends an enormous distance, from Telogia Creek to the Gulf of Mexico, it frequently loses its way.

New River is located in Apalachicola National Forest northeast of Sumatra. As with most of the small streams in the national forest, it is wise to check with the ranger district before paddling as the staff will know the water level.

From SR-65 in Wilma, a small community north of Sumatra, take Wilma Road east to FH-13 and go east to the bridge. A map of the national forest is available from either ranger district and highly recommended.

There are numerous camping options in this national forest.

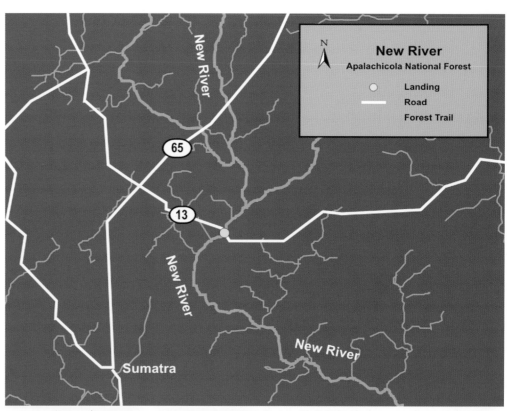

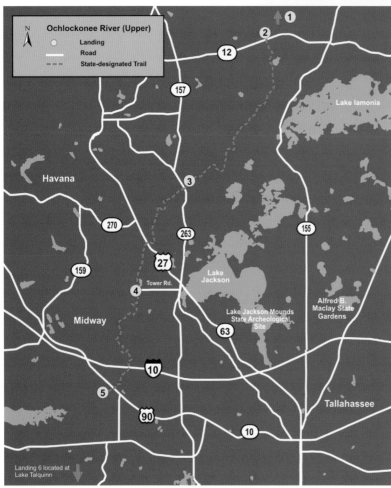

Above: The Ochlockonee River.

OCHLOCKONEE RIVER
(Franklin, Gadsden, Leon, Liberty, and Wakulla counties)

In Florida, this river separates the two ranger districts of Apalachicola National Forest. Most of the 102 miles of the river itself is divided into two state-designated canoe trails: Upper and Lower Ochlockonee. This refers to the areas above and below Lake Talquin Dam. Paddling is easy in normal water levels except for the length of trips.

Upper Ochlockonee canoe journeys end at Lake Talquin. The lake is long and broad, and it would easily require a day to navigate it. Wind could make it a chore. However, this lake is scenic, and Lake Talquin State Park and Lake Talquin State Forest offer camping.

Upper Ochlockonee waters look like hot chocolate. Only occasionally does a glimpse of a sand bottom break through. Below the dam the water is dark but clearer, like long brewed tea.

Lower Ochlockonee splits the national forest and is paralleled by SR-67 on the west and CR/SR-375 on the east. Forest Highway (FH)-13 runs east to west to cross both roads, but is often mis-labeled FR-113 on maps. Within the national forest, turning toward the river from either paved road on a variety of forest roads will take a paddler to the banks. The landings given below, therefore, are partial, and most have been long used in other guides, and as landings on the state-designated canoe trails.

Below the national forest, the river widens to perhaps a mile and enters the Gulf of Mexico at Ochlockonee Bay. Not many want to paddle there, but for those who want to experience the full expanse of the river, two landings have been added to the traditional ones.

Telogia Creek is a long tributary of the Ochlockonee River.

Telogia enters the river about 7 miles south of SR-20 and is crossed by SR-65 between Hosford to the north and Telogia to the south. This creek can be shallow and overgrown, and upper stretches pass through private land, thus it is not normally considered a paddling trip, although some brave souls have plowed into it. It is possible to paddle from the river up the creek a good distance when the water level is high.

POSSIBLE TRIPS AND LANDINGS - UPPER OCHLOCKONEE

Within the area of the Upper Ocholockonee, a number of roads change designation from CR to SR on various maps and in various guides. When such confusion exists, the road is given below as both county and state.

1. From Georgia SR-93 to Florida CR/SR-12, 15 miles. The beginning of the first Florida segment is south of Thomasville and east of Cairo in Georgia. From I-10, take US-319 north. At the intersection of US-319 and SR-93 (Jackie Robinson Parkway), go north on SR-93 to the bridge.

2. From CR/SR-12 (Fairbanks Ferry Landing) to CR/SR-157 (Old Bainbridge Road), 14 miles. CR/SR-12 is roughly parallel to the Georgia border north of Tallahassee. The bridge is located between CR/SR-155 to the east and CR/SR-157 to the west but closer to CR/SR-155. Coming from SR-93 in Georgia, turn west on an unmarked CR/SR in the small town of Meridian. It is the only road to the west between the SR-93 landing and US-319.

3. From CR/SR-157 (Old Bainbridge Road) to Tower Road, 6 miles. Go north on US-27 from Tallahassee. Turn east on CR/SR-157 and proceed to the bridge.

4. From Tower Road to US-90, 5 miles. From US-27 in western Tallahassee, turn south on Capital Circle. Tower Road is on the west side of the road and leads to the river. Watch out for the railroad tracks on the way to the landing and slow down before hitting them.

5. From US-90 to Lake Talquin, 6 miles.

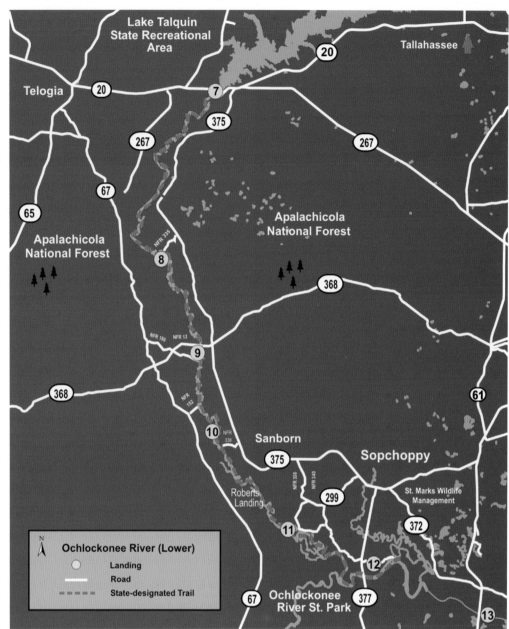

From the Tower Road Landing, turn south (right) on Capital Circle, then west (right) on US-90. Cross the bridge and the landing is on the southwest side.

6. Lake Talquin. There are at least seven landings within Lake Talquin State Park/State Forest. Some permit camping, others do not, and some are in private hands. Lake Talquin is a large, beautiful, man-made lake, and those wishing to paddle across it to the dam should arrange for camping in advance by contacting the recreation area or state forest.

CAMPING

Except for Lake Talquin, Upper Ochlockonee lands are largely private, and the banks at the landings are unfortunately littered with gross amounts of garbage. This litter problem does not disappear until after Tower Road. Thus, primitive camping options are very limited, but excellent at Lake Talquin. A lot of the east bank in the area of I-10 and US-90 is in Lake Talquin State Forest.

Maps. Ochlockonee River Canoe Trails, Office of Greenways and Trails. The 26-mile, state-designated trail begins at CR/SR-12 and ends at US-90.

POSSIBLE TRIPS AND LANDINGS - LOWER OCHLOCKONEE

7. From SR-20 (Lake Talquin Dam) to Pine Creek Landing, 15 miles. SR-20 is south of Tallahassee and can be reached by a number of I-10 exits, including Capitol Circle. Go west on SR-20 to the river. However, to miss the congestion, one might exit I-10 at CR-267 (Quincy) and take CR-267 south to SR-20, then east to the river.

8. From Pine Creek Landing to Lower Langston Landing, 13 miles. From Lake Talquin Dam on SR-20, go east a short distance to CR/SR-375, and turn south. A little more than 11 miles south, turn west on FR-335 and continue to the landing.

9. From Lower Langston Landing to Mack Landing, 6 miles. From SR-20, turn south on CR/SR-375 and proceed to FH-13. Turn west and proceed to SR-67 and turn south. Turn east on FR-152 and go to the river.

to the river.

10. From Mack Landing to Wood Lake, 12 miles. From SR-20, turn south on CR/SR-375 and proceed south over 20 miles to FR-336. A prominent sign announces the west turn to the river.
11. From Wood Lake to Ochlockonee River State Park, 11 miles. From Sopchoppy, go west on CR/SR-22 to SR-299. Go south to FR-338 and west to Wood Lake.
12. From Ochlockonee River State Park to Bald Point State Park, 16 miles. This wide, heavily boated section of the river is rarely paddled, but is presented for those who wish to follow all rivers to the ends. Ochlockonee River State Park is 4 miles south of Sopchoppy on US-319. It is also possible to break this trip by taking out at US-98 on the west bank.
13. Bald Point State Park. Bald Point is south of US-98 near the river. Turn south on SR-370, then east on Bald Point Road.

CAMPING

The Lower Ochlockonee and the sections beyond have excellent camping opportunities in Apalachicola National Forest and Ochlockonee River State Park.

Map. Ochlockonee River (Lower) Canoe Trail, Office of Greenways and Trails.

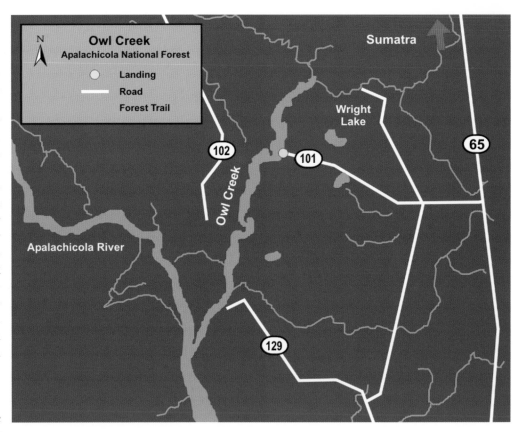

OWL CREEK
(Franklin and Liberty counties)

This is a 2-mile trip in Apalachicola National Forest. It begins at Hickory Landing and ends at the Apalachicola River. To return, paddle back upstream.

On SR-65 south of Sumatra, take FR-101 to the Hickory Landing sign. Turn south and proceed a little over a mile to the camping area. A forest map is available from either of the ranger districts in Apalachicola National Forest and is highly recommended. There are numerous camping opportunities in this national forest.

PERDIDO RIVER
(Escambia County)

This river is a boundary between Florida and Alabama and has 9 miles of state-designated canoe trail. The entire river is 58 miles long. Its name in Spanish means "lost," and is taken from Perdido Bay, where a Spanish explorer might have been lost 500 years ago. Indeed, paddlers looking for the northern remote landings and the southernmost launch may also find themselves feeling lost, as the landings are very hard to locate.

The river is usually sandy and lovely, and most of it is far from cities and in completely natural or rural settings. It is thus a fine paddle but unfortunately beset by access problems (see box on the next page).

For all but Panhandle Floridians, it is a long trip to the Perdido. This would be reason enough to call the local outfitter or paddling clubs in advance. With difficult access problems, calling in advance is more imperative.

In addition to access problems, at least three landings have some truly ugly signs which do not make a paddler feel welcome. Those signs state PRIVATE PROPERTY in very large letters, while in small print they announce that there is a public landing down the road. In fact, you cannot see the public landing information unless you first drive onto the private property. The signs in large print inform the visitor anyone found after sunset will be arrested. The Perdido River has had a problem with rowdiness. It is legal to use the landings during the day. During hours of darkness, remaining might draw suspicious locals and perhaps a sheriff.

The first two northern landings would be best approached by four-wheel drive. "Three Runs" has some sandy areas and little room to turn around. Old Water Ferry Landing had some serious standing puddles of water despite several rainless days before being visited. Both landings are on private property.

The river above the state-designated canoe trail had two substantial log jams when visited in 2001. Canoe clubs say they bypass by dragging-out 100 yards or more. Club members will undoubtedly chip away at the logjams.

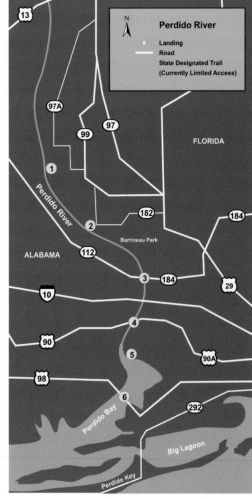

POSSIBLE TRIPS AND LANDINGS

1. From Jackson Springs ("Three Runs") to Old Water Ferry Landing, 5 miles. From I-10, exit on US-29 north and go west on CR-182 (Molino Road). At the dead-end, turn north on what becomes CR-99. Go west on CR-97A (Jackson Springs Road) at the Walnut Hill Water Tower. When visited, the county road was not marked, and the tower was the only saving grace.

2. From Old Water Ferry Landing to Adventures Unlimited, 9 miles. From I-10, exit on US 29 north. From "Three Runs" above, go south and west. When the road makes a sweeping hard left, the landing is a long way down a narrow dirt road.

3. From Adventures Unlimited to US-90, 10 miles. For Adventures Unlimited, take the last Florida exit, US-90A north. Take CR-99 north. Cross CR-184 and the outfitter is located on both sides of the road along the river.

4. From US-90 to Hurst Landing, 7 miles. From Pensacola, go west on US-90. The launch on US-90 is at a fishing camp by the river on the northeast bank just on the Florida side of the Florida-Alabama border.

5. From Hurst Landing into Perdido Bay. This landing is south of US-90 and substantially west of Pensacola. From US-90, turn south on CR-99. When you come to the stop sign, go straight ahead. Continue several miles to the end of the road at Hurst Landing.

6. Perdido Bay. There are no public landings indicated on maps of Perdido Bay. It is conceivable that a determined paddler could plow on until reaching Perdido Key State Park or even Big Lagoon State Park on Area. The water is wide (several miles at some points) and like the sea, thus the best course would be to skirt the land.

Should the Barrineau Park landing re-open, it is located by exiting I-10 on SR-29 north, and proceeding to CR-196, then northwest 2.5 miles. A map of the state-designated trail has not been included because it is presently meaningless without the Barrineau Park Landing.

CAMPING

The sole outfitter has a campground. There are plentiful sandbars on the river, but with all the unfriendly signs and public landings closed because of rowdiness, it might be better to consider this option. The outfitter is the best source of advice.

THE INACCESSIBLE STATE-DESIGNATED CANOE TRAIL

Only the presence of a private outfitter assures public access to this state-designated canoe trail. Barrineau Park, the starting point of the trail, was closed because of rowdiness. The outfitter has an arrangement with a private landowner to put paddlers in, but this agreement may change if the land is sold. The ramp at Muscogee Landing was also closed because of bad behavior. Both are cited in other canoeing guides.

In addition, the first two landings, Jackson Springs ("Three Runs") and Old Water Ferry Landing are on private lands. Access is presently allowed to paddlers, but this too should be checked with the local outfitter. The outfitter's business has been hurt by the closing of the park and landing, and unless something is done so the business can continue to aid paddlers, access to this state-designated canoe trail may vanish. This would be unfortunate because the river is a scenic joy.

POND CREEK
(Santa Rosa County)

Pond Creek is about a 5-mile paddle suggested by local paddling enthusiasts. It is narrow, fast, and winding, and recommended for the experienced. The put-in is at the Hamilton Road Bridge, 3 miles west of Milton, and the take-out is at Mayo Park on US-90 in Milton. From US-90 in Milton, go north on Glover Road and west on Hamilton Road to the bridge. Mayo Park is west of Milton on US-90.

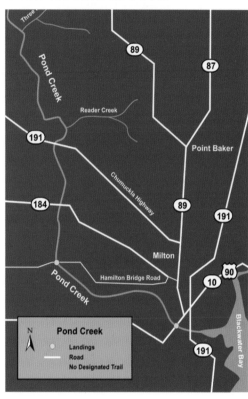

RIVER STYX
(Liberty County)

It is surprising, but there is more than one River Styx in Florida. In mythology, the River Styx led to Hades or Hell. This river is nowhere close.

Located along Apalachicola National Forest and lands of the Northwest Florida Water Management District, the river travels perhaps 3 miles to the Apalachicola River. The trip begins at White Oak Landing, located north of Sumatra. Take CR-379 north, and FR-115 west a little over 3 miles. At the fork, go right. It is 1 mile to the river, where there is a concrete boat ramp. A forest map is available from either of the ranger districts and highly recommended. There are numerous camping options in this national forest and anywhere on the water management district property.

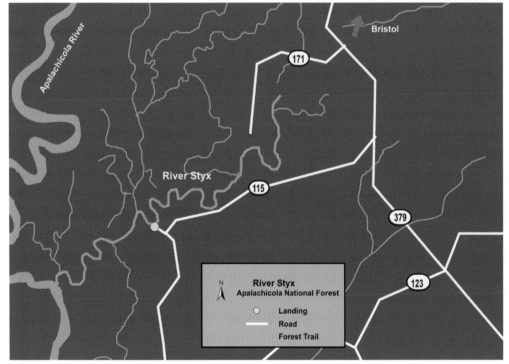

PC

Above: Time for a rest along a creek on Eglin Air Force Base.

ROCKY CREEK CANOE TRAIL
(Okaloosa and Walton counties)

Rocky Creek originates on Eglin Air Force Base, then flows south through Eglin, exiting at Rocky Bayou State Park on Rocky Bayou. The entire distance may be 10 miles, possibly less, but the base canoe trail (from RR-200 to SR-20) is 6.3 miles.

Base literature warns of many fallen trees and possible portages. The effort to overcome these obstacles will be rewarded by the wonderful scenery and wildlife. Base information also warns that it is possible to lose the way in the expanses near the end of the trail before Rocky Bridge is found.

Use of Eglin Air Force Base requires an annual pass at a modest fee. It can be obtained from Natural Resources at the Jackson Guard in Niceville on SR-85. A base map comes with the permit and is essential for finding one's way about Eglin. Eglin has camping options. Rocky Bayou State Park is a very popular camping site.

SHOAL RIVER
(Okaloosa and Walton counties)

The Shoal forms from small streams north of DeFuniak Springs. Along its path to the Yellow River, other streams feed in. Twenty-seven miles of the river are a state-

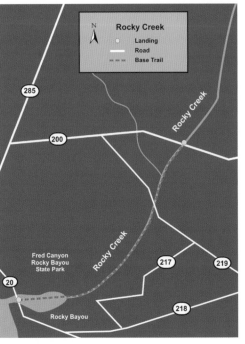

designated canoe trail.

At normal water levels, the trips on this river would be fairly easy paddles except for trip length and river width. Usually shallow and sandy, the Shoal is moderately wide from the SR-393 landing until it merges with the Yellow River near Gin Hole Landing on Eglin Air Force Base.

On Eglin, Titi Creek is a small and beautiful stream feeding the river. It and other Eglin paddles have separate accounts.

For the portions on Eglin Air Force Base, an annual permit at a modest fee is needed

from Natural Resources. This office is located on SR-85 at the Jackson Guard in Niceville south of I-10. A map of Eglin is exceptionally helpful for finding one's way.

POSSIBLE TRIPS AND LANDINGS

It is at times possible to paddle above CR-1087 depending on water level. A number of small creeks and streams flow into the Shoal. However, many of these are problematical since they are mostly accessed from private land and often too shallow.

1. From CR-1087 to SR-393, 10 miles. From US-90 west of DeFuniak Springs, turn north on CR-1087 and go to the bridge. This is a rugged, "unofficial" put-in, without any good space to leave a car. It is best to scout it beforehand, but the best put-in appeared to be on the southeast bank. Locals said there was access to the river from a dirt road to the west about 200 feet south of the bridge. However, at that time a 4-wheel vehicle was necessary to travel the road, and lacking one, this was not verified.

2. From SR-393 to US-90, 8 miles. From I-10, exit north on SR-85 in Crestview. Turn east on US-90, and go north at the junction with SR-393. Proceed to the Shoal River.

3. From US-90 to SR-85, 10 miles. From I-10, exit on SR-85 north in Crestview. Turn east on US-90 and proceed to the

Above: A scenic portion of the Wacissa River.

Shoal River. This landing is on the northeast side of the road at a picnic area.

4. From SR-85 to Gin Hole Landing, 8 miles. From I-10, exit on SR-85 south in Crestview and proceed to the bridge at the Shoal River.

5. Gin Hole Landing. From I-10 at Crestview, go south on SR-85 and cross the Shoal River. Turn west on RR-211 (Rattlesnake Bluff Road). Go 4 to 5 miles. A prominent sign announces the turn north to the landing.

CAMPING

Sandbars provide camping. There is an excellent, large sandbar at the SR-393 landing. Camping on Eglin is also possible; check in advance with Natural Resources. Camping is permitted anywhere on water management district lands.

SOPCHOPPY RIVER
(Wakulla County)

The Sopchoppy begins in swamp, meanders by limestone banks, and flows through 6 miles of Bradwell Bay Wilderness in Apalachicola National Forest. It is a beautiful river with a 15-mile state-designated canoe trail.

The Sopchoppy forms a portion of the eastern border of Bradwell Bay. It is a very wild place, with tangles in the forest off the river, and black bears. Bradwell Bay is not a bay as might think of a bay; rather it is a wet, swampy area where bay trees grow. For solitude and wildness, it is one of Florida's special places.

Being able to paddle the upper Sopchoppy portion is dependent on rainfall. During periods of drought, canoeing is questionable. There is a water gauge at Oakbridge Bridge on FR-346. If the gauge does not read at least 10 feet, the river is impassable.

A tributary of the Sopchoppy, Buckhorn

Shoal River

N

○ Landing

— Road

- - - State-designated Trail

New Harmony

Crestview

Defuniak Springs

Eglin Air Force Reservation

85

188

393

3

90

8

10

4

285

5

1087

1

2

Creek, flows into the river from the north in St. Marks National Wildlife Refuge. It is possible to paddle up Buckhorn Creek. The creek does have one remote landing. The combined waters flow into the Ochlockonee River.

A forest map is available from Apalachicola National Forest and is exceptionally handy for finding forest road landings.

POSSIBLE TRIPS AND LANDINGS.

These directions will become much clearer with the aid of the national forest map.

1. From FH-13 to FR-329, 10 miles. From Tallahassee, take US-319 south to Crawfordville and go west on Arran Road (SR-368). SR-368 becomes FH-13. Continue on FH-13 to the bridge.
2. From FR-329 to FR-346, 5 miles. From Sopchoppy go northwest on CR/SR-375, and turn east on FR-329. Proceed to the river.
3. From FR-346 to FR-365/Mount Beeser Church Bridge, 5 miles. From Sopchoppy, go northwest on CR/SR-375. Go 2.5 miles past the Sopchoppy River. Turn north (right) onto a small, graded road. Go to the bridge.
4. From FR-365/Mount Beeser Church Bridge to Myron B. Hodge City Park, 7 miles. From Sopchoppy go northwest on SR-375 to the junction with FR-343, then go north on FR-343 about 1 mile. Turn east (right) onto a small, graded road and proceed about .25 miles to the bridge.
5. From Myron B. Hodge City Park to Ochlockonee River State Park, 5.5 miles. From Sopchoppy, go south on US-319. Just outside town look for the post office. Immediately south of the post office is a sign indicating the park. Turn west and go to the "T," then turn south. The park is on the left.
6. From Ochlockonee River State Park. The park is south of Sopchoppy on US-319. There are meandering backwaters leading from the state park onto several rivers, including its namesake.

CAMPING

Ochlockonee River State Park is a first-class operation with canoe rentals and camping options. Apalachicola National Forest has many camping options. Myron B. Hodge City Park has restrooms, picnic areas, and allows camping.

Above: Sopchoppy River.

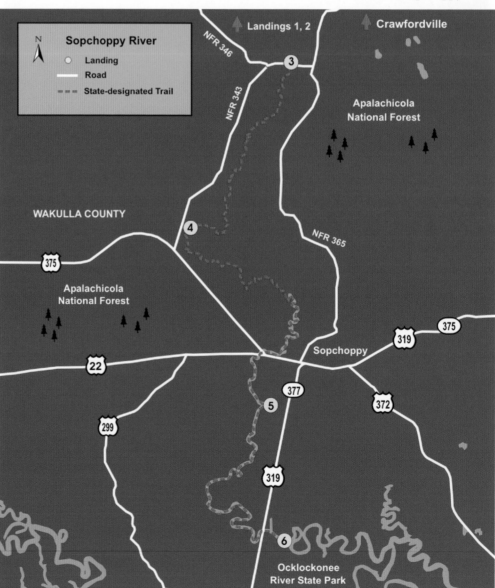

ST. GEORGE SOUND
(Franklin County)

While the beach at St. George Island is frequently voted among the best beaches in Florida (in fact in the United States), the scenery around the islands in the sound is equally gorgeous. The sound includes two large island kayaking destinations: St. George Island and (farther east) Dog Island. St. George Island has been cut for navigational purposes, creating Little St. George Island at the west end. Many along the coast believe that this cut allows sands from the Apalachicola River to wash to sea

and has caused erosion of natural beaches along the coast. Around Little St. George, the tides are also reported by local paddlers to be dangerous.

The distance from one end of these islands to the other exceeds 20 miles. Thus the kayaking explorer may wish to take them on one at a time. The islands have gorgeous dunes, coastal scrub, and estuaries. Charts are a must in this area and always a prudent safety measure when sea kayaking. Local marinas, including two in Apalachicola, are sources of information and charts.

There is a landing at Carrabelle Beach

Above: Spectacular dunes at St. George Island State Park are only one reason to visit. The beach is among the finest in Florida and coastal beach scrub flowers bloom in season, particularly along the east end.

on US-98 southwest of Carrabelle. Just east across Apalachicola Bay from "Apalach" are landings at Eastpoint, and it is possible to launch from two landings in St. George Island State Park.

Camping is available on St. George Island in that state park. Park officials requested that it be mentioned that Cape St. George Lighthouse is not on St. George Island but on Little St. George Island.

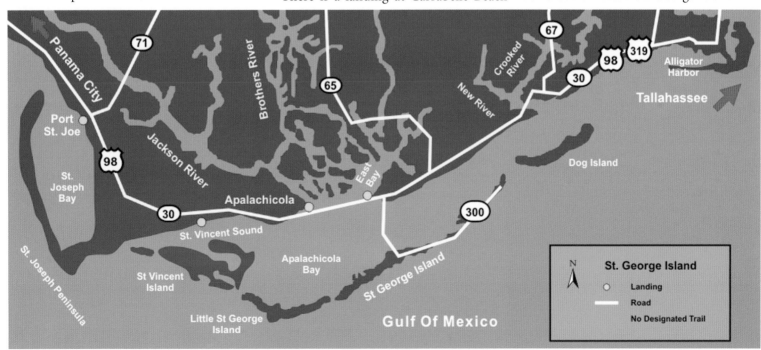

ST. JOSEPH BAY
(Gulf County)

The Nature Conservancy declared portions of this area an Endangered Biosphere for the large number of endemic species and the threat of development. Long term efforts have been underway by The Nature Conservancy and St. Vincent National Wildlife Refuge, which someday will hopefully result in preservation purchases. There have also been efforts to acquire land in the St. Josephs Buffers by the State of Florida.

Kayaking has grown into a popular activity in the area because of the protected and often very shallow bay. The bay is encircled by St. Joseph Peninsula, a former barrier island connected to the mainland by a bayhead, and by the mainland itself. North of Port St. Joe is the opening to the Gulf, while around the bay lie saltmarsh and small islands, with pines, wax myrtle, yaupon holley, and palms.

Paddling here is a delight. Hermit crabs, blue crabs, and horseshoe crabs abound. The bay is rich in fish, and it is easy to see stingrays. Alligators lie in grass clumps on the islands, which are rich in snakes, including rattlesnakes and Florida cottonmouths.

There is a landing on the mainland along SR-30A. SR-30E from the junction with SR-30A leads onto the Peninsula ending at St. Joseph Peninsula State Park, where putting-in is easy. From Apalachicola go west on US-98 and turn south on SR-30A, then go north on SR-30E. (There are many who consider SR-30A as CR-30A, but the according to park officials, the state took over this road because it is an evacuation route in case of hurricanes.) There is also a landing on Cape San Blas Road (SR-30E), which might be an easier put-in, but is a little hard to find. Ask the local outfitters or the state park for directions.

Navigational charts are available from two marinas in Apalachicola and one marina in Port St. Joe. There are generally higher tides in the summer and fall than in the winter or spring because of some unusual characteristics of the bay. Also, north winds can sometimes drive water from the bay.

CAMPING

St. Joseph Peninsula State Park has a variety of camping options. The beach at the park was selected in 2002 by the Laboratory for Coastal Research as the best beach in all 50 states.

St. George Island State Park is perhaps 20 miles to the east and also has an incredible beach.

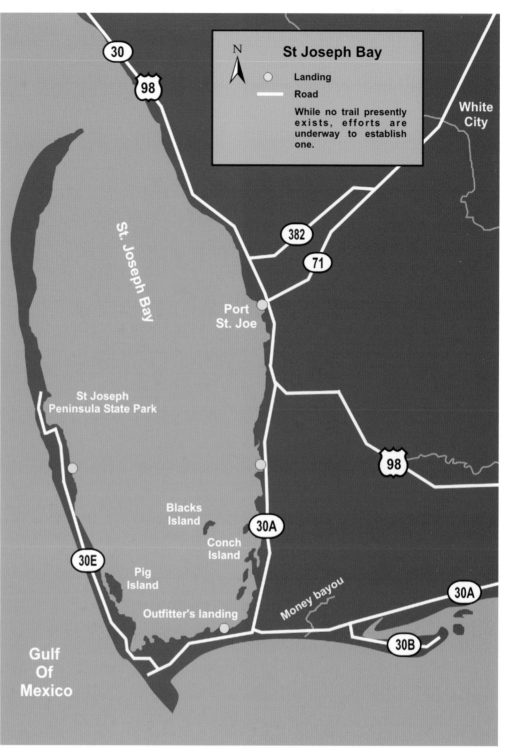

TIDES

St. Joseph Bay has some very unusual tidal fluctuations. In winter, in fact, there are many days, even up to a month or so, when there is not enough water for near shore paddling. North winds sometimes blow the water out of the bay. Some days St. Joseph Bay has one tide, other days two. Farther south two, three, or four tides are routine. There is further variation between low-low tide and high-high tide, although not often in St. Joseph Bay (shortened locally to St. Joe Bay) where sometimes the change in tides cannot even be noticed. Checking on tides is easy for internet users who can go to: www.saltwatertides.com. For weather: www.weather.com.

ST. MARKS RIVER
(Leon and Wakulla counties)

Although the 35-mile long St. Marks flows in from Georgia, its upper reaches are usually too shallow for paddling. Paddles take place above and below Natural Bridge. Its source is spring-fed wetlands west of Lake Miccosukee.

The St. Marks River flows from Horn Spring only to disappear underground at Natural Bridge. It re-emerges at St. Marks Springs, then flows to meet the Gulf near the town of St. Marks. The section beginning with St. Marks Springs has a decidedly tidal influence, with water backing up at high tide and dropping sharply as the tide goes out. The portion closer to the Gulf is brackish.

The river character is also different north

Above: The St. Marks River.

and south of US-98. Much of the river above the Newport Bridge on US-98 remains in natural condition, but there are some homes. South of the Newport Bridge there is much more human activity.

From Natural Bridge, it is necessary to paddle up to Horn Spring (which should be *springs,* since there are two, but isn't). From US-98, it is necessary to paddle upstream again to St. Marks Springs. The trip from Natural Bridge is a piece of cake, but going against the current while the tide is falling can be work from Newport Bridge on US-98. But rewarding work. It is beautiful.

Alligator snapping turtles can be seen at times. Sometimes manatees are seen also. The natural banks have many gorgeous trees, including tupelo.

POSSIBLE TRIPS AND LANDINGS

1. From Natural Bridge and back, 5 miles. From Tallahassee, travel south on SR-363 and turn east on Natural Bridge Road to Natural Bridge. Turn north on an unmarked dirt road and proceed about 2 miles.
2. From Newport Bridge and back, 12 miles. Newport Bridge is located on US-98 at Newport. There is a paved boat launch on the northeast bank.
3. From Newport Bridge to St. Marks, 5 miles. St. Marks Marina is in the sleepy

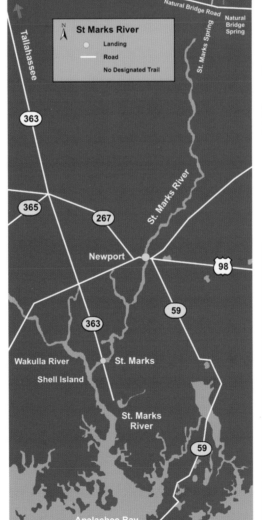

town of St. Marks to the south of US-98.

CAMPING

Nearby camping opportunities include Apalachicola National Forest and Econfina River State Park. There is also the lodge Wakulla Springs State Park.

TWO WALKED OUT

In 1766, the ship Tiger *struck a ledge at Cape St. George. Shipwrecked travelers from the ship* Tiger *were stranded for 81 days. Originally assisted by Native Americans, the Indians abandoned the small party on an island in the area. The marooned castaways dwindled to three: two men and a woman. They built a raft, made it to the mainland, where one of the men was killed and eaten by his companions. A forest fire later provided the two cannibals with cooked animals in place of human flesh. Those who are hungry now-a-days can just go to the convenience store.*

PC

ST. VINCENT SOUND
(Franklin County)

St. Vincent is a large barrier island and national wildlife refuge west of Apalachicola. Bay-side it has extensive saltmarsh and alligators. These bayous are rich estuaries, teeming with fish. Along the Gulf are extensive dunes and maritime forest where large congregations of wading birds and pelicans are seen.

Kayaking or boating are the only ways to access St. Vincent, a truly wild place. In fact, red wolves have been introduced to St. Vincent as part of a breeding program to produce pups for rehabilitation into the wild. The Sambar deer, a large elk, was brought to the island when St. Vincent was a private hunting preserve. The sambar remain and are frequently seen around at least one freshwater lake on the island. There are many snakes on the island, with pygmy rattlesnakes often seen along old lumbering roads. Feral hogs are prolific also.

From Apalachicola, go west on US-98 and make the south turn onto CR/SR-30A. Proceed to Indian Pass, where there is a landing next to an outfitter. While it is a relatively short trip across the pass, it can be difficult and dangerous depending on weather conditions. Charts are available from outfitters or one of the marinas in Apalachicola. Permission need not be

Above: Leaning palms line the Gulf side of St. Vincent Island.

obtained from the refuge for daytime visitors. There is no overnight camping on the island, in fact to do so is a felony. It is also a felony to take Native American artifacts which are found on the bay-side. Both restrictions are vigorously enforced.

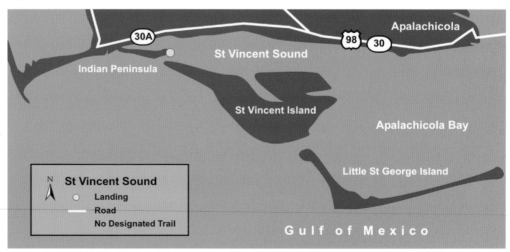

SWEETWATER CREEK
(Santa Rosa County)

Sweetwater is basically a struggle to reach Juniper Creek, a tributary of the Blackwater River. This effort has its rewards on gorgeous, scenic Juniper.

Various storms have felled many trees in Sweetwater. Only the dedicated efforts of paddling clubs have made the way passable. Storms may reverse the clearing of the river in the future, and it is best to check in advance with a local outfitter. Check about water level too, as the water can become too shallow to traverse. There is also the possibility that Blackwater River State Forest may not allow additional clearing of the northernmost stretch.

This little creek is for those who like to be "technical."

This means they can show-off their skills in maneuvering about obstacles, or their strength and balance climbing over them. In fact, there is one log with a notch cut out of it that you presently pass through rather than around or over. One canoe club member referred to this journey as not "technical" at all, but rather more "Rambo."

Sweetwater Creek joins Juniper Creek, which then makes a sharp south turn. The first take-out is on Juniper Creek at the Red Rock Bridge, just before the spectacular Red Rock Bluffs. It would be a shame to stop there, rather proceed on Juniper.

For directions and map, see Juniper Creek account, this section.

Right: Canoeing around obstacles on Sweetwater Creek.

PC

TUPELO

Tupelo trees (water tupelo) grow along rivers, around lakes, and in floodplains and swamps. In Florida, the tree is found primarily in the Panhandle, from Leon and Wakulla counties extending west. Another tupelo (ogeechee) is found in similar habitats from Hamilton to Walton counties. It is often difficult to tell the two trees apart until they bear fruit; then water tupelo sports a blue or purple drupe while ogeechee tupelo's drupe is red. The trunk of tupelo often seems similar to cypress in its complexities and width, but cypress has needles while tupelo has leaves. Florida's famous tupelo honey is produced from the ogeechee flowers in the spring. Ogeechee is often called ogeechee lime. That is because settlers used it like lemon in their drinks and to season their food.

PADDLES

Kayak paddles are quite different from canoe paddles. Not only do kayak paddles have a cupped paddle to capture the water, they also have an up and down side.

Although paddlers are often seen with arms at their side, paddling rapidly, the most effective way to grip a kayak paddle is with hands extended, spread slightly wider than your chest.

Kayak paddles are adjustable, and can be "feathered," which means adjusting the blade so that on the upstroke it does not catch the wind. This is more important to paddlers at sea, where wind is a significant factor.

Some kayak paddles are made of special materials. A carbon fabric paddle weighs next to nothing and cuts down on exertion.

Most kayak paddles lengths are adjustable.

Canoe paddles should feel comfortable in length. Wooden canoe paddles are preferred by some, but are much heavier than aluminum paddles. Thus, wooden paddles may wear some people down on long trips. Wooden paddles may also wear on the hands.

Having an extra paddle is an excellent precaution. If a person is paddling alone and loses a paddle, he may be stranded without a spare. Even when two people are paddling one boat, it is best ot keep at least one spare on hand in case a paddle is lost. It is not unusual to lose a paddle when striking an object, or when the paddler is distracted while having a drink of water, or while putting a paddle down to open a cooler or reach for a camera.

TITI CREEK CANOE TRAIL
(Okaloosa County)

This Eglin Air Force Base trail wanders 6.2 miles from RR-220 through beautiful county on Eglin Air Force Base to join the Shoal River. The take-out is at the SR-85 Bridge. This is a favorite paddle for local paddlers and a wonderful spot for those who love pure nature.

Use of Eglin Air Force Base requires an annual permit at a modest fee. This can be obtained from Natural Resources at Jackson Guard in Niceville on SR-85. A map of the reservation can be obtained there. Eglin offers camping options.

TURKEY CREEK CANOE TRAIL
(Okaloosa County)

This trail is given at 3.7 miles in Eglin Air Force Base literature, but when tracked by GPS was 5.5 miles. It is a trail leading from RR-232 to Niceville, ending at the Valparaiso/Niceville Chamber of Commerce. Just prior to the confluence with Juniper Creek is an area usually requiring a 150 foot portage due to shallow water. According to local paddlers, this trail rivals Titi and Boiling creeks which are fantastic paddles, so the scenery is very gorgeous and worth the extra 50 yards of canoe carrying at the end of the trip. The last 1.5 miles is bordered by private land.

Local paddlers do a section upstream from this trail. They take RR-232 to SR-233 (north) to the bridge across Turkey Creek. The put-in is called "The Hippie Hole," an intriguing name whose history we would like to know. Paddlers can take-out on RR-626 at two big culverts, or continue into Niceville near the Chamber of Commerce.

Use of Eglin Air Force Base requires an annual pass at a modest fee. This can be obtained from Natural Resources at Jackson Guard in Niceville on the east side of SR-85. A map is available there to help you navigate Eglin. Camping options exist on Eglin.

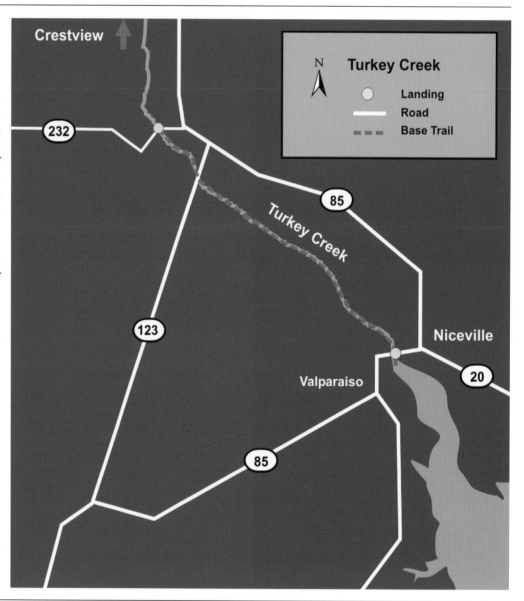

NAMING OF THE CREEK

The creeks of Eglin Air Force Base are aptly named. Boiling Creek has small boils, or mini-springs, which can be seen in branches off the creek. Titi Creek has titi trees or shrubs along its banks. Turkeys are sometimes seen along Turkey Creek, and Rocky Creek does have some rocks.

The members of local paddling clubs find all these steams places of great beauty, isolation, and wonderful paddling. It is likely that descriptions of these trails have never appeared in print before.

A great debt of gratitude is owed to Eglin Air Force Base for the maintaining the pristine quality of these streams and for allowing access to paddlers.

Eglin personnel provided the author with a very old and out-of-print map showing the canoe trails on the base. Those trails have been enhanced by graphic artists and are presented here as a service to anyone wishing to paddle Eglin's wonderful and overwhelmingly natural trails.

Above: Canoeing up a spring run of the Wacissa River.

WACISSA RIVER
(Jefferson County)

This 14-mile, state-designated canoe trail begins at Wacissa Springs in the town of Wacissa and goes through Aucilla Wildlife Management Area. The upper 2 miles of the river, near the town of Wacissa, has a dozen springs (Aucilla, Big, Big Blue, Cassidy, Hot, and Little Blue are some of the springs). The Wacissa is connected to the Aucilla by a cut called the Slave Canal.

Hell's Half Acre is a confusing area above Goose Pasture and below Welaunee Creek. The main path of the river lies to the left, and not in the several streams going to the right. Too far left, there are a few misleading streams, but they are against the flow.

The Aucilla and Wacissa provide some of the most glorious remote scenery in Florida. Paddlers often discussed the two in the same breath. Until they are joined by the cut, they come so close together below Goose Pasture that sounds from one river are sometimes heard on the other.

Several dirt roads lead to the Wacissa through Aucilla Wildlife Management Area. These roads might be used in an emergency. Goose Pasture includes a campground and is easily reached.

When the Wacissa ends, even experienced paddlers and guides sometimes have trouble finding the cut to the Aucilla River called The Slave Canal. The cut lies through a few feet of seemingly impenetrable wild rice. At present, there is a tree with white blazes at the entrance, but this may not be true after enough future

Above: A tricolor heron fishing along the Wacissa River.

storms.

POSSIBLE TRIPS AND LANDINGS

1. From Wacissa to Goose Pasture, 9 miles. The small town of Wacissa is southeast

Above: A view of the Slave Canal which connects the Wacissa and Aucilla rivers. The stone at the bottom of the photo has an inscription.

PC

of Tallahassee and best reached from US-27. From US-27, turn south on SR-59 and proceed to the river.

2. From Goose Pasture to US-98, 5 miles. Fourteen miles east of Newport, turn north on Powell Hammock Road (often modified by the locals to Pal Hammock) and follow it to Goose Pasture Road, which leads to the campground.

3. US-98. The US-98 landing is announced by a prominent launch sign on US-98.

CAMPING

Camping in Aucilla Wildlife Management Area is controlled by the Florida Fish and Wildlife Conservation Commission. Camping at Goose Pasture is controlled by the Suwannee River Water Management District.

Map, Wacissa River Canoe Trail, Office of Greenways and Trails.

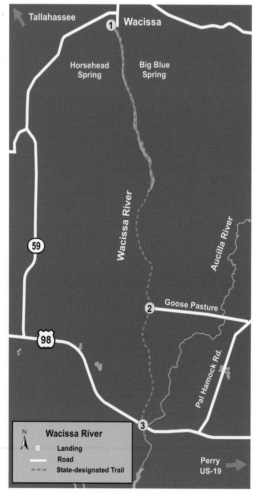

Tallahassee · Wacissa

1

Horsehead Spring · Big Blue Spring

Wacissa River

Aucilla River

59

2 Goose Pasture

98

Pal Hammock Rd.

3

Wacissa River

N

○ Landing

— Road

⋯ State-designated Trail

Perry US-19

WAKULLA RIVER
(Wakulla County)

This river flows from what is one of the mightiest springs in the world. The average outflow from Wakulla Spring might be 500 million gallons a day. Some days a billion gallons have been recorded. Enormous underwater caverns lie below the spring mouth and twist away for miles.

The stretch from US-98 to the Marina at St. Marks is a 2-mile journey but is more like being at sea or in a bay. Porpoise may leap up to join you, and powerboats may rip by where not restricted by manatee zones.

From the bridge at US-98, the 4-mile state-designated canoe trail does not lead into Wakulla Springs, since the way is blocked by a fence dating to the times of St. Joe Paper Company's Ed Ball and intended to keep the proletariat out of his sanctuary. Thus, it is also 4 miles back, the easier part of the journey, if you use a canoe from the local outfitter. If you take your own canoe, it is possible to avoid paddling against the mighty flow by putting-in at SR-365.

The water flow is great, and mother nature can turn on the spigot. If the tide is going out in the lower part of the river,

Above: A manatee mother with her calf in the Wakulla River.

falling water level can combine to make for a paddle which builds muscles. It is often rewarded by gently sighing manatees rising to the surface to breath. Timing the paddle with the incoming tide will make it much easier.

POSSIBLE TRIPS AND LANDINGS

1. From SR-365 to US-98 Bridge, 4 miles. The SR-365 bridge is 2 miles southwest of Wakulla, or 10 miles northeast of Crawfordville.
2. From US-98 Bridge to St. Marks, 2 miles. The local outfitter is located beside the launch on US-98 to the west of St. Marks. (Current materials from Greenways and Trails incorrectly state this is US-93.)
3. St. Marks Marina. It is in St. Marks at the end of SR-363, a south turn from US-98.

LODGING

Stays at Wakulla Springs State Park can include sleeping in the former lodge of powerful Florida businessman Ed Ball. The state park offers much to the public, including a dining room and a glass-bottom boat tour of the springs.

Map. Wakulla River Canoe Trail, Office of Greenways and Trails.

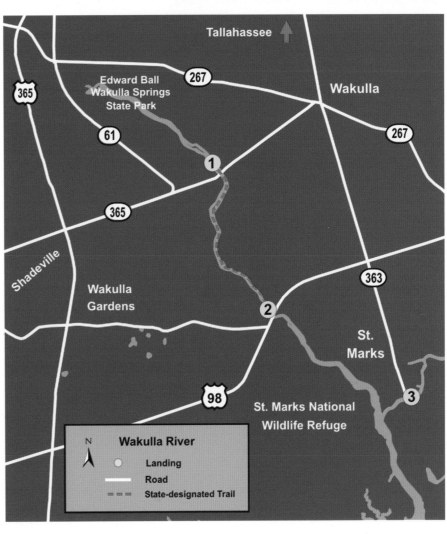

WEAVER CREEK
(Santa Rosa County)

Weaver Creek is located on Eglin Air Force Base. It runs northwest into the Yellow River Delta. It is a very short but scenic trip, a favorite of local canoe clubs. Camping is an option on Eglin Air Force Base.

Use of Eglin requires an annual permit at a modest fee. The permit can be obtained from Natural Resources at Jackson Guard on the east side of SR-85 in Niceville. A map is available and is essential for finding one's way about Eglin.

This creek's put-in and take-outs would be best approach with a 4-wheel drive vehicle.

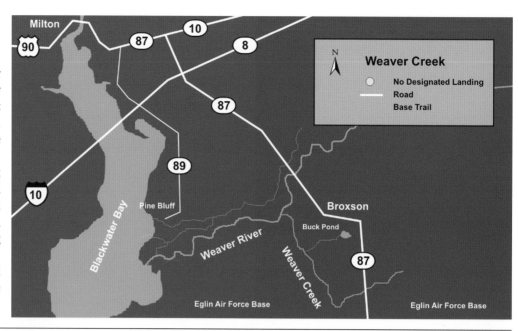

YELLOW RIVER
(Okaloosa and Santa Rosa counties)

This blackwater river flows south from Conecuh National Forest in Alabama and reaches 56 miles into Florida. Portions of the river border Eglin Air Force Base. The Yellow meets the Shoal River on Eglin, then turns sharply west. Paddling would be easy except the lower river is wide and thus subject to wind.

Within Eglin, a number of largely wild streams rush to meet the Yellow, such as Boiling Creek. Some of these streams are mentioned separately in this section. Bear are sometimes seen around the landings of the smaller streams; other wildlife is prolific.

The largest tributary of the Yellow is the Shoal River. The confluence is near Gin Hole Landing on Eglin. The Shoal is a shallower, sandy river, wide enough in the lower sections to feel the wind, while the Yellow is much broader.

Sections of the Yellow are at times filled with sturgeon that roll on the surface. The endangered fish were being trapped and identified by wildlife researchers at the time it was paddled. One sturgeon, said to weigh 142 pounds, executed a startling leap into the air as it woke from sedation.

A proposed dam north of I-10 would interfere with the sturgeon's spawning. This dam would be for drinking water retention. In addition to endangered sturgeon, the river also hosts rare freshwater mussels that could be threatened. The Nature Conservancy warns that the dam could also have a negative effect on Alabama map turtles, Florida bog frogs, and the black bear population.

Dams in general create backwaters, silt rivers, change hydrology above and below ground, and in general play havoc with the natural river system. It will be a tragedy if the dam is built, not just for sturgeon and

Above: The Yellow River.

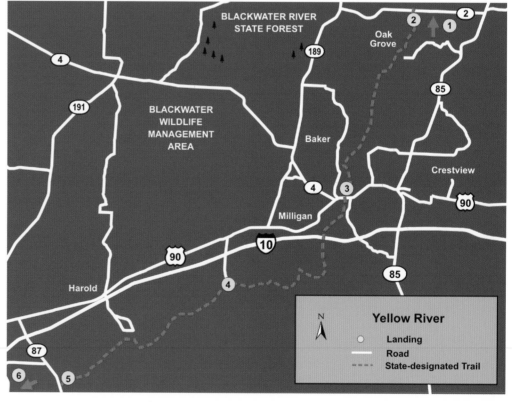

other wildlife, but for humans, as this beautiful river, forever altered, would further deplete wilderness. Unfortunately, conservation and alternative sources of drinking water have traditionally taken a backseat to intrusive and destructive dams.

As the Yellow approaches the Gulf, it forms a large delta, mostly saltmarsh, where the way could be easily lost. Thus, the paddling usually stops before the delta or Blackwater Bay is reached.

POSSIBLE TRIPS AND LANDINGS

1. From Alabama SR-4 to Florida SR-2, 10 miles. From I-10, exit north on SR-85 and continue through Crestview. In the small community of Laurel Hill, turn west on 3d Street (labeled on some maps as Old Ebenezer Road). Turn northwest on Murray Road which emerges at the landing on SR-4.
2. From SR-2 to US-90, 17 miles. From I-10, exit north on SR-85 and continue through Crestview. Go west on SR-2 to the bridge.
3. From US-90 to Gin Hole Landing, 10 miles. US-90 crosses the Yellow River a few miles west of Crestview.
4. From Gin Hole Landing to SR-87, 29 miles. From I-10, exit south on SR-85 at Crestview. Cross the Shoal River. Turn west on Rattlesnake Bluff Road (RR-211). A sign announces the turn north to Gin Hole Landing.
5. From SR-87 to Guest Lake Park, 3 miles The landing is on the southeast corner of the bridge on SR-87 about 4 miles south of I-10.
6. Guest Lake Park. From I-10, exit south on SR-89 just to the east of Milton. The park is located south at the absolute end of SR-89. It is possible to continue on into Blackwater Bay, but the bay is at least a mile wide.

CAMPING

During normal to low waters, some sandbars exist on the northern sections. Eglin provides exceptional camping opportunities, and Guest Lake Park is a Northwest Water Management District Land with room to camp and picnic tables. Most of the land along the Yellow belongs to the Northwest Florida Water Management District. It also owns the land across from Eglin. These areas are open to camping.

Map, Yellow River Canoe Trail, Office of Greenways and Trails. The 56-mile, state designated trail begins at SR-2 and ends at SR-87. The Northwest Water Management District also has a map of the Yellow River Basin.

Above: Paddling the Yellow River.

DEADHEAD LOGGING

Submerged longleaf pine and cypress logs more than a century old have been pulled from many northern Florida river bottoms. The logs were once floating down river to a sawmill. Lost logs, referred to as "deadheads," were then considered too much trouble to bother with, but now bring top dollar. The taking of "deadheads" has created a minor industry and opposition.

After so much time, the logs have become part of the natural environment, like fallen trees. Cypress and longleaf do not deteriorate while submerged. Yanking them out, particularly if there are a lot of them, is destructive to the river and the living things that depend upon it.

Some deadhead harvesters illegally cut paths to the river to make removal easier. Deadhead harvesters argue they are merely clearing the waterways while providing a product in great demand.

MERMAIDS IN THE WAKULLA

While most spring runs attract manatees in the colder months, manatees are apparently in the Wakulla River in all seasons. If you stop paddling, and sit among them, you can hear them softly breaking the surface, and gently taking a breath before re-submerging.

Ancient mariners are said to have confused manatees with mermaids. While this might appear a far reach, even for love-starved sailors long at sea, these large marine mammals demonstrate grace and agility in the water.

Even the fastest, most-skilled kayaker, trying to pursue a manatee mother with a calf, will be unable to keep up, or make the same maneuvers.

PC

ALAPAHA RIVER
(Hamilton County)

This is potentially the most dangerous river in Florida. It is certainly one of the most intriguing. It varies from dry to placid to violent. One cannot just set a date and go paddle it, especially in its entirety. Rather, consult with the local outfitters.

Mysterious and capable of dramatic change, the Alapaha is furious at flood stage. It blasts into Florida from Georgia and rushes to the Suwannee River. Flood stage usually occurs in spring, but flooding also occurs with hurricanes. During such times, even experienced guides have been known to "crash and burn" a canoe into tree canopy. Riding the river then must be a little like being on the front of a speeding locomotive.

While almost all rivers can be dangerous during exceptionally high water, the Alapaha has two remarkably dangerous spots at times of low or medium water levels. At such times, the Alapaha no longer even reaches the Suwannee directly. Instead, it disappears into underground sinks. These pathways through limestone take the water away from the river, so that south of Jennings Bluff the river bottom becomes a sandy path on which four-wheel jeeps drive.

These sinks have various names depending on who you talk to. The more northern sink area lies to the south of Jennings on the east bank and has been called The Suck Hole and Devil's Den, among other colorful names. It draws water continuously.

The southern sink is 0.5 miles north of Jennings Bluff. This sink is called The Siphon or Dead River. At the proper water levels, half the river appears to be sucked off into a channel on the west bank. The water in the channel is immediately whitewater in nature. The channel twists and turns through limestone banks, over limestone boulders, for perhaps a quarter mile. Then, *whoosh,* it is sucked underground. This is a startling sight when water levels allow it to be witnessed. Someone careless enough to put themselves in front of this when the water level is just right *might be sucked underground and underwater!*

Paddling into The Siphon would be foolhardy anyway because of the violence of the rapids and large fallen logs in the path. It is possible to put-out on the west bank of the channel, climb up the cliff, and walk along the edges of the fury.

Where these sinks go is something of a mystery. Many say they reappear at the Alapaha Rise and Holton Creek. Others say no one knows. Are they dangerous? You bet. Do not approach them; pass them by. No long monstrous arm will reach out, but exceptionally careless adventurers could be in danger unless the water is high. If the water level is high, the river is dangerous too for its violence, and the siphons may not even be noticed.

Stunning in its wild beauty, the Alapaha has it source in Georgia. Springs flow in

Top: A calm section of the Alapaha.

Opposite page, top: Large rocks along the banks of the Alapaha River, Jennings Bluff Tract.

Opposite page, bottom: The rushing waters of the Alapaha along the approach to The Siphon.

from its walls, and limestone shoals complement the rocky banks. Swallow-tail kites can be seen circling, plunging, and skimming at times. Green anoles, skinks, black racers, water snakes, and deer are also abundant.

When the river is down, Jennings Bluff has a 40 foot overlook which can be descended cautiously with not much effort. Climbing up Jennings Bluff, however, is another matter.

The river flows south from Lakeland, Georgia. In the Peach State, the river is crossed by a number of roads. According to local guides, it is possible to put in at any of these roads, although there are no official launches.

POSSIBLE TRIPS AND LANDINGS

1. From Georgia SR-94 to CR-150, 11 miles. This is not an official landing. From Jasper, Florida, take US-129 north, turn west on Georgia SR-94, and proceed to the river.
2. From CR-150 to Jennings Bluff Conservation Area, 4.5 miles. From I-75, take CR-143 east to Jennings. After passing through the Jennings stoplight, make a right on poorly marked CR-150. The road is heading east, although at first it appears to be going south. The entrance is on the northeast side of the bridge, but be careful. Two very steep exits have been cut by adventuresome four-wheelers and should not be attempted by sane people.
3. From Jennings Bluff Conservation Area to US-41 Bridge, 5 miles. Take the Jasper exit of I-75 and proceed east through Jasper on US-41. Several miles beyond Jasper take Jennings Bluff Road (NW 25 Lane) east to the water management property. Turn onto the water management land at the gate and follow the road to the landing. The embankment is steep but short.
4. From the US-41 Bridge to Suwannee Take-Out, 11 miles. Although US-41 is a north-south road, it essentially goes west from Jasper. As it does, it crosses the Alapaha. The put-in is on the apparent southwest side of the road. This section will look like miles of sand when the water level is drawn-off by the siphons.
5. Suwannee Take-Out. The first take-out on the Suwannee is a few hundred yards on the Suwannee to a county park near CR-249, a north road from Live Oak, a town easily accessed from I-75 and I-10. The Alapaha Rise is beyond this a few hundred yards.

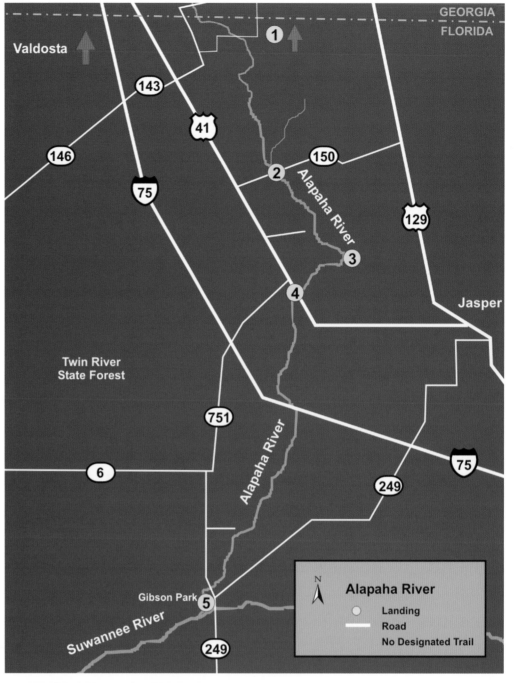

SAFETY TIPS

A river like the Alapaha causes one to think of safety tips for paddlers. In addition to a personal flotation device (called a PFD), an extra paddle is always a good idea, in case one is lost or broken. Even on day trips, it might be wise to carry a flashlight in case something goes wrong. Whistles are routinely handed out by some outfitters. Also, when two to a craft, only one person should stand at a time, whether trading places, embarking, or departing. On long trips and overnights, adequate gear should be taken, including medicine. Sun block, insect repellent, Benadryl spray (or the equivalent), and plentiful water should always be on hand, as well as that emergency roll of toilet paper, for which (at awkward moments) some paddlers will kill.

CAMPING

At low water levels, you can almost camp in the river. At high water levels, you may be up in the trees. Check with Suwannee River Water Management District prior to using any lands within their boundaries.

Above: The dry bed of the Alapaha River at the US-41 Bridge north of Jaspar.

Right: The rushing waters of the Alapaha River flowing into the The Siphon.

MICHAEL WARREN/SI

ALEXANDER CREEK
(Lake County)

Alexander Springs is one of Florida's 27 first-magnitude springs. In terms of average discharge, it is one of the smallest, but in terms of beauty, it is off the scale.

This trail begins at Alexander Springs Recreation Area and passes through Alexander Springs Wilderness. It is glorious and wild along the way, a great scenic trip. Large alligators, peninsula cooters, redbelly turtles, various herons and egrets, and deer are all likely to be seen. The river is fairly wide, requiring sun block for about 5 of its 7 miles, then it narrows considerably.

Fair numbers of limpkins are seen. They blend into the adjoining banks, their brown and black markings providing camouflage. Among other things, limpkins eat apple snails, plentiful in the creek. Like the Everglade (or snail) kite, limpkins have down-curved bills suited for snails. Limpkins are almost unique to Florida, rarely found outside the Sunshine State.

The concession at Alexander Springs has canoe rentals for a 7-mile journey. The take-out point for the concession ends on fenced-in, leased, private property, so it is not possible to take your own boat out there.

If you take your own craft, the take-out point is different, but you can put-in at Alexander Springs. The take-outs have changed in the past, because of insufficient space for all users, and it is best to consult with the concession.

The creek runs for 7 miles beyond the take-outs to reach the St. Johns. This is described as difficult by forest service literature, and no one keeps the way cleared.

Visiting any national forest is aided by having a forest map. This can be obtained in advance or at any of the visitor centers.

Above: Paddling Alexander Springs Run.

This national forest has many camping opportunities.

Ocala National Forest lies between I-75 and I-95. SR-40 cuts through the forest from both interstates. From SR-40 in Astor Park, turn south on SR-445 and continue 4 miles to the prominently announced entrance to Alexander Springs Recreation Area.

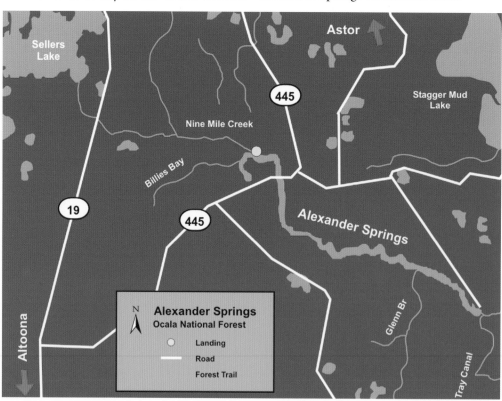

PADDLING IN THE OCALA NATIONAL FOREST

Paddling trails within or passing by Ocala National Forest include Alexander Creek, Juniper Creek, Salt Springs Run, and the Ocklawaha and Silver rivers. The first three provide canoe rentals from recreation areas, while the Ocklawaha and Silver rivers have excellent outfitters.

All are influenced by powerful springs. Alexander pours into Florida's longest river, the St. Johns, and Juniper Creek and Salt Springs run into Lake George, Florida's second largest lake and part of the St. Johns. The Ocklawaha River is fed by the Silver River.

The recreation areas have entrance fees, but annual permits are available.

AMELIA RIVER
(Nassau County)

The Ameila River is largely surrounded by saltmarsh on the land side of Fernandina Beach. On the north end of Amelia Island, the put-in is at Fort Clinch State Park. On the south end, it is possible to put-in from Amelia Island State Park. Traveling about this large barrier island is generally a kayaking adventure. There are many miles to explore, including the mouth of the St. Marys River. Some kayakers also cross Cumberland Sound to Cumberland Island, Georgia. Cumberland Sound, however, is deep water and used for shipping.

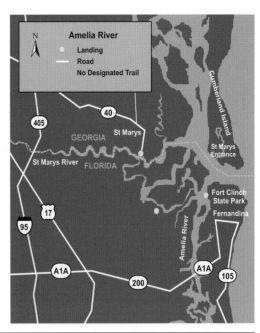

PADDLING WITH ALLIGATORS

William Bartram, the famous naturalist, wrote this account of an alligator attack on the St. Johns in 1832. "I was attacked on all sides. I expected every moment to be dragged out of the boat and instantly devoured."

There is no reason to believe in a coordinated alligator attack, so many believe Bartram's account fanciful. Still alligators should inspire caution.

Alligators are a common sight on many rivers. Both alligator and human populations are escalating. Florida growth is running 15% a decade. More humans are paddling than ever before. Man and gator are in closer proximity than at any time in modern history.

All alligators should be considered dangerous, no matter how small or large. Tendencies to treat a gator like "Fluffy" or "Barney" are ill-conceived and dangerous.

Here are some safety suggestions. Boat as far away from visible gators as possible. Do not disturb them. Do not come between them and the water, as that is their likely escape route. Do not swim in waters with gators in sight. Do not swim in murky waters. Never disturb an alligator nest unless you want to meet Psycho Mom in person. Bringing a dog into alligator country is inviting a potential tragedy for our best friend. Never leave small children unattended near any water, gators or not, and do not allow small children into water with alligators.

The most dangerous alligators are those that have been fed. It is said they lose their fear of humans, but a good question is: did they ever really fear us? Feeding them, however, does teach them to come to us, drawing them too close for safety.

Florida law provides for a $500 fine and 60 days in jail for feeding alligators.

While alligator attacks are rare, they do happen. While the risk is mathematically small, it is a real risk, and alligators have attacked kayaks, although it is not clear for what reason.

Above: The entrance to the Alapaha Siphon is to the left while the main river flows to the right.

SE

Above: Black Creek.

BLACK CREEK
(Clay County)

The river has two prongs. The south prong trail begins near Camp Blanding, a National Guard Training area along SR-16, and wanders about until it emerges on the broad, lower St. Johns south of Jacksonville. It is a pleasant paddle, sometimes shallow at first, with great overlooks, pitcher plants, and playful otters. Final portions of it are quite wide, even before what is customarily the last canoe take-out on SR-209. From SR-209 to the St. Johns is really wide and subject to a lot of wind.

The North Prong of Black Creek from Jennings State Forest is paddled, too. This trip is largely within Jennings State Forest. Upper stretches of the North Prong can lack for sufficient water and when paddled, were not cleared. Trips within the forest presently proceed from McNights or Nights Landing, although there are plans to expand landings.

POSSIBLE TRIPS AND LANDINGS - SOUTH PRONG

1. From SR-16 to SR-218, 7 miles. From Starke, go east on SR-16 about 18 miles

to the bridge. This is in the tiny community of Black Creek and to the west of the small town of Penney Farms. The landing is on the southeast side and would be best approached with a four-wheel drive vehicle, although this might be done with caution using two-wheel drive. The put-in has a steep carry but is not impossible.

2. From SR-218 to SR-209, 7 miles. From SR-16 in Penney Farms, turn north on SR-218. The landing is on the southwest side. A short carry downhill is necessary.

3. SR-209 to Old Ferry Road, 8 miles. From Penney Farms, go north on SR-218 to SR-739, which veers and continues north. At SR-209, turn east and proceed to the bridge.

4. From Old Ferry Road to Magnolia Springs, 1-2 miles. There is a paved, gated, public boat landing from SR-209 at the end of Old Ferry Road. SR-209 is a chore to find because it wanders and is not clearly identified at times. From US-17/15 north of Green Cove Springs on the St. Johns, turn northwest on SR-209. Old Ferry Road will be on the right in 2 to 3 miles.

5. Magnolia Springs is on the west bank of the St. Johns. It is possible to continue from Old Ferry Road to Magnolia Springs. It is broad paddling, hard in the wind and subject to some surf and boaters.

CAMPING

There are two campsites within Black Creek Ravines Conservation Area with use controlled by the St. Johns Water Management District. Jennings State Forest has camping options.

BLUE SPRINGS
(Volusia County)

There is a short canoe trip on a portion of the spring run to the St. Johns, and canoes can be rented in very busy Blue Springs State Park. This trip is a must, not for scenery, but for manatees. On cold winter days, manatee concentrations may reach 60 or more, all visible and easy to observe in the crystal clear waters. One can, of course, paddle onto the St. Johns and visit nearby Hontoon Island State Park.

Exit I-4 north onto US-17/92 as close as possible to Orange City. US-17/92 has many I-4 exits, and some are quite far from the park. In Orange, turn onto French Avenue. The turn from French Avenue to the park is marked by signs. Camping and cabins are available at the park.

FIRST-MAGNITUDE SPRINGS

Precisely what is a first-magnitude spring? It is one with an average daily outflow of at least 64.6 million gallons. About 80% of the discharge from all Florida springs comes from the 27 first-magnitude springs listed below. The two springs not associated without navigable rivers are in Apalachicola National Forest: Kini Spring, located northwest of Wakulla Springs, and River Sink Spring, part of Leon Sinks Geological Area, a natural marvel which includes series of sinks.

First-Magnitude Springs	County	River
Alapaha Rise	Hamilton	Suwannee
Alexander Springs	Lake	St. Johns
Blue Springs	Jackson	Chipola
Blue Spring	Madison	Withlacoochee (North)
Blue Spring	Volusia	St. Johns
Chassahowitzka Springs	Citrus	Chassahowitzka
Crystal River Springs	Citrus	Crystal
Falmouth Springs	Suwannee	Suwannee
Fannin Springs	Levy	Suwannee
Gainer Springs	Bay	Econfina Creek
Homosassa Springs	Citrus	Homosassa
Hornsby Spring	Alachua	Sante Fe
Holton Spring	Hamilton	Suwannee
Ichetucknee Springs	Columbia	Ichetucknee
Kini Spring	Wakulla	
Manatee Spring	Levy	Suwannee
Natural Bridge Spring	Leon	St. Marks
Rainbow Springs	Marion	Withlacoochee (South)
River Sink Springs	Wakulla	
Silver Springs	Marion	Ocklawaha/St. Johns
Silver Glen Spring	Marion	St. Johns
Spring Creek Springs	Wakulla	Spring Creek
St. Marks Spring	Leon	St. Marks
Troy Spring	Lafayette	Suwannee
Wacissa Spring Group	Jefferson	Wacissa
Wakulla Springs	Wakulla	Wakulla
Weeki Wachee Springs	Hernando	Weeki Wachee*

Sometimes spelled as one word.

Above: A canoeist pauses to admire the manatees. On cold winter mornings, up to 100 manatees may be found in Blue Springs.

PC

Above: Three to a canoe along Alexander Creek.

BULOW CREEK
(Flagler and Volusia counties)

This is a 13-mile, state-designated trail that departs from Bulow Plantation Ruins State Historic Site. The first trip is upstream and back. In the summer months, take sun block and perhaps a hat, especially for the saltmarsh areas.

POSSIBLE TRIPS AND LANDINGS
1. From Bulow Ruins State Historic Site upriver and return, 7 miles. The site is south of St. Augustine. Exit I-95 east at SR-100 and take the first road south. This is Old Kings Road, although it appears as CR-2001 on many maps. The historic site is on the east side of the road.
2. From Bulow Plantation Ruins Historic Site to Walter Boardman Lane Bridge, 3 miles. From the historic site, go south to Old Dixie Highway, turn east and go 0.5 miles to Walter Boardman Lane. The bridge crosses the river.
3. From Walter Boardman Lane Bridge to High Bridge Park, 3 miles. Continue east on Walter Boardman Road to High Bridge Road. Turn south and go 3 miles to High Bridge Park.

CAMPING
Tomoka State Park.

Map. Bulow Creek Canoe Trail by Office of Greenways and Trails

PC

CEDAR KEYS NATIONAL WILDLIFE REFUGE
(Dixie and Levy counties)

"The soul and spirit of this area are in the water. There are substantial fishing and oyster industries around Cedar Key that are dependent on water quality. Sport fishing is more than a pastime here; for many it is a way of life." *Florida's Fabulous Natural Places, 1999.*

The town of Cedar Key is at the Gulf-end of SR-24, a west turn from US-19 north of Crystal River. It is encircled by 14 keys that can entice the ardent kayaker. There are rentals at the docks in Cedar Key, and it is possible to put-in from there. There is also a landing on the land side of SR-24 just after leaving Gulf Hammock.

One favorite paddling destination from Cedar Key is Atsena Otie Key, once the home of pioneer settlers. It lies south of Cedar Key and north of Snake Key.

Turning north from SR-24 on CR-347 leads to CR-326. Then go west to another landing staring out toward Hog Island. There is saltmarsh north and south to explore, and several additional islands in both directions.

No entry is allowed on some of the islands where birds nest. It is best to check with the refuge before proceeding.

Below: Kayakers resting on a beach in the Cedar Key area.

Above: Sunrise along the road to Cedar Key.

There is more than enough kayaking here to accommodate many months of exploration, if not years. Charts and tidal information are very important in this area. Low tide can come suddenly and leave the paddler stranded, sometimes among unpleasant oyster beds. There is also a short but painful yellow fly season to avoid. These are small inconveniences for some very beautiful island paddling.

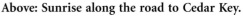

PC

DEEP CREEK
(St. Johns County)

There are several rivers with the name "Deep Creek" in Florida, none of them particularly deep. Two which are popular with paddlers are this one and another on the Suwannee River in Columbia County.

The two Deep creeks are quite different. While the Suwannee journey is filled with limestone, the St. Johns' Deep Creek is largely a paddle in a beautiful, wide floodplain and swamp.

Many paddlers use the landing at Federal Point Boat Ramp. From SR-207 in Hastings go west on Church Street to Federal Point Road, and follow it to the end at the Federal Point Boat Ramp.

Paddles are from the ramp and back and can exceed several miles depending on water level.

DEEP CREEK
(Columbia County)

Located upstream from Big Shoals on the Suwannee River, this Deep Creek might be easily overlooked. The creek is very scenic but is not suitable for the inexperienced or unskilled paddler. The creek has eroded limestone bluffs and can be dangerous when the water level is high.

Go south from White Springs on US-41 to CR-246. Turn left on CR-246 and proceed to US-441, a distance of about 5 miles. Turn left on US-441 and go about 3.5 miles to Deep Creek. A dirt drive on the right leads to a parking area at the creek.

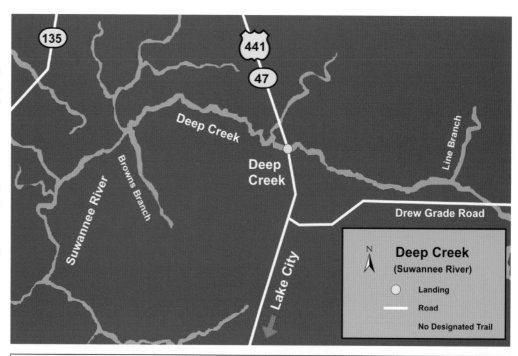

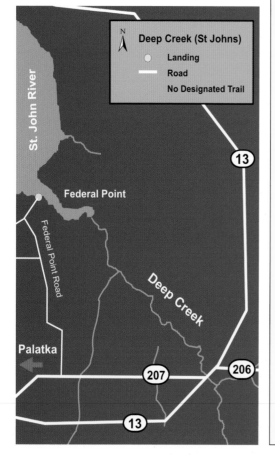

THE FINE ART OF BEING A CANOE GUIDE

Shown above are Randy Smith and Randy's dog, Goldy. Randy, along with Graham Schorb, are guides at Canoe Outpost at Spirit of the Suwannee Music Park. They take adventurers on area rivers. Among the highlights of these trips are bumping over the rocks at Melvin Shoals on the Withlacoochee River, traveling up the Suwannee, and viewing the Alapaha Siphon. The Siphon is one of the wonders of Florida's natural places. However, it would be dangerous and foolhardy to enter the run leading to The Siphon in a canoe. Sometimes these river adventures include the occasional spill which can damage expensive camera gear.

After crossing Melvin Shoals without a spill on one fine day in spring, the canoe which Graham was handling bumped-up against a log. Graham took hold of the log in an attempt to push-off, but in the fast-flowing Withlacoochee River (North), the canoe capsized. Graham's passenger, a professional photographer, was tossed into the water along with a cooler containing expensive camera equipment. The photographer held his precious gear aloft in the cooler while kicking furiously with his feet. However, kicking in this position was useless.

Fortunately, Graham, whom Randy would describe as a "big man," swam rapidly ahead of the photographer to the shore line, gained ground, then reached-out from the bank with a powerful arm and snagged his passenger, thus saving him, his gear, and his photos.

DE LEON SPRINGS
(Volusia County)

Canoes can be rented from a concession in De Leon Springs State Park for a paddle down Spring Garden Creek to Lake Woodruff, one of the large lakes in the St. Johns Drainage. Lake Woodruff National Wildlife Refuge adjoins the recreation area. Paddling onto the lake can lead to many miles of paddling, so trip length is up to the individual. The state park is in De Leon Springs on US-17. From I-95, exit west on SR-40, and turn south on US-17.

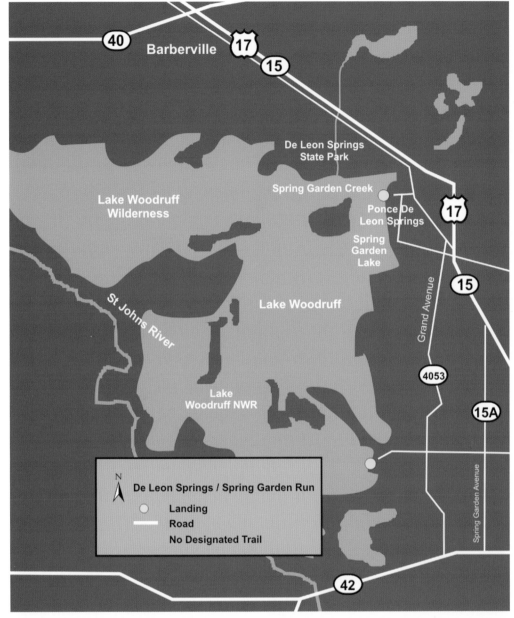

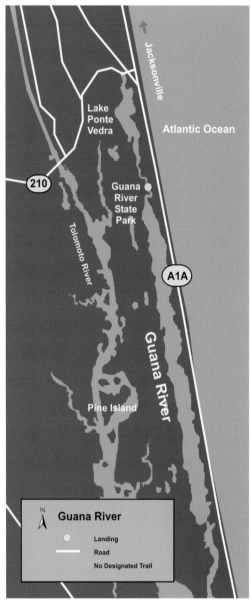

GUANA RIVER
(St. Johns County)

The river is really an estuary located between a narrow strip of beach on A1A and a strip of marshy mainland which borders the Tolomato River farther inland. It is possible to launch from several areas of Guana River State Park and within the wildlife management area. This area has extensive saltmarsh, some maritime forest, and high dunes on the beaches. The state park lies along A1A, south of Jacksonville and north of St. Augustine.

Left: Paddling on the Guana River.

HOLTON CREEK
(Hamilton County)

Only a half mile long, it is easier to walk the banks of Holton Creek than to canoe in it. The banks are lined with gorgeous cypress along the short distance to the Suwannee River.

Where the creek spills into the Suwannee, there is a set of shoals, unless the water level is exceptionally high, in which case the paddler might be shot out onto the Suwannee like a bullet. It would be wise to scout the shoals before making a trip.

Since there is no official landing, dangerous shoals, and the run is short, the water management district does not feel this is suitable for paddling.

CR-751 crosses Holton Creek where there is an "unofficial" landing. One could then paddle downstream to Suwannee River State Park. CR-751 is a south turn from SR-6 less than 10 miles west of Jasper.

HONTOON ISLAND
(Lake and Volusia counties)

Hontoon Island sits on the edge of three rivers and several scenic canals. The rivers are: Dead River, Hontoon River, and the St. Johns. Paddling in the area is gorgeous and rewarded with manatee sightings and lots of alligators. Take SR-44 for 6 miles west from Deland, then CR-4410 south to its dead-end at a marina.

ICHETUCKNEE RIVER
(Columbia and Suwannee counties)

One of the most wonderful spring runs in Florida, the Ichetucknee surges from underground springs, down a narrow channel to the Santa Fe River, and from there into the Suwannee.

Ichetucknee Springs are considered together as one of Florida's first-magnitude springs

Cold and brisk, its waters invite thousands upon thousands of tubers in the summer months, so paddling is best when it is cool. Because there is a limit on the numbers allowed on the river, some paddlers on busy weekends go in early, explore side branches and backwaters, waiting until the parking lot is closed-off because it is full. They then paddle an empty spring run in the wake of happily tubing hordes.

A place of magic, the Ichetucknee brings about something rather difficult to accomplish. It draws together people of all ages, races, and backgrounds to float on its waters.

Above and below: Tubing on the Ichetucknee is very popular, and the river can be a bit crowded on a hot summer day.

Opposite page: Blue Spring at Ichetucknee River.

POSSIBLE TRIPS AND LANDINGS

1. From Ichetucknee Springs State Park to US-27, 3.5 miles. From I-75, take the first High Springs exit north of Gainesville (US-441). Take US-27 northwest to Ft. White. From Ft. White, go north on SR-47 and west on CR-238 to the park.
2. From US-27 to the Santa Fe River, 2.5 miles. From I-75, take US-441 to US-27. Take US-27 northwest to the Ichetucknee Bridge.
3. Additional Trip. It is possible to continue down the Santa Fe River to landings on the Suwannee. There are two landings on the Santa Fe and one on the Suwannee within 4.5 miles of the confluence. As always, check with local outfitters about conditions.

Above: The Ichetucknee River.

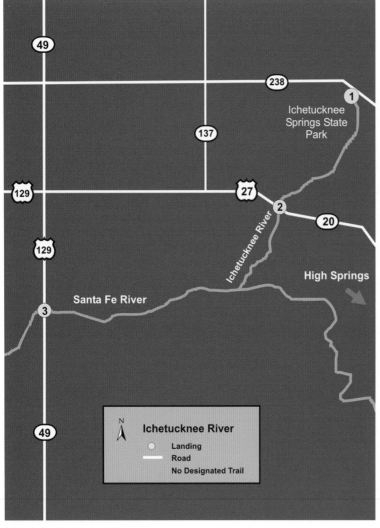

Right: A sinkhole in the forest surrounding the Ichetucknee River.

Above: Paddling over the shallow, sandy bottom in the Juniper Springs Run.

JUNIPER SPRINGS RUN
(Marion County)

This is a popular, attractive canoe run in Ocala National Forest. Formed by waters from Juniper and Fern Hammock springs, it is fed by smaller springs along the way to Lake George, Florida's second largest lake and a wide place in the St. Johns.

The trail begins at Juniper Creek Recreation Area and is narrow and winding. At times the creek widens, but it is largely 7 miles of twists and turns to the bridge on SR-19. It is an additional 3 miles to Lake George, but the canoe trail ends at the bridge, and those 3 miles are said to be shallow and not maintained.

Halfway Landing is at 3.5 miles along Juniper Creek but is not a take-out or put-in, rather a dock at a place to rest or picnic. Until this landing, the creek is bordered mostly by floodplain. After this landing, the creek widens in an area something like an oxbow where there is marsh.

Before reaching the bridge on SR-19, the creek passes below modest banks with sandpine. Most of the trail passes through Juniper Prairie Wilderness. There are alligators, frogs, peninsula cooters, plentiful deer, snakes, and all manner of waterbirds.

At Juniper Springs Recreation Area, the visitor should take the time to walk the short trail, including Juniper Springs and

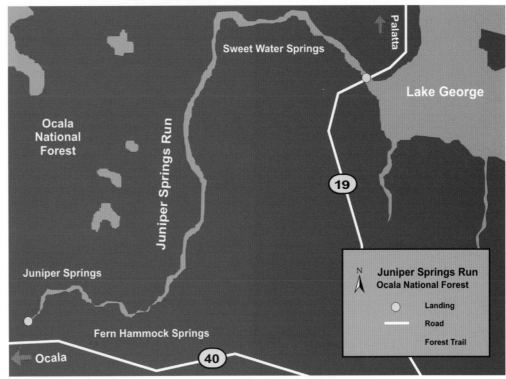

the bridge over Fern Hammock Spring.

Canoes can be rented at the recreation area. Transportation is provided between the area and the pick-up at the SR-19 bridge. Those bringing their own canoes or kayaks can also take advantage of this service.

Ocala National Forest is between I-75 and I-95. SR-40 runs through it. Juniper Creek Recreation Area is located on the

north side of SR-40 and is prominently announced by signs. The 7-mile trip ends at Juniper Creek Bridge which is 4 miles north on SR-19 from SR-40, to the east of the recreation area.

Visits to any national forest will be enhanced by using a forest map. This is available in advance or at any visitor center in the forest. There are numerous camping opportunities available in this forest.

LOWER SUWANNEE NATIONAL WILDLIFE REFUGE CANOE TRAIL

Three trails totaling 8.75 miles are located to the southeast of the town of Suwannee. The trails cross over the Suwannee River at two locations, then travel along Demory Creek, Lost Creek, Magnesia Pass, and Shingle Creek. Information on these trails is available from Lower Suwannee National Wildlife Refuge. In addition to marina landings, there is a public boat ramp at the end of McKinney Drive. From US-19 in Old Town, take CR-349 apparent west (actually south) into Suwannee, then turn left on McKinney Drive.

CAMPING

There are two camping areas adjacent to the refuge. Details are available from the refuge.

MATANZAS RIVER
(Flagler and St. Johns counties)

The river is really a long inlet starting at St. Augustine and running quite some distance south behind Anastasia Island and other beach areas. It is primarily for kayaking, as much of it is broad sea, while other portions are saltmarsh. There are a few launches along A1A, but the put-in from Salt Run in Anastasia State Park is popular. From I-95, exit into St. Augustine. In St. Augustine, take the Bridge-O-Lions from downtown to Anastasia Island, and choose either from putting-in at the state park or along A1A.

Below: A scene along the Sante Fe River.

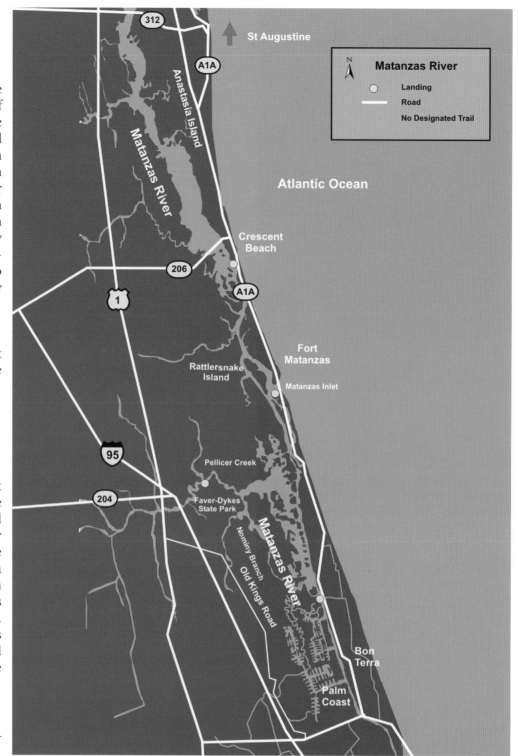

OCKLAWAHA RIVER
(Marion and Putnam counties)

Perhaps the most joyous portion for the paddler is the absolute wilderness between Gores Landing and the Blue Hole. This 8 mile stretch, turn after turn, is numbing in its beauty, and bristling with alligators and waterbirds. Along the way is some surprisingly high, rolling land.

Sometimes spelled without the "c," as in OKLAWAHA, this 79-mile river flows north into the St. Johns River, another north-flowing river. The Creek word that gives the river its name means "muddy," and the Ocklawaha is a muddy, sand-bottom river.

The Ocklawaha has its source in several lakes (Dora, Eustis, and Griffin) and springs, including one of the more powerful of Florida's 27 first-magnitude springs, Silver Springs.

The Ocklawaha has been tremendously impacted by engineering, primarily for the ill-fated Cross Florida Barge Canal. A remnant of that ill-conceived project, Rodman Dam, stops the Ocklawaha journey and creates a large backwater. Because the trees were taken down before the backwater was created, there are plentiful cypress stumps which bass like and which makes bass fishing remarkable.

Bears are sometimes surprised on the Ocklawaha banks by quiet paddlers. This area, bordering Ocala National Forest, is prime bear country.

Between Gores Landing and Ocklawaha Outpost, Cedar Creek is a twisty, naturally gorgeous side trip to the northeast. It adds at most 1 hour to the journey to linger there, time well spent.

POSSIBLE TRIPS AND LANDINGS

1. From Moss Bluff Dam to SR-40 Bridge, 13 miles. From Ocala, east on SR-40, then south on SR-314A to Moss Bluff Lock and Dam.
2. From SR-40 to Gores Landing, 10 miles. The Ocklawaha River Bridge is east of Ocala on SR-40. On this section, the paddler will usually make the right decision by following the current or going to the left.
3. From Gores Landing to SR-316, 8 miles. From SR-40, east of Ocala, turn north on SR-315. After 5 miles, there is a sign indicating Gores Landing to the east. Follow the signs.
4. From SR-316 to Cypress Bayou, 8 miles. From SR-40, east of Ocala, turn north on SR-315, and east on SR-316 to the landing at the bridge. This enormous bridge was intended to allow passage of barge traffic in the intended canal.
5. From Cypress Bayou to Orange Springs, 10 miles. From SR-316 just to the west of the bridge over the Ocklawaha, turn north on Mill Pond Road. This is also Daisy Road on some maps. Follow this dirt road north to the landing.
6. Orange Springs is located on SR-315 to the east of the junction with SR-21. SR-315 is a north turn from SR-40. The landing is on the west bank to the east of SR-315 down a series of roads.

Additional Trip. There is good paddling at the Rodman Dam. Leave from the ramp on the southeast side of SR-19. It is possible to paddle to the St. Johns River and back, a trip of 8 miles. Or paddle up to Caravelle Wildlife Management Area, public land along SR-19.

CAMPING

Camping is generally allowed wherever not specifically forbidden along the banks. Nearby Ocala National Forest has many camping options off the river.

RODMAN DAM

Plans to remove Rodman Dam, if implemented, could result in a restored river and more paddling. The dam has changed the character of the river and sturgeon can no longer reach spawning grounds.

At present, some Florida legislators are trying to retain the dam, which is vigorously defended by those who catch lunker catfish below the dam, or lunker bass on the backwater. A long string of governors have wanted to take the dam out.

An annual "Save Rodman Dam" fishing tournament is drawing increasing participation from bass fishermen. One recent fund raising event was the raffling of a two-foot long lure.

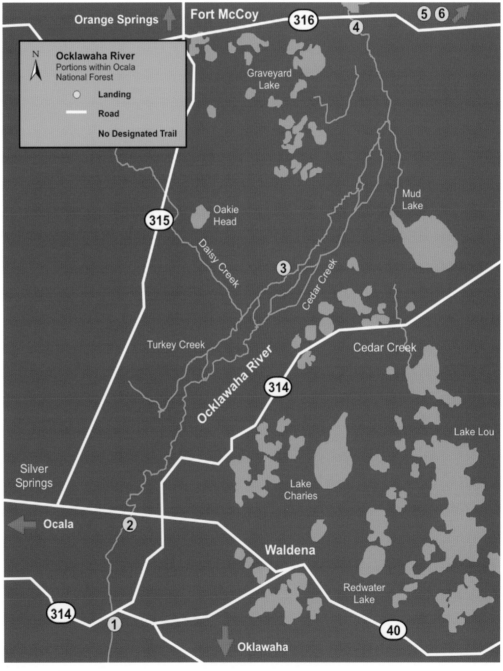

SE

Above: A kayaker glides through the crystal clear waters of the Ichetucknee River.

PELLICER CREEK
(Flagler and St. Johns counties)

This 4-mile, state-designated canoe trail can be paddled west from Faver-Dykes State Park and back, making the trip 8 miles, or two cars can be positioned in the park and at the US-1 Bridge. However, this traditional landing at US-1 should be checked before trying this. When last visited, access was blocked.

This is largely a trip through saltmarsh.

Traveling east, the way leads quickly into the Matanzas River.

Faver-Dykes is south of St. Augustine. From I-95, exit on US-1, proceed north less than 0.5 miles, and turn east at the prominent sign. Go south on US-1 to the bridge.

This trail is too short to require any overnights. However, Faver-Dykes offers camping options and is a great place.

Map. Pellicer Creek Recreational Canoe Trail, Office of Greenways and Trails.

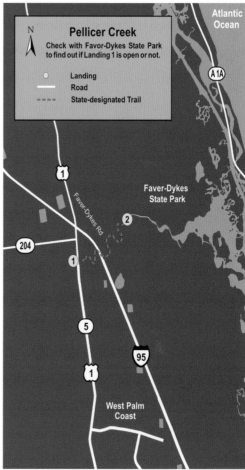

Left: Canoes for rent in Faver-Dykes State Park on Pellicer Creek.

RAINBOW RIVER
(Marion County)

However you get to the Rainbow River, it is a worthwhile experience. The waters are exceptionally clear and water quality good. The river is deep and free of obstacles. Despite dwellings primarily along the west bank, wildlife is plentiful. Many waterbirds are seen and are easy to observe, perhaps habituated to humans. Otters are exceptionally easy to spot, perhaps for the same reason. The wading and fishing birds often do not take flight when you approach.

Rainbow River is a tributary of the Withlacoochee River (South). Where they meet, the river is wide, the flow powerful, and the banks populated city. It is likely you will also pass some logs loaded with large numbers of turtles.

From the headwaters at Rainbow Springs, one of Florida's more powerful first-magnitude springs, to the confluence with the Withlacoochee River is 7 miles, but the trip is rarely done that way. Canoes can be rented in Rainbow Springs State Park, at the headwaters, but this requires the paddler to paddle back upstream against the flow, unless other arrangements have been made with an outfitter. Outfitters put paddlers in below the springs at K. P. County Park (for Knights of Pythias), so to experience the entire river, it is customary to paddle upstream about 1 mile, then return downstream 1 mile, expanding the trip to 8-9 miles. Bringing your own canoe to the state park requires a long carry down a steep slope, so few people do that, although it is allowed.

Camping is available at the state park.

POSSIBLE TRIPS AND LANDINGS

1. From Rainbow Springs to K.P. County Park, 1 mile. For those who do not mind a long, long carry down a steep hill, Rainbow Springs State Park is located on the east side of US-41 north of Dunellon.
2. From K. P. County Park to US-41 Boat Ramp, 6 miles. The park is to the east of US-41, north of Dunnellon, accessed by 99th Place.
3. The first take-out on the Withlacoochee River is at the US-41 Boat Ramp in Dunnellon just after passing under US-41. The landing at CR-484 Bridge is for tubers and rafts only. The US-41 Boat Ramp is heavily used but has ample parking.

Above: The Rainbow River, which pours out of Rainbow Springs, is pristine despite the construction of many houses along its west bank.

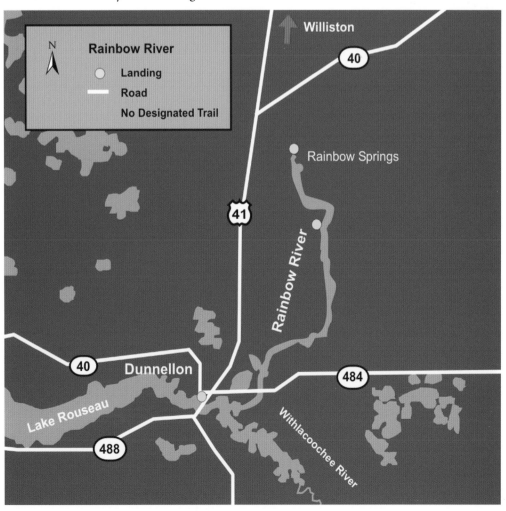

JP

SALT SPRINGS RUN
(Marion County)

Lake George is worth the effort to paddle this wide run. Scenic vistas trail off along the banks. Sit quietly for a few moments and listen to birds and pig frogs call. The birds, including redwing blackbirds in season, flit back and forth. Various fishes, including mullet and bass, churn the surface.

It is a 4.5-mile trip from Salt Springs Recreation Area, in Ocala National Forest, to Lake George, Florida's second largest lake, and a wide spot in the St. Johns River.

Canoes can be rented from the concession, as can pontoon boats and skiffs. There is no take-out on the run, so it is necessary to canoe 4.5 miles back upstream against an average flow of 54 million gallons of water a day.

For most of the journey, the river is wide, and powerboaters fish on the river and lake. The final mile or so of the river narrows, but it is a no-wake zone, so powerboats should not be troublesome. Paddlers should probably avoid venturing too far out on the lake. When the wind is up, whitecaps can form not far from shore.

The salty quality of the water comes from ancient mineral deposits formed when global seas were much higher than they are now. The salt pours into Lake George and flows north on the St. Johns River. Saltwater fishes, like pinfish, are present in the springs, and one shark species even enters Lake George. From Palatka north, the St. Johns is considered a marine estuary.

Salt Springs Recreation Area is on the east side of SR-19 in the northeastern part of the national forest. From I-75, exit east on SR-40 and proceed through the national forest to SR-19, then go north.

A forest map is very helpful for exploring Ocala National Forest. It can be obtained in advance or from any of the visitor centers. The forest offers numerous camping opportunities.

Above: Salt Springs Run.

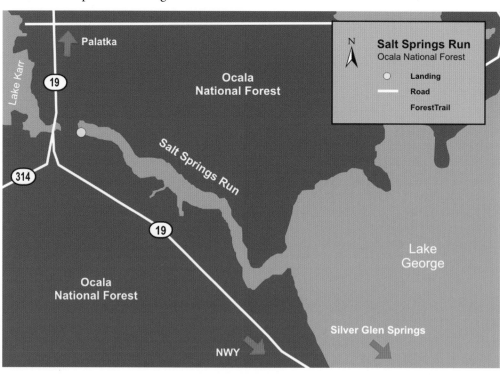

SANTA FE RIVER
(Alachua, Bradford, Columbia, Gilchrist, Suwannee, and Union counties)

A major tributary of the Suwannee, the Sante Fe is one of Florida's most intriguing rivers. It goes underground at O'Leno State Park and pops up at River Rise State Preserve. When it comes back up, much more water is in the river than before it went under. It is obviously fed by underground waterways.

The river above the rise is tannin-colored and often appears "stained." Below the rise, the water is usually clear, and becomes clearer as a number of springs flow into it. About 15 miles below the rise, the Ichetucknee River flows into the Sante Fe, another blast of pure, clear water.

Below the rise, many springs rush in. Some sources say 35 springs. One outfitter says 45 springs. In reality, it is hard to tell where some of the springs leave off and others begin. Sometimes the same underground flow is coming up in two spots on opposite sides of the river.

Like the Alapaha, the river has areas called The Siphon and The Suck. They are also called Little and Big Awesome. These are areas where the river is sucked underground. It is difficult, in fact, to keep the canoe out of even Little Awesome even with paddles firmly on the limestone bottom attempting to anchor it. These two siphons pop back up in areas referred to as Black Crack and Myrtle's Crack. Some have tried to sanitize these traditional bawdy references by, for example, making it Myrtle's Fissure.

Some of the springs include Blue, Columbia, Ginnie, Hornsby, Lily, and Poe springs. Ginnie Springs is a popular campground and dive site located down river from Rum Island Spring, which takes its name allegedly because demon Rum was once made there.

Poe Spring has a pleasant county park with canoe rentals. At one time, Poe was a first-magnitude spring.

The river is 76 miles long, flowing east to west, and sometimes north as its snakes toward the Suwannee. It is the boundary between Alachua and neighboring Bradford, Union, and Columbia counties. Its origins lie in Lake Santa Fe and Santa Fe Swamp.

The entire path of the river below the rise is wide and attractive, while above it is twisty and narrow. While there are many homes on the banks below the rise, there are pristine areas with plentiful wildlife and numerous turtles. Deer are frequently seen along the banks, and they often do not shy away, but may be seen reclining on the banks. Otters are spotted easily, as are brown water snakes, and more rarely, Florida

Above: The Santa Fe River has a number of spectacular springs for paddlers to explore.

DOUG PERRINE/SEAPICS.COM

cottonmouths (water moccasins).

Both O'Leno State Park and River Rise State Preserve are natural treasures. O'Leno has camping options and numerous trails to explore. It also has a reputation as the tick capital of Florida. The reputation is deserved. Especially in dry months, come prepared.

In the stretch between US-27 and SR-47, an unusual individual has gained notoriety by living naked on the river. He is referred to as The Naked Guy or Naked Ed. He does not come up to the river to assault the senses, but if one paddles up to his property it could be a shock for those with sensitive feelings about nudity. He is located near Lily Spring.

POSSIBLE TRIPS AND LANDINGS - ABOVE O'LENO STATE PARK

There are several sections to the east of Worthington Springs (especially the Brooker {CR-231} to Worthington Springs) that are very pretty and popular with paddlers. However, they seldom have sufficient water. The sections above O'Leno are fairly technical in places, and often too low for comfortable paddling. Easier sections lie below O'Leno State Park.

1. From Worthington Springs to SR-241, 6 miles. Worthington Springs is north of Gainesville on SR-121. The bridge is south of Worthington. This section is questionable at low water levels; it is a

tough, tangled paddle under the best conditions.

2. From SR-241 to O'Leno State Park, 5 miles. SR-241 leads north from Alachua, an exit of I-75. Although SR-241 is traditionally mentioned in guides as the landing, it is not an official landing, and it requires parking on the roadside. This trip is best down from Bible Camp Road Boat Ramp. For that landing from High Springs, go 6 miles north on US-441, and make the right hand turn toward O'Leno State Park. About 100 yards after that turn, turn right onto Bible Camp Road and follow it 3 bending miles to the boat ramp. Olustee Creek to Bible Camp Road always has water because of a large spring. From SR-241 to Olustee Creek usually has a lot of downfall and low water.

3. O'Leno State Park. North of High Springs, the park is located on US-41/441. There are prominent signs.

POSSIBLE TRIPS AND LANDINGS - FROM HIGH SPRINGS US-441 BOAT RAMP.

There are numerous landings, so not all have been included. See landing 7 for how to obtain a free map which includes those additional landings if desired.

4. From High Springs to US-27 Boat Ramp, 3.5 miles. From I-75, exit west on US-441 toward High Springs. At NW 210 Lane, turn west to the boat ramp. It

Above: The gray colors of winter along the Sante Fe River.

Below: Canoeists at Ginnie Springs with the tent of campers in the background.

HELPFUL SANTA FE MILEAGE

The following distances are provided by Ken Kramer, an ardent paddler and now a guide based in Tampa, and Lars Anderson, an outfitter and author. Things come pretty fast on some stretches of the Santa Fe and such a mileage guide is very helpful in telling what wonder has been encountered.

From	Total Miles From Origin
US-41/441	0
US-27	3.5
Poe Springs	5.25
Lily Springs	6.5
Rum Island	7.25
Blue Spring	7.5
Ginnie Spring	8.75
Big Awesome	10
Little Awesome	10.5
Black Crack	11
Myrtles Crack SR-4712	11.25
Hollingsworth Bluff	12.5
Ichetucknee River	21.5
US-129	26.25
Sandy Point	26.75
Suwannee River	28.5

Above: A view of the Ichetucknee River which is a tributary to the Sante Fe River. Both rivers are fed by powerful and scenic springs.

is usually possible to go upstream 2.5 miles to River Rise, but this route was blocked by rafts of water hyacinths in fall of 2001.

5. From US-27 Boat Ramp to SR-47 (Santa Fe River Park), 7 miles. (A number of landings between the two highways are not included, such as Rum Island, Ginnie Springs, and Poe Springs.) The bridge is 3 miles west of High Springs on US-27.

6. From SR-47 (Santa Fe River Park) to US-129, 13 miles. (There are a number of landings between these two points which are not included, such as Hollingsworth Bluff, Ira Bea Oasis Ramp, and Sandy Point Ramp.) From High Springs, go west on Poe Springs Road (Highway 340) and turn north on SR-47. The park is at the river on the east bank.

7. From US-129 to Suwannee River, 2.25 miles. From High Springs go northwest on US-27. Turn south on US-129 and proceed to the river.

8. Suwannee River. There are numerous take-outs, public and private, along the Suwannee River. A map is available from the Suwannee River Management District showing 52 public landings (see Appendix for address).

CAMPING

Suwannee River Water Management District allows camping by permit on many of its lands. O'Leno State Park offers camping. Ginnie and Blue springs have campgrounds.

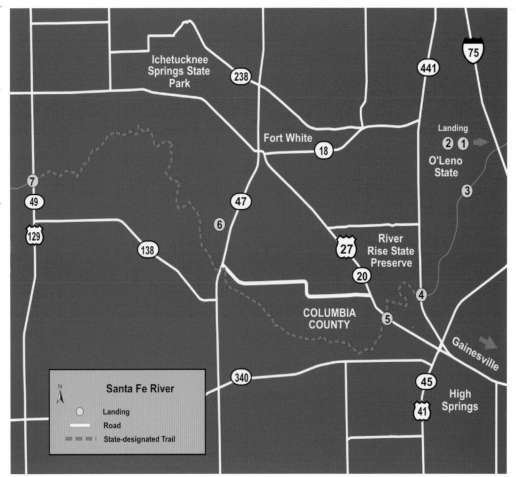

Map. Sante Fe River Canoe Trail, Office of Greenways and Trails. The designated canoe trail is 26 miles, running from US-41/441 to US-129.

SILVER RIVER
(Marion County)

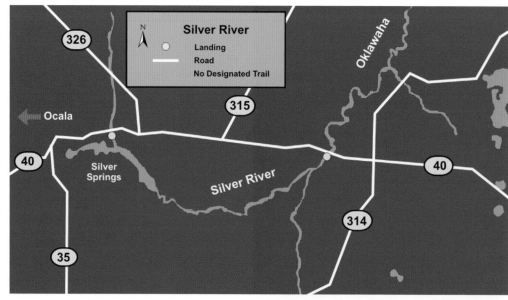

If you are limiting yourself to a handful of paddles, this is certainly one that would be in your top ten, probably top five. The river is exceptionally scenic, with sand and eel grass bottom, fish swimming about, and plentiful wildlife, including some interesting exotics.

Tourism in Florida began shortly after the Civil War. Original tourists were not drawn to theme parks in Central Florida. Rather, Florida's tourism industry began with steamboats chugging from Jacksonville south down the St. Johns, into the Ocklawaha, ending at Silver Springs, the source of the Silver River. The Silver River is a 8-mile tributary of the Ocklawaha.

While it is possible to put-in at Silver River State Park, this requires a long carry, perhaps 0.75 mile, so most mortal paddlers put-in on the Ocklawaha River and paddle upstream, then return downstream. The trip back downstream is an easy one because of the outflow from Silver Springs, one of the state's more powerful first-magnitude springs. The trip upstream is liable to be a chore because of the flow, but most people won't mind at all, since there will be beautiful sights and they will almost surely be amused by otters.

The tourist attraction at Silver Springs has been frequently filmed, and many black- and-white Tarzan movies were produced along Silver River. Esther Williams also swam for Hollywood in Silver Springs, and a boat was sunk near the main spring in the making of that movie. The remains of a steamboat from the 1800s also lie conspicuously in the river closer to the Ocklawaha.

Wildlife likely encountered includes monkeys, otters, alligators, large gar, and bass. Mud fish can be spotted on the clear bottom, and alligator and spotted gar reach epic size. Did I say monkeys? Yes, monkeys. Some have even reported lemurs.

There are camping options at the state park.

THE SILVER RIVER MONKEYS

Four Rhesus macaques, popularly known as Rhesus monkeys, were put on a river island in the mid-20th Century. Fuzzy-headed thinking said the monkeys would never escape. Today, large bands of monkey descendants frequently come to the bank to gaze at paddlers. Undoubtedly they spice up alligator diets from time-to-time. Officials seem to take turns tolerating the monkeys and threatening to remove them because they are not native.

Groups of up to 100 monkeys, from nursing tots to alpha males, have been known to stare from the banks at visitors. It would be wise to avoid eye contact with the alpha males. The dominant males make their presence known by coming clearly to the forefront of the troop. When upset, they are something like drivers during road rage, with no manners at all.

Locals report that spider monkey escapees from Ross Allen's famous attraction also roam freely but are more secretive. Supposedly 100 were released by mistake. While no biologist will confirm this, with all the exotics brought in over the years to the Silver Springs attraction, there is no reason to doubt it, or that other exotics might be found in the area.

The monkeys range at least as far as 40 miles from the attraction. With a natural corridor, they may well expand to other areas.

Above: The beautiful Silver River is one of the premier paddles in Florida.

Above: Paddlers on the Ichetucknee River.

SILVER GLEN SPRINGS
(Marion County)

Silver Glen Run is short, about 0.5 mile, from Silver Glen Recreation Area in Ocala National Forest to Lake George, Florida's second largest lake and part of the St. Johns. Fairly large boats frequently spend the night in the shelter of the run and travel up and down it. Naturalist William Bartram also traveled into the springs from Lake George.

Canoes are rented in the recreation area. Otters frequent the river and are easy to view because they are somewhat habituated to humans. At times, Florida black bears have been seen, even climbing the trees near the recreation area.

Silver Glen Recreation Area is on the east side of SR-19. From I-75, exit east on SR-40 through the national forest, then turn north on SR-19. Or from I-95, exit west on SR-40.

Above: Spring Warrior Creek.

SPRING WARRIOR CREEK
(Taylor County)

Spring Warrior is a gorgeous creek in splendid natural condition. From Spring Warrior Camp, it is a 5-mile trip to the Gulf. For the start of the trip, turn west on CR-361 in Perry, and proceed to Spring Warrior Creek. For the Gulf, proceed south from Perry on Jefferson Street which becomes CR-361A. Take CR-361A to the dead-end.

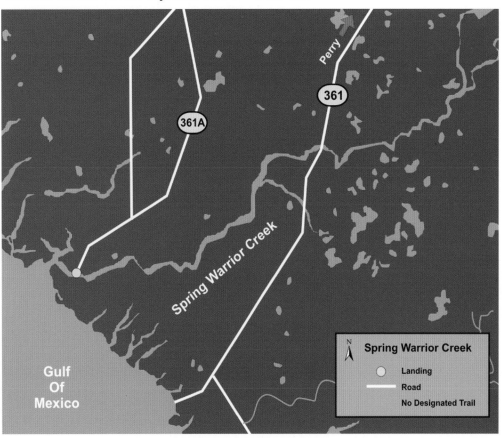

SPRUCE CREEK
(Volusia County).

This paddle begins and ends at Strickland Bay. The official state-designated trail is 16 miles, 8 each way, but one can also paddle around the bay. Parts of the trip closer to the Atlantic are through saltmarsh. Inland, the paddle is freshwater. To reach the trail, exit I-95 on SR-421 (Dunlawton Avenue) east and go 1 mile to Spruce Creek Park.

Map. Spruce Creek Canoe Trail, Office of Greenways and Trails.

THE FENHOLLOWAY RIVER
Immediately south of Perry, the first river encountered is not Spring Warrior or Steinhatchee. Rather it is the Fenholloway River. This river, once a source of drinking water, was tested and found to have 200 times the allowable levels of dioxin, a known carcinogen. This pollution is the result of paper manufacturing.

Once again the need for jobs and the protection of the environment are on a collision course. The area around Perry is remote, the economy sluggish. Thousands of workers depend on the paper industry for their living.

Waters from the Fenholloway enter the Gulf of Mexico in a remote area of the Big Bend. Fishermen in the area reported they had been pulling in good numbers of redfish or trout, when there were suddenly no more strikes. Waters from the Fenholloway had drifted into the area and the fish had fled.

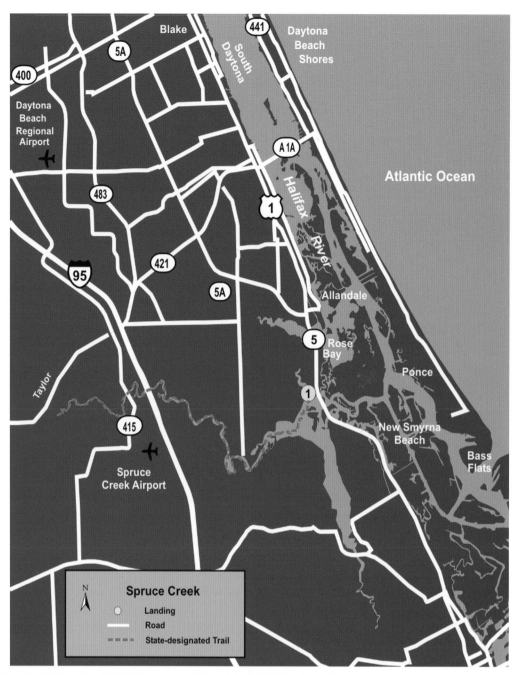

Below: The very popular Sante Fe River.

ST. JOHNS RIVER
(Brevard, Clay, Duval, Flagler, Indian River, Marion, Nassau, Orange, Putnam, Seminole, St. Johns, and Volusia counties)

At 273 miles, the St. Johns is the longest river in Florida. However, "river" may not be the right word. Native Americans called it *Welaka*, or chain of lakes, but even this might not be an accurate description.

This river is so long and extensive it is divided into three areas reversed from the normal logic because of the northerly flow: Upper (southern), Middle, and Lower (northern). The Upper St. Johns begins in marsh, where seepage and rainwater are the main source. The Middle St. Johns passes through a number of lakes and is fed by many of the river's springs. Over 50 named springs flow into the St. Johns. Systems within the St. Johns Drainage include the Wekiva. The Lower St. Johns is essentially a wide estuary and arm of the sea.

Although the famous naturalist, William Bartram, traveled over much of the river, modern paddlers are generally more interested in specific areas (like the Wekiva System, Ocklawaha River, or Black Creek) rather than the entire river. This is because it is broad in many of the lakes and also toward its mouth on the Atlantic. For this reason, paddlers are subject to wind and even whitecaps. This is also the domain of powerboats.

Those paddlers who wish to paddle the broad river will not want for landings, as there are many, both public and commercial. The recreational guide of the St. Johns Water Management District will be of assistance, as will DeLorme's *Florida Atlas and Gazetteer.*

Among lakes included in the St. Johns Drainage are Lakes George, Harney, Jessup, Monroe, Norris, and Blue Cypress. (Blue Cypress Lake, a gorgeous lake located along SR-60 to the east of the Florida Turnpike, has been listed in at least one paddling guide as a fine journey unto itself.) Lake George is Florida's second largest lake, and Salt Springs Run pours into it, increasing the salinity of the river. In fact, from Palatka north, the Lower St. Johns is considered a marine estuary, and a species of shark even penetrates it at times.

St. Johns River Water Management District is so large it is divided into three regions: South, Central, and North, corresponding to the Upper, Middle, and Lower St. Johns. The water management district holds much public land in trust, and a substantial amount of that is open to camping. A recreation guide is free from the water management district.

Florida environmental journalist Bill Belleville explored the entire St. Johns and wrote an excellent book, *River of Lakes* (University of Georgia Press, 2000). Anyone interested in understanding or exploring the St. Johns in greater depth would do well to acquire this book. There are so many landings on the St. Johns River that none are shown on the small map at right.

Above: Boaters from Salt Springs Run entering Lake George, a part of the St. Johns River.

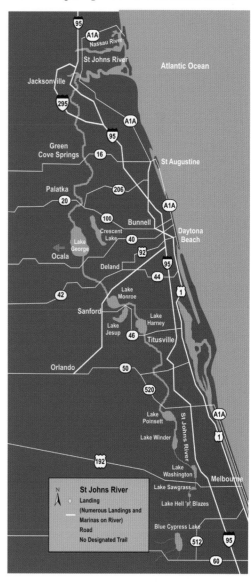

PC

ST. MARYS RIVER
(Baker and Nassau counties)

For most paddlers, the section of the river which will be of interest is that within the state-designated canoe trail. That trail runs from the SR-121 Bridge north of Macclenny, Florida, to Scotts Landing, besides Ralph Simmons Memorial Forest. This trail is stated at 51 miles by the state, but appears to be longer when measured by GPS. It would be a good idea to check with the sole outfitter in Appendix A to make sure there is sufficient water. This section is remote, mostly natural, with lots of timber plantations. At low water, the river is beautiful and the camping great; however, paddling portions during low water is a little problematic

Other guides traditionally list paddling opportunities on upper reaches of the river. Three prongs form the St. Marys: Middle, North, and South. The South Prong is said to be impassable, and certainly appeared to be. The North and Middle Prong flow out of the Okefenokee Swamp in Georgia. Contrary to what is in print, the river is not spring-fed. When last visited, the upper reaches of the North Prong were narrow and shallow. A former outfitter, Hidden River Ranch, located on the upper northern portion has changed to Hidden River

Resort, a nudist resort, in part because there have been a number of years with insufficient water for paddling. The Middle Prong is wild and tangled, but probably passable for the independent, adventure-loving paddler. It too is narrow and shallow, and could not be paddled when last visited. Part of the Middle Prong passes through Osceola National Forest. Most of the way is gorgeous wilderness, including some fine slopes and floodplain.

Beyond the state-designated trail, indeed before it is over, the river widens and deepens considerably. It may be one hundred yards wide beyond Trader's Hill, and by the time it flows past the town of St. Marys, Georgia, it is more than a mile wide. With wind and tidal influence, the river above Trader's Hill is not necessarily a good paddle for many of us. On weekends especially, from Trader's Hill onward, jet skis and boats roar by.

The river exits to the Atlantic between the islands of Amelia to the south in Florida and Cumberland to the north in Georgia. Cumberland Island is a National Seashore, and the extensive areas of saltmarsh before it is reached provide some interesting paddling. Indeed, paddlers sometimes cross the channel from Amelia to Cumberland, however be warned this is not for everyone and is potentially dangerous. The water is

Above: The cliffs along the St. Marys River lie on the Florida side. At this point, the St. Marys is a very wide river. The cliffs can be seen in the distance from the town of St. Marys, Georgia. The river upstream from Trader's Hill, Georgia, however, is not wide, but narrow and twisting with many sandbars. It is excellent paddling.

exceptionally deep and tidal rip can be significant. There are large boats on this section of the river.

This 130-mile river is a boundary between Florida and Georgia. Like the Suwannee River, portions of the St. Marys originate in Okefenokee Swamp. The 130 mile distance is the length given by the St. Johns River Water Management District and the St. Marys River Management Committee. The length of the river in various reference publications is given from 97 to 127 miles. In a newspaper article, The Florida Times Union described the river as 150 miles long. Take your pick.

While many portions have sandbars for camping, canoes should not be overloaded on this river as it is usually shallow, and there are sometimes frequent carries requiring wading. At times, this has been a grueling trip for even experienced, primitive-camping canoeists.

For those going fishing on their paddle,

consider that the St. Marys River lies in two states. Based on drainage, about 60% lies in Florida while 40% is in Georgia. Fishing licenses of both states are honored within the main channel of the river. However, going up a Georgia stream leading off from the main river with only a Florida license is not a good idea.

In the early 1990s, the St. Marys River was nominated by Congressmen William Bennet to become a Wild and Scenic River, a National Park Service designation which helps to protect the river. The distinguished and respected congressman probably considered this a no-brainer. Unfortunately, county governments and local property holders stopped this from happening. From the controversy, a river management committee was established which has a good record for proposals to protect the river, as well as providing education.

Areas along the St. Marys have a population of Florida-Georgia bears. There is plentiful native wildlife, and at least one member of the local outfitter's staff swears that escaped tigers are found across the Georgia border in a nearby swamp.

Many landings along the St. Marys tend to be very rural. They were not particularly well-marked when visited, and the roads also were sometimes difficult to distinguish. Those intending to use the landings would be well advised to talk to the sole local outfitter located on the river. A map will be exceptionally helpful to understanding the directions below. It is also easy to confuse SR-121 and CR-121 in this area.

POSSIBLE TRIPS AND LANDINGS - MIDDLE PRONG

1. From SR-250 to SR-127, 10 miles. SR-250 extends north and east through Osceola National Forest and to the river.
2. From SR-127 to North Prong, 2 miles. From SR-2 after the west bank of the North Prong, turn north on SR-127 and proceed to the bridge.

POSSIBLE TRIPS AND LANDINGS - NORTH PRONG

Note: Thompkins Landing is sometimes given as Tompkins Landing.

3. From SR-2 to SR-120, 5 miles. SR-2 crosses the North Prong. Go north on SR-125 from Glen St. Mary. Turn north on SR-127. Turn east on SR-2 and continue to the bridge.
4. From SR-120 to SR-121, 12 miles. Near Sanderson, take SR 127 north, then go east on SR-120 to the river.
5. From SR-121 to Stokes Bridge, 11 miles. The landing is 5.5 north of Macclenny on SR-121 at the northwest side of the bridge.
6. From Stokes Bridge to SR-2, 14.5 miles.

Go 6 miles east from Macclenny on US-90 to SR-121 and turn north. After about 6.5 miles, turn west on Stokes and go to the bridge.
7. From SR-2 to Thompkins Landing, 21 miles. From CR-121, go west on SR-2 to the bridge.
8. From Thompkins Landing to Trader's Hill, 8.5 miles. Thompkins Landing is west of Hillard and north on CR-121. There was no launch sign when visited, and it took several tries to find the landing, another reason to rely on the sole outfitter located on the river.
9. From Trader's Hill to Scotts Landing, 5.5 miles. From US-301 and Georgia SR-121, go south on SR-121 for 3.1 miles and turn east to Trader's Hill Recreation Area.
10. From Scotts Landing to Kings Ferry, 13.25. Just before US-301 leaves Florida, turn east in Boulogne onto Lake Hamilton Road. The landing is on a side road before you reach the state forest sign.
11. From Kings Ferry to US-17, 15.75 miles. From US-301 in Boulonge, go west on Lake Hamilton Road to Kings Ferry. This

is at the junction of Highways 121A and 115A.
12. Beyond US-17. The last landing the outfitter serves is at US-17 as it leaves Florida north of Yulee. Beyond US-17 the area is wide and consists of extensive saltmarsh followed by sea.

Additional Landings. There are presently 23 landings on the river. Some are private. A few are illegal. Some are too close together to be of much good for day paddling. A map of the river is available from the St. Marys River Management Committee.

CAMPING

From SR-121 north of Macclenny, to Trader's Hill on the Georgia side, there are numerous sandbars. Shortly after Trader's Hill, there is tidal influence. Ralph Simmons Memorial Forest is a St. Johns River Water Management District land.

Map. St. Marys River Canoe Trail, Office of Greenways and Trails. The 51-mile, state-designated canoe trail begins at SR-121 Bridge, north of Macclenny, and ends at US-301.

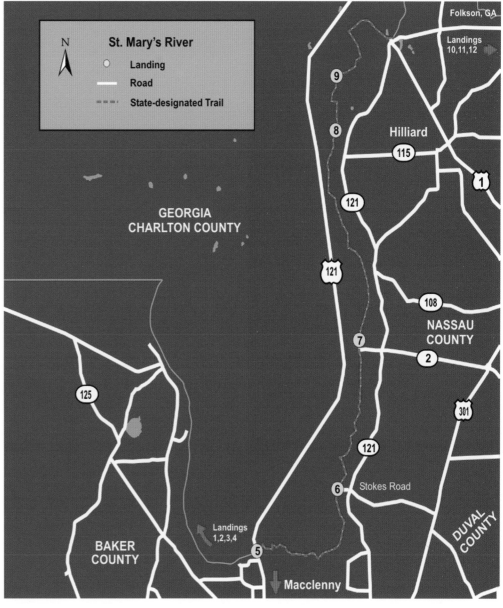

PC

Above: A placid portion of the Steinhatchee River above the falls.

STEINHATCHEE RIVER
(Dixie, Lafayette, and Taylor counties)

All rivers between Anclote Key and Ochlockonee Bay are seen by scientists as one huge drainage and estuary. Spring-fed and affected greatly by rainfall, the Steinhatchee River lies in the midst of this vast area.

The Steinhatchee River serves as a boundary between Dixie and Taylor counties, and forms from Mallory Swamp in Lafayette County. It is fed by inflows from: Boggy, Eight-Mile, Kettle, and Rocky creeks.

Perhaps the river is best known for Steinhatchee Falls, a short waterfall that provides a two-to-three foot plunge (which feels like six-to-ten if you are in the front of the canoe). This usually results in a large splash and a little swamping.

At times, paddlers have spilled if they did not approach correctly. Although it may change in time, the best path is presently to the right. As with whitewater, look for the V sign on the water's surface and shoot for the middle. Or take-out. There are landings just above and below the falls for those who wish to take-out before and put-in after.

While the river has deeper holes, the depth is usually six or seven feet. It is another of Florida's disappearing rivers. A

PC

FLORIDA WATERFALLS

Above: A natural waterfall on Falling Creek, south of White Springs. The yellow color is due to the wearing away of soil.

Steinhatchee Falls is one of a handful of tiny waterfalls in the Sunshine State. They would hardly count in a state like North Carolina. Another tinier fall is located on the Peace River. But Florida's best falls are not located on rivers. Falling Waters State Park has a fall of over 50 feet from a lake into a sink. Torreya State Park's weeping ridge is interesting only after heavy rainfall. Florida once had a spectacular waterfall along the Caloosahatchee River emerging from Lake Flirt, but this was destroyed with the making of the Disston Canal in the 1890's.

sign on US-19 states that you are crossing the Steinhatchee River, but the river is not there unless there is flooding. The river has gone underground on the east side of US-19 and has a rise a short ways to the west.

The community of Steinhatchee sits on Deadman's Bay. It is thought that Steinhatchee meant Deadman's River to Native Americans. Deadman's Bay is part of the Big Bend Paddling Trail. The town has excellent seafood restaurants with fried mullet fresh from the bay and famous Steinhatchee scallops.

Although it is spelled **Stein**hatchee, it is pronounced **Steen**hatchee. Some state maps show the Steinhatchee River as a state-designated canoe trail.

POSSIBLE TRIPS AND LANDINGS

1. From CR-137 to Bennett Grade, 4 miles. From US-19 south of Perry, turn left or apparent east on SR-51. Proceed to CR-137, and turn right to the bridge. There are landings to the right and left of the bridge.

2. From Bennett Grade Road to east of US-19, 5 miles. From US-19 south of Perry, turn east on SR-51. Turn right at Bennett Grade Road. Turn left at the Suwannee River Water Management District sign and proceed to the landing.

3. East of US-19. From US-19 to the south of the Steinhatchee Bridge, turn apparent east and follow the signs to the landing.

4. From Steinhatchee Falls to west of US-19, 1 mile. From US-19 south of Perry, turn apparent west (actually south) on SR-51. Turn "south" (actually east) or left at the Suwannee River Water Management District sign and proceed to the falls.

5. From Steinhatchee Falls to Steinhatchee to Steinhatchee Landing Resort, 7 miles. This is in "downtown" Steinhatchee at the west end of SR-51.

Above: The small, but lovely, waterfall on the Steinhatchee River.

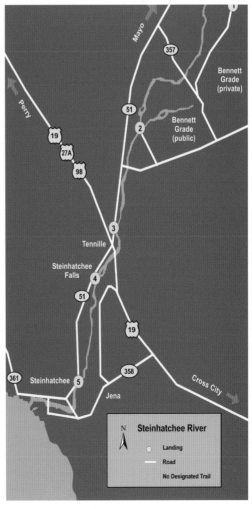

SUWANNEE RIVER
(Columbia, Dixie, Gilchrist, Hamilton, Lafayette, Levy, Madison, and Suwannee counties)

Portions of the Suwannee River are visually stunning. Its northern banks reveal limestone cliffs, worn away by thousands of years of moving water. Stare at the reflected banks long enough, and you may develop vertigo and wonder which is up and which is down.

Suwannee River serves as the boundary between many counties. It seeps forth from the Okefenokee Swamp, and along the southwesterly way to the Gulf, it is fed by numerous springs.

The Suwannee is also Florida's second longest river after the St. Johns, 177 miles versus 273. It is the paddle of a lifetime. Serious Florida paddlers and legions of scouts seek to make the trip from Stephen Foster Park (at Okefenokee Swamp in Georgia) to the Gulf near Cedar Key. Those who do not have this much free time - perhaps a week - may take the entire trip in weekend bites or even day trips.

Suwannee River is usually thought of in terms of Upper, or northern, and Lower, or southern. The Upper Suwannee reaches from the state line to Suwannee River State Park, but the 69-mile state-designated canoe trail begins at SR-6 Bridge. The Lower Suwannee includes a 52-mile, state-designated canoe trail from Suwannee River State Park to Branford.

With the exception of whitewater areas, the Suwannee is generally easy paddling except when the water level is very high. There are three prominent whitewater areas: Big Shoals, Ellaville, and Little Shoals. Ellaville Shoals lies to the west of Suwannee River State Park. Big Shoals is between Cone Bridge and US-41. The shoals are spectacular whitewater for Florida. Paddlers will hear the shoals before seeing them. Although some have gone over them in an inner tube, the three whitewater areas on the Suwannee require good paddling skills. Inexperienced paddlers will want to take-out. The instructions on the pamphlets from The Office of Greenways and Trails advise "portage around."

One of the most scenic single segments of the Suwannee River begins at Spirit of the Suwannee Music Park in Live Oak and ends at Suwannee River State Park. During normal to low water levels, large limestone outcrops lie around each bend.

At high water, the river is furious and sometimes dangerous. Then the confluence with the Withlacoochee (North), which occurs at Suwannee River State Park, is a sight to behold. The Withlacoochee is a long, powerful river in its own right. It

Above: A rocky outcrop on the Suwannee River. The northern portion of this river has considerable limestone along its banks. This rock is exposed during periods of low water.

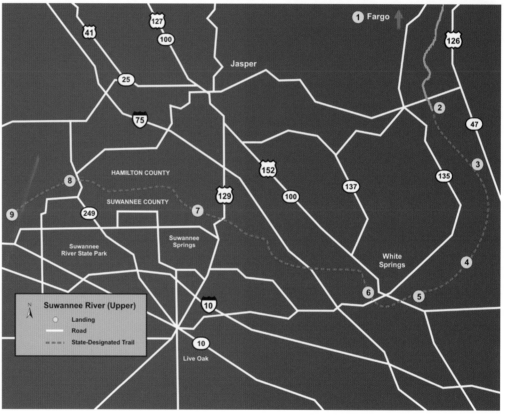

rushes into the Suwannee from the north, and springs along the banks spill out violently. Other significant Suwannee tributaries include the Alapaha and Sante Fe rivers.

There are many landings along the Suwannee. Some are private, including fish camps, and others are public. A publication is available from the Suwannee River Water Management District detailing directions to 52 landings on the Suwannee River, five landings on the Withlacoochee River, and twelve landings on the Santa Fe River.

POSSIBLE TRIPS AND LANDINGS - UPPER SUWANNEE

1. From Fargo, Georgia, Boat Ramp to SR-6, 21 miles. From I-10, exit on US-441 north at Lake City. Proceed across the Georgia border until reaching the Suwannee River. The landing is on the northeast side of the Suwannee. A Georgia State Park is being constructed at this landing as of March 2003. In fact, the park was largely underwater due to heavy rains and outflow from the Okefenokee Swamp.

2. From SR-6 to Cone Bridge, 10 Miles. From I-10, exit on US-441 north at Lake City. Turn west on SR-6 and proceed to the bridge.

3. From Cone Bridge to Big Shoals Public Lands, 10 miles. From I-10, exit on US-441 north at Lake City. Cone Bridge is announced by a launch sign indicating a west turn. Follow the dirt road to the landing.

4. From Big Shoals Public Lands to US-41, 6 miles. Exit I-75 on SR-136 east to White Springs. Turn south on US-41.

Take CR-135 north to Big Shoals Public Lands.

5. From US-41 to SR-136, 2 miles. Exit I-75 on SR-136 east at White Springs, turn south on US-41 in town, and proceed to the US-41 Bridge.

6. From SR-136 to Suwannee Springs (US-129), 19.5 miles. The SR-136 bridge is located within White Springs.

7. Suwannee Springs (US-129) to SR-249 Bridge, 15 miles. From I-10 near Live Oak, exit north on US-129. Suwannee Springs is on the east side of US-129 just before the river.

8. From SR-249 Bridge to Suwannee River State Park, 7.6 miles.
   From Live Oak, take SR-249 north to the bridge.

Map. Upper Suwannee River Canoe Trail, Office of Greenways and Trails.

SUWANNEE RIVER WILDERNESS TRAIL

In 2002, Florida's Department of Environmental Protection and the Suwannee River Water Management District, along with businesses located on the Suwannee River, announced a Suwannee River Wilderness Trail. The purpose of this trail was to create one-day journeys the length of the river which might encourage paddling and ecotourism. Information can be found on MyFlorida.com and www.dep.state.fl.us, or by writing DEP or the district (see Appendix B).

PADDLING IN THE OKEFENOKEE

Two prongs of the Suwannee River actually flow through the Okefenokee National Wildlife Refuge. They are considered the Middle Prong and the river itself. In actuality, the whole swamp can be considered part of the Suwannee and the St. Marys rivers. The refuge has constructed a series of camping platforms with toilets to aid paddlers in a wilderness experience.

In addition, some camping takes place on islands, in one case (Floyds Island) in a cabin. Reservations for using these trails and camping facilities are sometimes needed months in advance. The prime time is in the cooler months. Those interested can contact the Okefenokee Wildlife Refuge (see Appendix B) or outfitter Okefenokee Adventures (see Appendix A, under Suwannee River).

Georgia Landing. Stephen Foster Park in Okefenokee Swamp is the traditional beginning of the canoe journey.

POSSIBLE TRIPS AND LANDINGS - LOWER SUWANNEE

9. From Suwannee River State Park to SR-250 Bridge, 14.7 miles. One of Florida's premier state parks, it is located off both I-10 and I-75 and announced by prominent signs. It is northwest of Live Oak.

10. From SR-250 Bridge (Dowling Park) to SR-51 Bridge, 14.6 miles. Dowling Park is southwest of Live Oak at the junction of CR-136 and SR-250. The landing is on the east bank of the river.

11. From SR-51 Bridge to US-27 Bridge (Branford), 22.4 miles. From US-27 in Mayo, turn north on SR-51 and proceed 2 miles to the bridge.

12. From US-27 Bridge to SR-340 Ramp, 18 miles. The US-27 Bridge is in Branford.

13. SR-340 Ramp to Hart Springs Ramp, 14 miles. From Branford, take US-27 east to US-129/SR-49. Go south to CR-340 and west to the river. The park is on the south side of the road.

14. Hart Springs Ramp to Fanning Springs,

9 miles. From Branford, take US-27 east to US-129/SR-49 and go south across CR-340 and through the community of Bell. South of Bell, turn west onto CR-232. This road makes a right-hand south turn. After it does, make a west turn onto CR-344 which leads to the launch.

15. From Fanning Springs to Manatee Springs State Park, 9 miles. Fanning Springs is on the southwest bank where US-19 crosses the river in the community of Fanning Springs to the north of Chiefland.

16. Manatee Springs State Park to Suwannee, 20 miles. Manatee Springs State Park is in the north part of Chiefland, a west turn on SR-320 from US-19, prominently announced by signs.

17. Suwannee. The small community of Suwannee, with some excellent seafood restaurants, is located at the absolute dead end of CR-349. This is a south turn (apparent west) from US-19 in Old Town, 3 miles north of the Suwannee River.

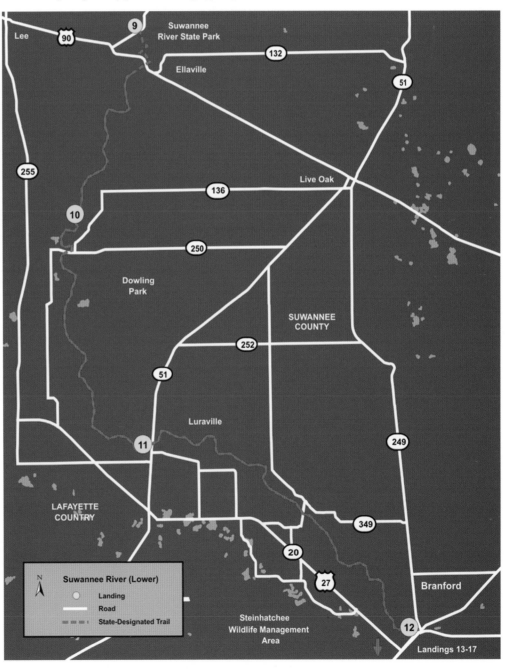

CAMPING

The Suwannee River is surrounded by much public land and many fish camps. Some of the public land which offers best camping options is managed by Suwannee River Water Management District. Big Shoals Public Lands, Suwannee River State Park, and Twin Rivers State Forest are located along the river in the Upper Section. Spirit of the Suwannee Music Park, a private campground, offers an option near Live Oak. In addition, the Lower Suwannee includes Manatee Springs State Park.

Right: Bathtub Spring along the Suwannee River.

Below: A side channel in the limestone along the bank of the Suwannee River.

Opposite page: The rapids at Big Shoals are one of three permanent rapids on the Suwannee. The other two are at Ellaville and Little Shoals. At low water levels, other runs may appear, but these three are permanent, except during periods of very high water.

WHITEWATER

Surprisingly, whitewater exists on several Florida rivers. Paddlers frequently refer to the "class" of whitewater. This means how difficult it is. Classes are rated from the easiest, Class I, to the most difficult, Class XI (in the extreme range). Florida has nothing more difficult than Class I or II, both of which are considered easy. Tell that to the novice facing whitewater areas such as Big Rapid on the Aucilla and Melvin Shoals on the Withlacoochee (North).

TO

SWIFT CREEK
(Hamilton County)

Above: Sand and limestone are found around the bends along much of the northern portion of the Suwannee River. Swift Creek is a small tributary of the Suwannee.

Fast and dangerous, local outfitters caution that Swift Creek is not for beginners.

A tributary of the Suwannee River, this creek was recommended by a member of the Apalachee Canoe and Kayak Club. Swift Creek flows into the Suwannee from the northeast between Suwannee Springs to the west and White Springs to the east.

Right conditions, as always, mean a lot. During high water, this creek can be difficult. At low water, there is an exposed limestone shelf. In between, conditions are perfect.

Swift Creek is crossed by US-41 and CR-25A. The put-in is northwest of White Springs on CR-25A. The next official take-out is on at Suwannee Springs, nearly 5 miles downstream. Suwannee Springs is north of I-10 on the east side of US-129 just before the river. However, some scout "unofficial" landings to shorten the trip.

Club members were curious if the trip could be paddled from US-41 to CR-25A. Any paddlers who do this are welcome to provide an update.

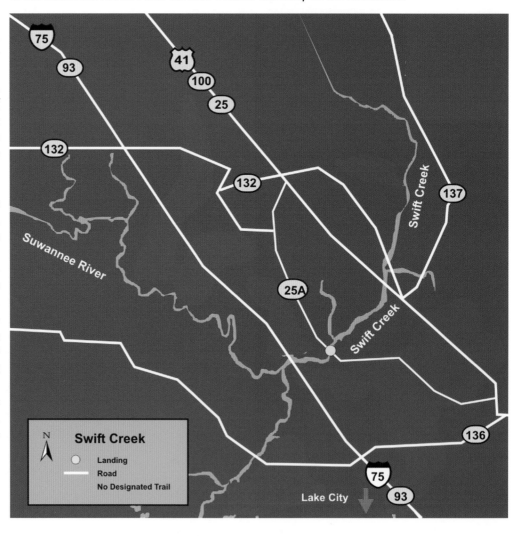

TOMOKA RIVER
(Volusia County)

This state-designated canoe trail starts at SR-40 near Ormond Beach and ends at Tomoka State Park. The trip can add up to a little over 13 miles. Many paddle upstream from SR-40 and back as one day trip, then SR-40 to Tomoka State Park as another. However, in times of drought, it may not be passable very far south on the river.

Inland, the Tomoka River is cypress dominated, but by the sea, it is largely in saltmarsh. At Tomoka State Park, the river has become wide and merges with the Halifax River, an inland waterway that can be rough and sea-like when the wind is up.

POSSIBLE TRIPS AND LANDINGS

1. From SR-40 south and return, 4 miles total. This mileage varies greatly with water level. At some point south, the river becomes impassable. From I-95 near Ormond Beach, turn west on SR-40 and go to the bridge.
2. From SR-40 to US-1, 4.5 miles.
3. Tomoka State Park. From I-95, exit east on Old Dixie Highway, passing Bulow Plantation Ruins Historic Site, and follow the signs.

CAMPING

Tomoka State Park.

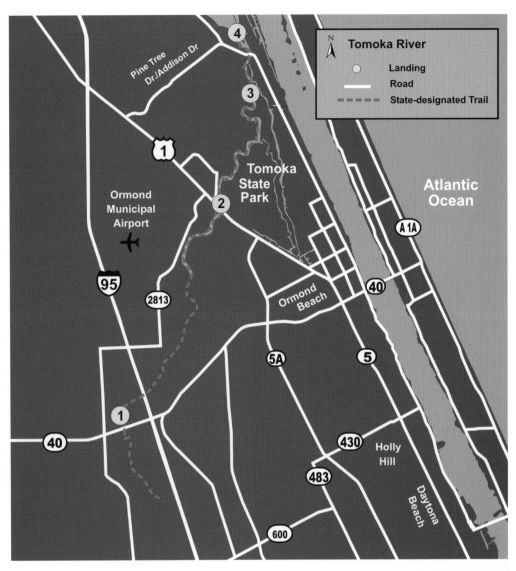

Below: Guides carrying canoes down the sandy banks of the Withlacoochee River (North).

WACCASASSA RIVER
(Levy County)

An annual canoe race, originally "Wild Hog Canoe Race," on the Waccasassa between SR-24 and US-19 has become known popularly as the "Waccasassa Mud Race." That stretch of the 29-mile blackwater river is shallow and twisty, with many log jams.

From US-19 going west, paddling becomes more bearable. The river continues narrow and twisty until it opens up in the Gulf Hammock area, before the river empties into Waccasassa Bay.

Those enjoying the Big Bend Paddling Trail can experience Waccasassa Bay also. Tides in this area can leave a paddler unexpectedly high and dry, so it is very important to check the tides. At the junction of the river and US-19, many people park under the overpass and put-in from there.

POSSIBLE TRIPS AND LANDINGS

1. Above US-19, problematical
2. From US-19 to CR-326 Landing, 5 miles. US-19 crosses the Waccasassa River just to the south of Otter Creek, and considerably north of Crystal River.
3. From CR-326 to Waccasassa Bay and Return, 8 miles or more. From US-19, turn west on CR-326 and follow it to the landing.

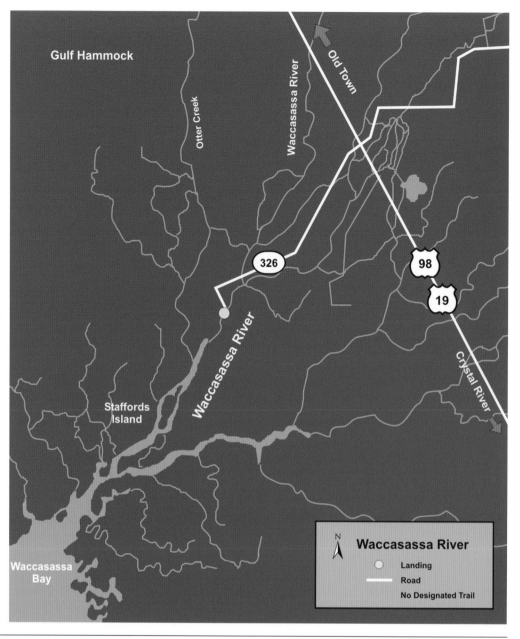

Below: Canoeist on the Santa Fe River pauses to examine a large cypress.

PC

WITHLACOOCHEE RIVER
(North) (Hamilton and Madison counties)

Withlacoochee North is one whale of a river and a great ride. Water level is everything on this river, and most of the time, there are shoals after shoals, with a finale at Melvin Shoals, a whitewater area a few miles above Suwannee River State Park, and the confluence of both rivers.

Florida has two Withlacoochee Rivers, North and South. Withlacoochee is a Creek word which means little and big water. The other Withlacoochee is in Central Florida, and referred to as the Withlacoochee (South) to avoid confusion. The Withlacoochee (North) is both blackwater and spring-fed. It flows past Valdosta in Georgia.

This is arguably the finest 32 miles of river in Florida. At least it should be rated in the top five of Florida rivers. It is a favorite of many scout troops, who canoe its total length. In Georgia, there are 70 additional miles of river flowing from the headwaters.

Two prominent springs are Blue Springs near the SR-6 landing and Suwanacoochee on the west bank before Suwannee River State Park.

This is also a super river for wildlife.

Sturgeon and spotted-gar churn the surface. Mullet make spectacular leaps. Alligator snapping turtles are sometimes seen, usually on the bottom, and snakes, including banded water snakes, swim on the surface and sometimes dive. Alligators are present, and deer sightings are frequent.

Going over Melvin Shoals is a thrill. For whitewater enthusiasts, it is a short thrill,

Above: The Withlacoochee River.

but a thrill none-the-less. Those who do not want to take this risk should take-out before the shoals and walk the boat through with a rope attached. It should be a long rope. Carrying the canoe or kayak up the slopes and back down might be worse than crossing the shoals. In actuality, these are rough waters and require a tough boat.

PC

Above: Crossing Melvin Shoals on the Withlacoochee River (North).

89

POSSIBLE TRIPS AND LANDINGS

1. From SR-145 to SR-150, 4 miles. This launch is at the Georgia border 18 miles northeast of Madison on SR-145. Most outfitters make the trip from SR-145 to SR-143 in one day and avoid taking out at SR-150.

2. From SR-150 to SR-143, 8.5 miles. SR-150 crosses the Withlacoochee at the Hamilton and Madison county lines to the east of the small community of Pinetta. In Pinetta, turn east from SR-145 onto SR-150 and go about 5.5 miles to the bridge.

3. From SR-143 to SR-6 (Blue Springs Canoe Launch), 2 miles. This landing is above SR-6. From SR-6 north of Live Oak, turn north on SR-143. The water management district directions then say to turn left on the second dirt road. A little exploration is then in order. The landing is not truly on SR-143.

4. From SR-6 (Blue Springs Canoe Launch) to Suwannee River State Park, 12 miles. Blue Springs is on the south side of SR-6. When visited, Blue Springs was in transition, the springs itself closed, and an alternative landing in use. It would thus be wise to check with local outfitters before proceeding if taking your own craft. (Road maps, guides, and road signs differ as to whether this is SR-6. The directions from Office of Greenways and Trails states county road.) It was reported by local guides that Blue Springs was to become a state park.

5. Suwannee River State Park is west of Live Oak on US-90. There is a marked exit on I-10 for the park.

Additional Landing. Wiggins Landing, not cited on material from Greenways and Trails or in other guides, lies between Blue Springs and Suwannee River State Park.

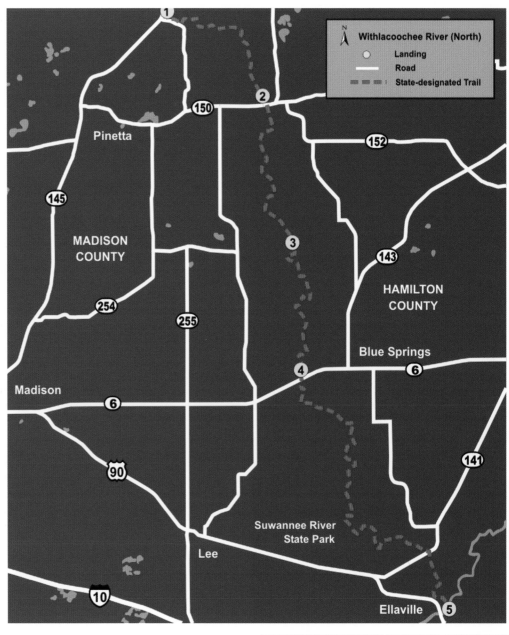

Map. Withlacoochee (North) Canoe Trail, Office of Greenways and Trails.

CAMPING

In Florida, the river passes through much land held by Suwannee River Water Management District.

Above: Falls on Steinhatchee River.   **Opposite: The floodplain along the Sante Fe River.**

SPILLED!

Without a doubt, if you paddle long enough, you will spill. It is therefore important to know how to reenter, a canoe or a kayak. (For kayaks that are sit-on-tops, it is more like remount.)

A spill in a river like the Withlacoochee (North) can be very dangerous. Rushing waters could quickly carry a paddler away from the canoe and assistance. A life jacket should always be worn, especially on non-swimmers and those with little stamina, like children.

In many rivers, the banks are nearby, and the river is shallow, so the easiest thing to do is to drag the craft to shore, dump the water, and climb back in.

Before taking that first canoe or kayak trip in broad waters, however, ask the outfitter for a brief class on reentering.

Kayaks are often turned 360 degrees in deep water to right a spill. In fact, some kayakers do "rolls" just for fun. Before trying a "roll," be sure to get instruction. Rolling is usually for the sea, not Florida's rocky rivers.

PC

ALAFIA RIVER
(Hillsborough and Polk counties)

Crossing the Alafia River on I-75 south of Tampa, it is easy to get an inaccurate impression of the river. To the west, the river is wide and brackish, with saltmarsh. Jet skis often zip on its surface on weekends. Motorized pleasure boats head to sea. To the east is a pretty little island in the midst of a wide river.

The state-designated canoe trail, however, is twisty and winding. It passes over limestone shoals. In times of low water, one is even likely to grind to a halt on a submerged limestone shelf, or smack into a limestone boulder. In times of high water, it is a rip. In-between, it is sometimes lazy paddling.

A typical visit may include an impressive display of wildlife: alligators, barred owls, catbirds, great blue herons, little blue herons, coots, four species of ducks, among others. The lower part of this 25-mile, blackwater river is rich in catfish, mullet, redfish, sheepshead, and trout. The Alafia

Banks, two spoil islands at the mouth of the river, are a nesting ground for 16 species of birds in congregations of thousands.

The outfitter's signature trip is to put-in at Alderman-Ford and take-out at their business, or put-in at their business (see Appendix A) and take-out at the last landing. Both Alderman-Ford and Lithia Springs are outstanding county parks worth visiting.

At times, the river above Alderman-Ford County Park has been clogged by logjams. At other times, the water level has also been too low for paddling. Until this section is cleared, checking with the canoe outfitter is a good idea before putting into those sections.

The Alafia exits into Hillsborough Bay. There the Alafia Banks support rookeries for 16 species of birds.

Some paddlers avoided the Alafia for a long time both because of past catastrophic phosphoric acid spills and rowdiness. Its banks have something of a reputation for bad behavior. Sadly, this reputation is well-earned, at least in the past, but the situation

Above: Canoes on the Alafia River at Alderman Ford Park.

appears to be resolved, and order restored on the river. Some years ago, families and casual paddlers on weekends were harassed (and even bombarded with thrown objects) by rowdy elements on the shore. This was unfortunate because there is much beauty on the river.

POSSIBLE TRIPS AND LANDINGS
1. From Keysville Bridge to Alderman Ford Park, 7 miles. The Keysville Bridge is on CR-676 approximately 1.5 miles east of the intersection with SR-39. SR-39 stretches between I-4 and SR-60.
2. From Alderman Ford Park to CR-640 Bridge, 9 miles. Alderman Ford Park is located on both sides of SR-39 south of Plant City and I-4.
3. From CR-640 Bridge to Lithia Springs Park, 2 miles. From I-75, exit east on SR-60 in Brandon. Turn south on CR-640 and proceed to the bridge.
4. From Lithia Springs Park to Bell Shoals Road Bridge, 12 miles. Lithia Springs

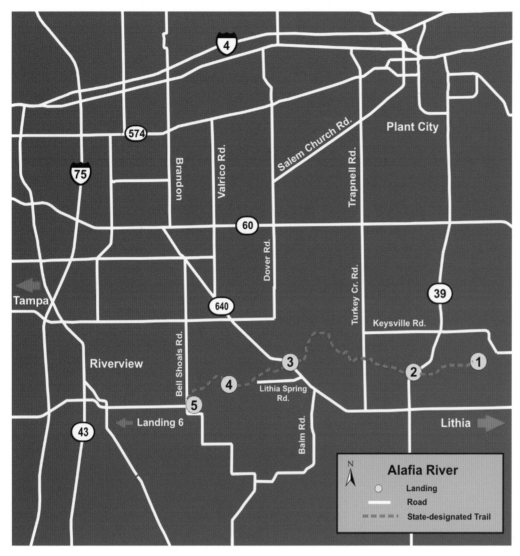

Map legend:
Alafia River
○ Landing
— Road
- - - State-designated Trail

Park is located on Lithia Springs Road. To reach it, go south of Plant City on SR-39 to CR-640 (Lithia-Pinecrest Road). Go west on Lithia-Pinecrest then follow the directional on Lithia Springs Road.

5. From Bell Shoals Bridge to Alafia Ramp, 3 miles. From SR-60 in Brandon, turn south on CR-640. The road forks to Bell Shoals, Lithia, and Durant Road. Take Bell Shoals to the bridge.

6. Alafia Ramp. It is possible, of course, to paddle beyond this Alafia ramp into Tampa Bay. From the intersection of Bell Shoals Road and Bloomingdale, go west on Bloomingdale for 1.5 miles. Turn south (left) onto Kings Road. Go 0.75 miles and turn west (right) onto Center Street. The ramp is located at the end of Center, about 0.25 miles.

POSSIBLE TRIP ON SOUTH PRONG

A South Prong Canoe Trail is being cleared by volunteers from a launch site to a camping area within Alafia River State Park. At present, the paddler can go a short distance north down river before hitting lift-overs, but this will change in time. The paddler can also go south to Hurrah Lake, a wide spot in the river, for about 1 mile. The launch is located at the end of Thatcher Road. From the junction of SR-60 and SR-39, go south on CR-39 for 12 miles and turn east onto Thatcher Road. It is 0.5 mile to the bridge. The park is on Thatcher Road and open from 8:00 mornings to sunset.

Map. Alafia River Canoe Trail, Office of Greenway and Trails. The 13-mile, state-designated canoe trail ends at Bell Shoals Road. This landing has been closed for quite some time because local landowners complained to police about after-hour activities. Allegedly, there was even an attempt to set fire to a private dock. Re-opening of this landing is a possibility and has been a matter of debate between paddlers and local homeowners. Checking with the local outfitter is the best course at present to find out what is open and what is closed. Or, just proceed the extra 3 miles to the Alafia Ramp.

Above: A DEP inspector atop Piney Point, an abandoned phosphogypsum stack. See adjoining box.

ALAFIA AND PHOSPHATE

In the late 1900s, a very large phosphoric acid plume drifted down the Alafia river killing millions of fish and other living organisms. Mulberry Phosphates took full blame and promised to clean up the damage. The company has since gone out of business without repairing the damage. The state has been stuck with operating the phosphate business so that further damage does not occur to the river. This is expected to deplete the phosphate trust funds raised by a tax on every ton of phosphate mined.

On December 31, 2002, an abandoned phosphogypsum stack located at Piney Point which had been part of Mulberry Phosphates was in danger of bursting and releasing over 100 million gallons of untreated waste water into Tampa Bay. A catastrophic spill was narrowly avoided. In order to drain this "stack," two controversial methods were employed by Florida DEP: treated waters were taken into the Gulf of Mexico by barge and were also released directly into Bishop Harbor, an aquatic preserve of Tampa Bay.

Phosphate provides jobs for many economically stricken areas of Florida. Industry proponents say that they are feeding the world. Fertilizers they produce guarantee large crops. After meeting most US needs, a large amount of Florida's phosphate presently goes to China. Running out of lands to mine, the industry wants new areas opened.

Industry opponents object to any expansion of the mining areas. They point to the dangers of phosphogypsum stacks created from the production of fertilizer and the clay settling ponds from the mining. They argue that mining changes the hydrology of the earth and increases radioactivity in water, fish, and birds. They also criticize award-winning restoration efforts as not returning the earth to its original state.

Clearly jobs and the environment are on a collision course over the issues of phosphate mining. Most of the mining proposed for Central Florida lies in little Hardee County, with a population of less than 30,000 and a relatively tiny budget.

There is no guarantee that another phosphate mining company operating phosphogypsum stacks will not go out of business. Over 200 phosphate mining companies operated at the dawn of the phosphate era. As of this writing, there are only three. Accidents can never be elimnated, as they are often the result of human error.

ANCLOTE KEY/RIVER
(Pinellas County)

This area off-shore from Tarpon Springs is a favorite paddle for sea-kayakers. Launching from Anclote River Park, there is a power plant to the north; its warm-water effluent attracts fish, and fishing from kayaks is very productive. In the distance is Anclote Key with smaller Dutchman Key in front of it. Perhaps 15 miles of Gulf kayaking can be enjoyed around the islands.

From Alternate US-19 in Tarpon Springs, turn west on Anclote Boulevard. Go to Bailie's Bluff Boulevard where the park is located.

Another access is from Howard Park easily pin-pointed by prominent signs on Alternate 19 in Tarpon Springs. From Howard Park, it is a 3 mile paddle to Anclote Key.

The Anclote River in portions is meandering, fairly wide, with saltmarsh. It begins east of Tarpon Springs near Lake Tarpon. The river has an interesting section with numerous bends in natural condition that make paddling by development and through boating fishermen worthwhile. These bends lie east of the public launch to the south of the junction of Alternate 19 and SR-582. A newly created trail lies in the saltmarsh at the river's mouth.

Right: A narrow part of the Pithlachascotee.

SHARKS AND KAYAKING

At times, warnings have been issued for large shark congregations near Anclote Key. On one occasion, 100 sharks were observed feeding nearby. This is a normal event, as sharks do congregate from time-to-time. However, such an event can become a media circus and chase people from the area.

While terrifying and sometimes tragic, shark attack is rare, and the odds against it are in the millions. Despite the movie Jaws, *it is exceptionally rare for a shark to attack a boat. Sharks do attack swimmers who are mistaken for fish.*

After kayaking in the summer sun, a swim is a great way to cool down. Here are some safety suggestions. When swimming, leave jewelry behind, as the flashing might imitate the flash of prey. It is not a good idea to go off the kayak into murky waters, where a shark cannot tell a person from a fish. Night, dawn, and dusk are the times sharks are most active. Of course, if a shark is seen, it is imperative to get out of the water. Amazingly, a number of people have taken to swimming with sharks as a new nature adventure. This hardly seems wise.

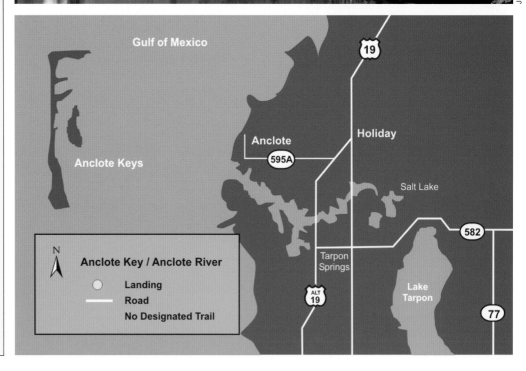

ARBUCKLE CREEK
(Highlands and Polk counties)

Arbuckle Creek connects Lake Arbuckle to Lake Istokpoga, Florida's fifth-largest lake. Istokpoga is about 1/17th the size of Okeechobee, Florida's largest lake. The creek passes through some fine, often remote country. Two large creeks flow into Arbuckle: Moran Hole Creek to the east above CR-700A and Carter Creek to the west below CR-700A.

The first 10.5 miles pass by Avon Park Air Force Range. Not to worry about bombs falling along the creek, as it is far from the range, but during hunting season, the same as many places in the great outdoors, wear orange.

Permission is not needed from Avon Park Air Force Range to canoe the creek, as long as vehicles are parked outside the base. However, in times of drought base personnel considered the section adjacent to the base impassable. Then, cows walked across the puddles in Arbuckle Creek onto the bombing range. It is also weed-clogged. Personnel on the base recommend instead putting-in considerably to the south at Arbuckle Creek Road during times of low water. Then, it is possible to paddle upstream or down to Lake Istokpoga. If in doubt, it might be wise to call the base, or go have a look and then make a decision.

During the period August to March, there is greater likelihood of having sufficient water on the upper stretches. Like everywhere in Florida, it is often deluge or drought.

As far as wildlife, this area is sufficiently remote to have anything on it, including panthers. Wild pigs and deer are commonplace mammals in this area. Lake Arbuckle is usually bird filled, with various snakes seen on its banks, and the fish are so plentiful they attract fishermen from some distance.

All landings are given, but check water levels. Having gone through the effort, from US-98 it is only a short paddle to say you have been on Lake Istokpoga.

POSSIBLE TRIPS AND LANDINGS
1. From Lake Arbuckle to Arbuckle Road, 3 miles. From US-27 in Avon Park, considerably south of I-4, go east to the end of CR-64. Put-in from the fish camp.
2. From Arbuckle Road to Arbuckle Creek Road, 12.2 miles. There are county boat landings at both Arbuckle Road and Arbuckle Creek Road. Arbuckle Road is an east turn from CR-64, a few miles from the end.
3. From Arbuckle Creek Road to US-98, 9 miles. In Avon Park, go south on SR-17 about 7 miles to CR-17A. Turn east and go about 6 miles to the bridge.
4. From US-98 to Lake Istokpoga and return, 2 miles. There is a landing on US-98 without any really good reference point.

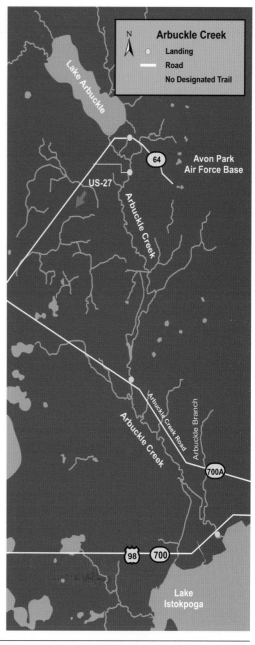

BISHOP HARBOR
(Manatee County)

The harbor is an open area surrounded by mangrove, with a mouth opening toward the Sunshine Skyway Bridge. It is located near Port Manatee.

Within its friendly confines, large concentrations of stingrays can be seen. Sometimes the curious rays, relatives of the sharks, come up to an idle kayak and stare with apparent curiosity at the humans in the strange atmosphere above.

At low tide, this harbor is very shallow, with only inches of water in places. Some mangroves sprout from oyster beds. Red and black mangroves, as well as buttonwood, are found. Waterbirds are plentiful. Hermit crabs abound on the bottom.

A 3-mile, marked loop trail has been established as part of Manatee County's Blueway. It is one of seven sections in the 75-mile marked trail. This area can be paddled by both canoe and kayak, providing the surf is calm.

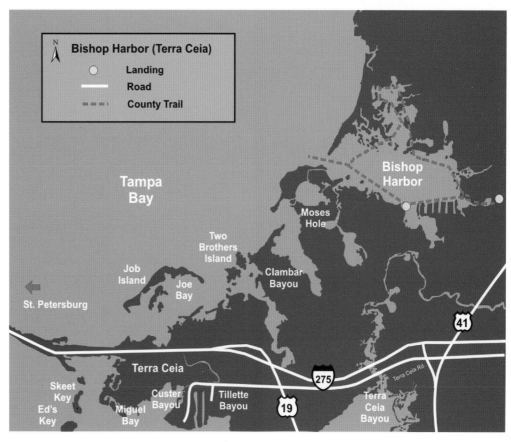

Unfortunately, the Piney Point gypsum stack has been at times drained-off in 2003-2004 into the Harbor. Phosphogypsum is by-product of making fertilizer from phosphate. How long this process will continue until the stack is dry and inactive is difficult to tell. There are already signs of unnatural enrichment in the harbor. The water leaks out of Bishop Harbor into Tampa Bay.

From I-75 between Tampa and Bradenton, turn north/west on I-275. Exit at US-41, the last exit before the toll for the Sunshine Skyway Bridge. Go north/east on US-41 and turn left at the light on Bishop Harbor. There is a launch on the right within a half mile. A little farther down the road is a second boat launch.

BLACKWATER CREEK
(Lake County)

This is one of the four rivers in the Wekiva River System, and its waters make their way into the St. Johns River. One popular journey is made by traveling 5 miles down the creek from Seminole State Forest and 4 miles south and upstream on the Wekiva to Katie's Landing. It also possible to paddle beyond the convergence with the Wekiva north onto the St. Johns and take-out at the first landing on the east side. Upper portions of Blackwater Creek are considered by local outfitters to be too shallow and blocked for most paddlers.

Katie's Landing is located on the north side of SR-46 down a dirt road. Exit I-4 west of Sanford. Within a few miles there is a large billboard advertising Katie's Landing that announces the turn north. Seminole State Forest is located farther east on SR-46 and can also be accessed off SR-44. The St. Johns' landing is at the west end of High Banks Road, a westerly turn off US-92/17 in DeBary, Volusia County.

CAMPING

Although short enough to be a day trip, camping in Seminole State Forest off SR-46 is very pleasant.

Above: Canoeists passing Morris Bridge Wilderness Park on the Hillsborough River.

BRADEN RIVER
(Manatee County)

Braden River is a fine river, with birds (particularly black-crowned night herons) and other wildlife year round. It is divided by a dam, so journeys are either above the dam or below it. Below the dam, there is great tidal influence. The paddle from SR-64 is part of the Manatee County Blueway.

A long-reported canoe trip above the dam is usually made between Linger Lodge Landing, at the end of Linger Lodge Road, and Jiggs Landing near SR-70. Sometimes the river, which downstream is blocked by a dam, has little flow, or even some slight flow to the east, but usually the flow is to the north-northwest from Linger Lodge. Depending on water levels, it is possible to paddle a short distance to the east of Linger Lodge, but usually the river turns shallow, and eventually water to paddle in runs out. Just before Jiggs Landing the dam creates a large, backwater lake. The dam is north of Jiggs Landing, impeding the journey. Folks at Jiggs Landing warn that the area around the dam is dangerous because of rocks.

It is also possible to paddle between SR-70 to SR-64, a distance of about 5 miles. At the SR-70 landing, the put-in is on Gap Creek. This is not a trip for canoes, but for kayaks, for the river widens out to a mile or more as it proceeds to join the Gulf near the Manatee River.

Linger Lodge is unique. It has a restaurant where the first thing encountered, other than a friendly waitress, is a stuffed Florida black bear. Dozens of mounted rattlesnakes adorn the walls. Other stuffed animals include a bobcat, otter, raccoon, and even what appears to be a Florida panther. These animals, with the exception of the snakes, were collected as road kill. Florida crackers did not create this; Linger Lodge is the product of a Yankee who moved south. Jiggs Landing, on the other hand, is like a trip back into old Cracker Florida.

Like most rivers, high water is a breeze during the rainy months. In low water, wild hog piglets walk across the river to be fed at Linger Lodge. The entire river is subject to boating. When visited, there was no launch fee at Linger Lodge, but there was a small fee at Jiggs Landing.

Within a mile or so of Linger Lodge, paddlers pass under two spans of the Braden Bridge on I-75. The sound is deafening for about a quarter mile from each side.

POSSIBLE TRIPS AND LANDINGS

1. From Linger Lodge Landing south, problematic miles. Linger Lodge lies at the wandering end of Braden River Road. Exit I-75 west on SR-70, and turn south on 63d Street East, also marked as Braden River Road. If you miss this, you can turn south at the next light. Continue on Linger Lodge Road to the end.

2. From Linger Lodge Landing to Jiggs Landing, 4-5 miles.

3. Jiggs Landing. Jiggs Landing is at a sharp curve on the way to Linger Lodge. The directions are the same except Jiggs Landing comes first.

3. From SR-70 to SR-64, 5 miles. Exit I-75 west on SR-70 and proceed to 51st Street East. Go north to Braden River Park.

4. SR-64 Landing. From I-75, go east on SR-64. Although two landings are shown on the Gazetteer, there is one good landing on the southeast bank.

5. It is also possible for the ardent kayaker to paddle farther on the Braden to the Manatee River, then west to Emerson Point Park to the west of Palmetto. The park is located west from Business US-41 in Palmetto on 10th Street. This trip is wide water, heavily boated, and at least 7 miles long.

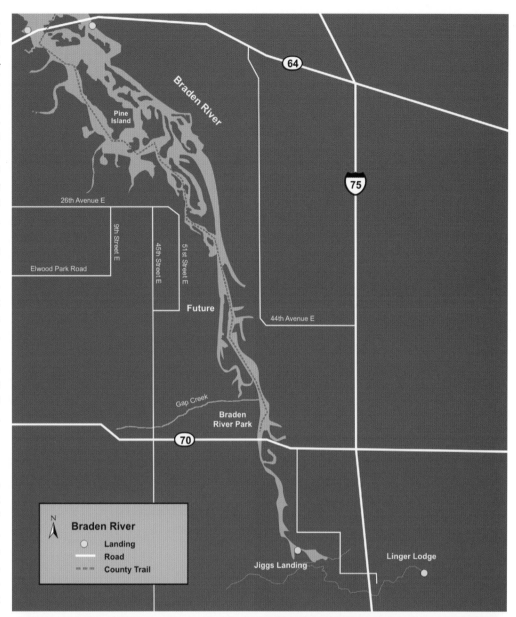

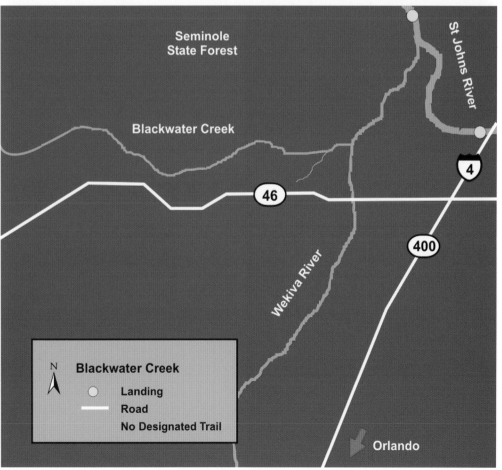

CALADESI ISLAND
(Pinellas County)

Many kayakers simply put-in from the causeway leading to Honeymoon Island to the north of Caladesi. Honeymoon Island is a state park. Because of shifting sands, Caladesi has for a long time been attached to Clearwater Beach to the south, and all this land shelters bay-side kayakers.

Access to Caladesi, itself a state park, is by ferry from Honeymoon Island State Park. Or just paddle over. The causeway is part of SR-586. Go south of Tarpon Springs and north of Dunedin on Alternate US-19 and turn west on SR-586.

A 3.25-mile canoe trail has been created by Caladesi Island State Park, part of the Gulf Islands GeoPark. The trail travels through mangroves on the east side of the island. Cafe Caladesi offers a limited number of sit-on-top kayaks for rent.

In 2002, the Laboratory for Coastal Research selected the beach at Caledesi as the fifth best in the entire 50 states.

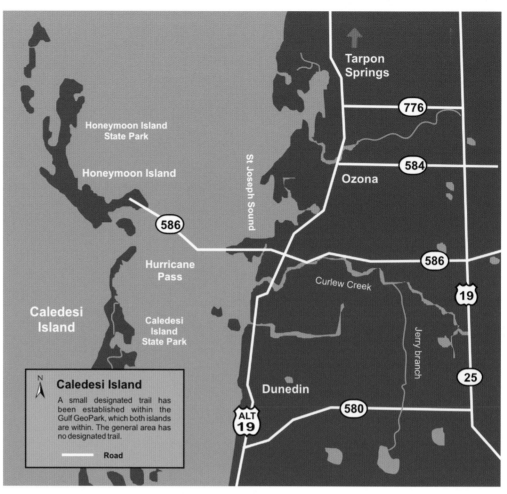

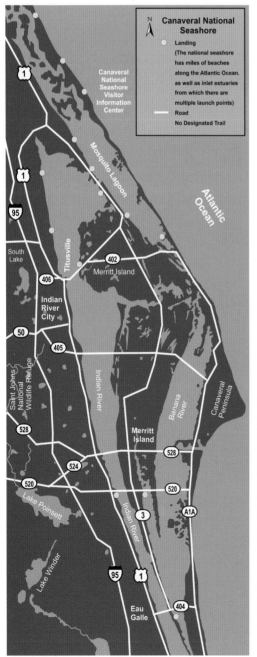

CANAVERAL NATIONAL SEASHORE
(Brevard and Volusia counties)

More than 20 miles of uninterrupted beach in a pristine condition attracts many for a stroll or a swim. In addition to a usually tranquil back bay for kayaking, "surf" kayakers love the seashore when the surf is up. Gulf Coast kayakers frequently make the cross-state trip so they can zip toward the beach on magnificent waves. Take the Titusville exit east from I-95 and go through the city. Cross the Indian River on SR-406 and follow the signs.

Mosquito Lagoon, between the national seashore and Merrit Island National Wildlife Refuge, is also a popular kayak paddle and has its own account in this section. To access the north end of Canaveral National Seashore, take the New Smyrna Beach exit east from I-95, go through the city to A1A, and follow A1A south.

Anyone wishing to paddle in this area, would be wise to call in advance. During shuttle launches, large areas are closed to the public for safety.

Above: A night heron hunting along a river bank.

CHASSAHOWITZKA RIVER
(Citrus County)

Possibly the loveliest small river in Florida, the Chassahowitzka flows west from several large springs into the Gulf. When the tide is going out, moving against the spring flow is made more difficult. Chassahowitzka is a first-magnitude spring system.

The put-in is beside Chassahowitzka Spring, once a favorite swimming hole, complete with floating dock, which has vanished. Miss Maggie's bait house is gone, replaced with a more substantial store, but the road is named Miss Maggie Road. Another spring is near the railroad trestle remnants. Farther west another spring run flows in from the north.

A small population of Florida black bear struggles for existence in this general area. They frequently come surprisingly close to suburbia and urban sprawl, but are rarely seen. The river also attracts manatees, and their enemy, fast, propeller-driven boats.

There is but one landing where Miss Maggie's Bait House stood for years. On US-19, 9 miles south of Homosassa Springs, go west at the only Chassahowitzka road available, and follow it to the dead end. For at least 40 years, this road has been marked by a blinking yellow light, but times may change as the population swells in this area.

If proceeding out of the main river, charts of the area are exceptionally helpful and may be purchased at local marinas in Homossasa and Crystal River.

The Chassahowitza River is part of the Nature Coast Canoe Trail. This trail connects three sister rivers: the Chassahowitza, Crystal, and Homosassa rivers. Some officials called it the Citrus County Paddling Trail, but that is not the correct designation.

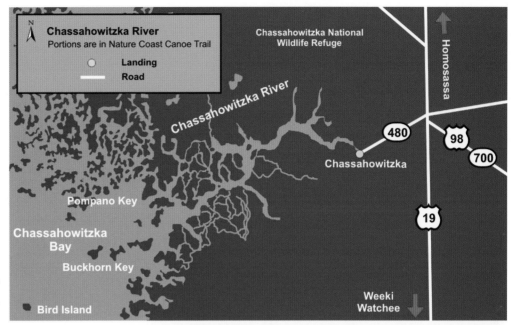

COCKROACH BAY
(Hillsborough County)

The two paddling trails, Horse Shoe Crab and Snook, twist through mangroves and some open water. The shorter Horse Shoe Crab Trail loops north from the landing, while longer Snook loops south. It is perhaps 1 mile on the shorter trail and 3 on the longer. The trails wind back and forth through mangroves but are thankfully marked with pipes. Both trails are rich in waterbird sightings.

Mangroves are now greatly reduced on Tampa Bay, so these trails are an indication of what once was extensive, rich estuary. Both red and black mangroves are found here, the black mangroves on higher ground inside the tangles.

At low tide, the trail can require some walking in the mud under a few inches of water; this too is a joy, but come prepared.

From I-75 south of Tampa, exit at Sun City and go west to US-41. Turn south on US-41 and turn west on Cockroach Bay Boulevard.

Above: A red mangrove in Cockroach Bay. The function of the roots is not clearly understood. Some scientists believe they add support, others think they help the plant cope with its environment by processing salt.

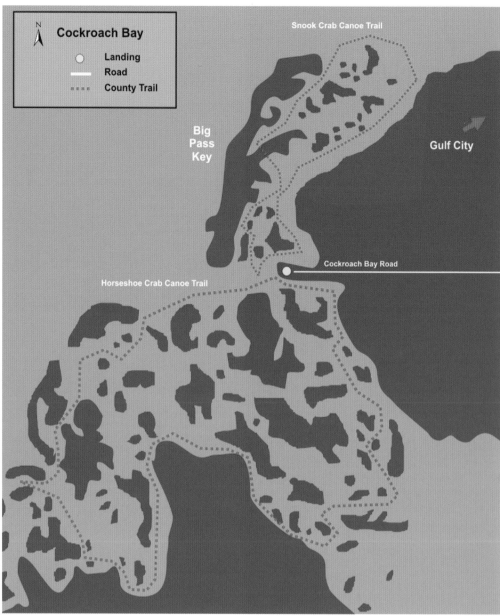

CRYSTAL RIVER
(Citrus County)

Known primarily for its manatee congregations, Crystal River flows 7 miles to the Gulf from a series of powerful springs. In fact, Crystal Springs are among the most powerful first-magnitude spring systems in Florida. Of the 30 springs in the river, 28 are located in the headwaters at Kings Bay. Some of the springs have colorful names; in addition to Idiots Delight, Shark Sink, and Gator Hole, there is American Legion and Three Sisters springs.

From Kings Bay, the river flows into the Gulf through South Pass. St. Martins Marsh Aquatic Preserve is along the north bank adjoining Crystal River Archaeological State Park. Crystal Bay and a number of islands are located south of the river. Charts of the area are available from local marinas.

Most winters, several hundred manatees take shelter from the cold in Crystal River National Wildlife Refuge. With the exception of an office, the refuge is entirely in the water. However the river is traveled, there are zones in which humans are

forbidden. Locally there is a small industry taking humans to dive with the manatees, and there have been times that divers have outnumbered manatees 10-to-1.

For an interesting view of how humans have impacted Florida, drive north of Crystal Springs on US-19 to the summit of the large bridge over the defunct Cross Florida Barge Canal, and then gaze west towards the nuclear power plant.

There are ramps at the Dockside Trading Company on the west side of US-19 in Crystal River across from the fire department; at Fort Island Trail Park, a west turn on West Fort Island Trail from US-19 in Crystal River; and at Fort Island Gulf Beach at the dead-end of West Fort Island Trail. The Nature Coast Canoe Trail runs from Chassahowitzka to Crystal River.

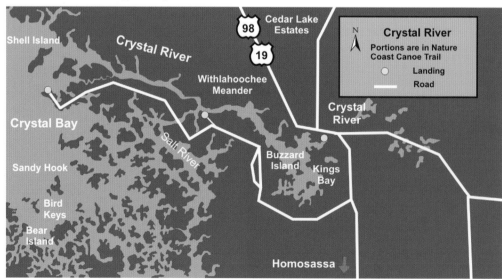

Above: A canoe approaches a snorkeler in the Rainbow River.

ECONLOCKHATCHEE RIVER
(Orange and Seminole counties)

This 36-mile blackwater river lies east of Orlando and is a major tributary of the St. Johns. Nineteen miles of the river are state-designated canoe trail. The water level varies considerably with rain.

Until the Little Econlockhatchee merges with the Econlockhatchee, there is often insufficient water for paddling. Locally the river is called the "Econ." Its waters eventually reach Lake Harney in the St. Johns Drainage.

The first section of the trail is often avoided during periods of drought and can be a technical, arduous journey under those conditions. Being able to travel this leg is a matter of "hitting it right."

The two additional segments are usually easy paddling. The river begins by flowing north, but makes a right-hand turn east before Snowhill Road. Snowhill Road, an important road for reference, is spelled both as Snow Hill and Snowhill on maps, signs, and in guides.

While the population in the general area makes the roads clogged and slow going, there is considerable conservation land along the river. Thus, the journey is pleasant and wildlife viewing often very rewarding.

The important towns in this area for reference are Oviedo, Chuluota, and Titusville.

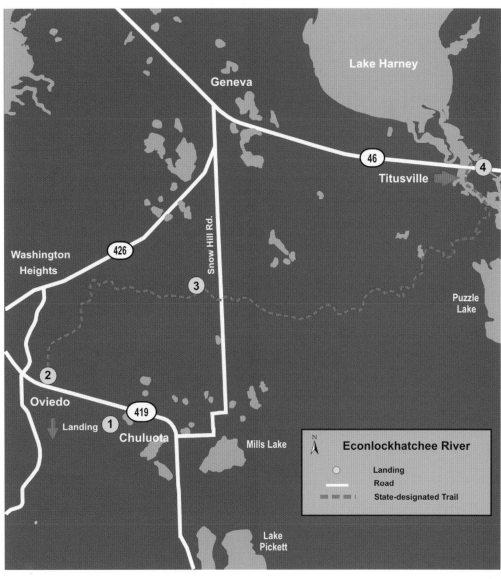

PC

POSSIBLE TRIPS AND LANDINGS

1. From SR-50 to CR-419, 8.5 miles. From I-4 in Orlando, take Toll Road 408 east to SR-50. Continue east on SR-50 to the river.

2. From CR-419 to Snowhill Road, 8 miles. From the put-in on SR-50, travel east to CR-419, turn north, and proceed to the bridge.

3. From Snowhill Road to SR-46, 11 miles. From I-95 near Mims, go west on SR-46 to Snowhill Road in Geneva. Go south 4 miles on Snowhill Road.

4. The take-out is at SR-46 and on the St. Johns River. Paddlers will see this as a canal near the bridge.

CAMPING

Little-Big Econ State Forest permits camping on the west side of the St. Johns River. On the east side lies the Seminole Ranch Conservation Area of the St. Johns Water Management District. Tosohatchee State Reserve is also nearby along the St. Johns River.

Map. Econlockhatchee River Canoe Trail, Office of Greenways and Trails. The state-designated canoe trail is from CR-419 Bridge to SR-46 Bridge.

Above: With shorebirds along the water's edge and the Skyway in the background, Ft. Desoto Park is a lovely place to paddle. Many serious sea kayakers cross from Ft. Desoto to Egmont Key to visit that state park with its historic ruins and pristine beaches.

LIGHTNING

Thunderstorms are frequent in Florida, a land often described (albeit incorrectly) as the lightning capital of the world. Perhaps this false assumption is because lightning sometimes claims more lives in Florida than elsewhere in the US, and to Americans the US is often wrongly thought of as the capital of the world.

On land one knows what to do when strikes abound, but where to hide on the water? The answer is to get off the water when bolts are jolting around. Take-out and seek shelter. Some paddlers take the additional measure of staying low to the ground. Most Florida thunderstorms pass quickly. Make sure the storm has fully passed before paddling on, as deadly strikes also occur on the back side of storms after people have dropped their guard.

FT. DESOTO PARK
(Pinellas County)

The park is located on Mullet Key in the mouth of Tampa Bay and overlooks the Sunshine Skyway Bridge. To the south of Ft. Desoto lies Egmont Key and to the north are Cabbage and Summer Resort keys, and two islands that make up Pinellas National Wildlife Refuge. Passage Key is another favorite trip for sea kayakers. Egmont Key, closer to Anna Maria Island, has a lighthouse, and sits in the approximate middle of the bay's mouth.

Ft. Desoto is a busy park with an outfitter providing kayak rentals. The beach was selected in 2002 by the Laboratory for Coastal Research as the fourth best in the entire US including Hawaii. In St. Petersburg, from I-275, take the Bayway Exit west and follow the signs.

Paddling about Ft. DeSoto can be a pleasant and easy trip. There is an established trail.

Some sea kayakers cross the bay on their journey about Florida; this crossing is far from easy. Those who venture into the currents or would cross over the bay are hopefully experienced sea kayakers who know what they are doing because this is a dangerous crossing. Such a journey is not for the weekend warrior. This is a shipping channel. Its waters are frequently vigorous and violent, its currents strong. The Sunshine Skyway Bridge is over 200 feet high to allow large boats to pass.

The park is named after Spanish Explorer Hernando DeSoto, so it is fair to ask if DeSoto actually landed here. No one really knows, although historical records indicate he probably did land somewhere in the Tampa Bay area. Some historians believe the first Spaniard to die in the New World passed away on Egmont Key, just across the pass from Mullet Key on which Fort DeSoto Park sits. Other historians believe it was in Charlotte Harbor that this unfortunate explorer met his fate. It must have been like dying on Mars would be for us.

HALLS RIVER
(Citrus County)

This is a small, spring-fed river, which flows 3.5 miles into the Homosassa River. It is much like the Chasshowitza, Crystal, and Homosassa rivers in that it has convoluted turns in vast coastal marsh areas, as well as hammocks with cedar and palms, and in the winter may have congregations of 100 or more manatees. Other frequently-sighted wildlife includes otters, snowy egrets, great blue herons, alligators, and various kinds of turtles and snakes. It is a rich estuary, with lots of fish, including redfish and trout, and jumping mullet.

Areas of the river are brackish and it is affected by tidal fall. It meanders in many directions, but for a trip with a start and finish, it may be best to use the services of the local outfitter.

It is a marvelous natural paddle, but there is no shade out there anywhere. Sun block, a hat, and plentiful water are essential, especially in the summer months. A good map is a fine precaution also, because it is often hard to find the way.

The river can be traveled from Riversport Kayaks, and this outfitter has located its business on a canal leading into the Halls River. The outfitter has an aerial map which would be exceptionally helpful. Another benefit of using the outfitter is that they will put you in at their location off US-19 and pick you up in downtown Homosassa Springs. The outfitter also does moonlight cruises.

Though very shallow in spots, Halls River is used by both boaters and airboaters. When visited, both the airboaters and boaters seemed to be using caution and watching out for smaller boats and paddlers.

HILLSBOROUGH RIVER
(Pasco and Hillsborough counties)

Portions of the Hillsborough River are among the most scenic in Central Florida. This blackwater river has its headwaters in the Green Swamp, historically a large and wild watershed, and it is spring-fed along its flow, most notably by Crystal Springs, the same spring which supplies the commercially-bottled water of the same name. The springs' outflow is an average 40 million gallons daily.

Of its 54 miles, the portions of the Hillsborough most used and raved about by nature lovers are from Crystal Springs Preserve near Zephyrhills to above the dam at Hillsborough Reservoir in Tampa. The area south and west of the reservoir is used by powerboats, and not considered very good paddling. It also becomes largely a walled canal through Tampa. Portions immediately below the dam for several miles are in an area of the city troubled by crime. In this area, lies Sulphur Springs with odorous sulfur waters.

Hillsborough River above the reservoir, where it is wild and free, truly meanders. On many runs, before the journey is finished, the paddler finds him or herself heading hither and yon to all four points of the compass. A large number of small creeks drain into the river, including Cypress, Blackwater, Flint, and Trout creeks,

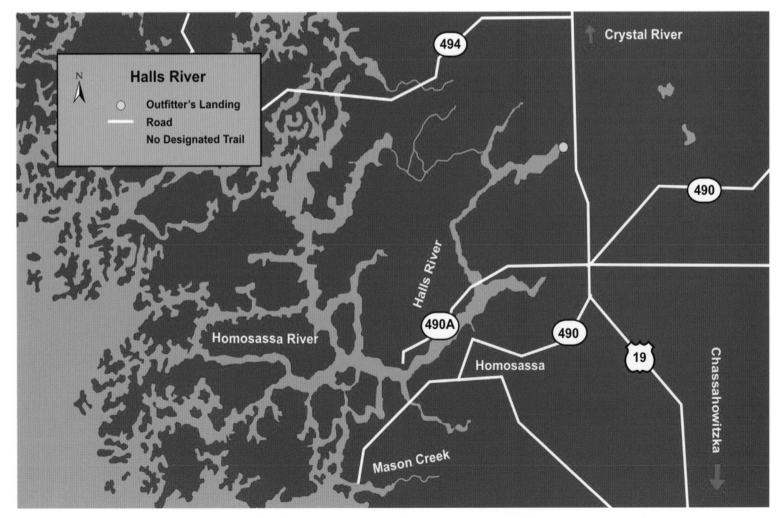

and the New River.

Most of the river is under tree canopy: cypress, live oak, red maples, sweet gum. The floodplain in places stretches considerable distances. On sunny days, shafts of light burst through the trees and greenery to shine like spotlights on the shaded ground, where cabbage palms and thick ferns rule.

With the exception of one stretch called the "Seventeen-Runs," and the short Hillsborough Rapids, it is easily paddled. There is great tranquillity on its waters in those Seventeen-Runs and there are rarely humans, perhaps the cause and effect. The Seventeen-Runs lies between Dead River Recreation Area and Sargents Park.

The stretch between Sargents Park and Morris Bridge Wilderness Park is heavily paddled daily. This section is the most popular trip of local outfitters. It is kept free of obstacles, has plentiful wildlife, and is generally easy paddling. Paddlers come along at fairly frequent intervals.

There are many alligators along the river, some very large. Wading birds and deer are plentiful. Deer and herds of wild pigs sometimes thunder-off on the shore. Otters show up at unexpected times in unexpected places.

It is mesmerizing to sit on a bench in the state park and watch the Hillsborough Rapids pour over the limestone. While many have bounced through the rocks in canoes and kayaks, portage is recommended. Walking over the rocks on the banks is very slippery and caution should be used.

POSSIBLE TRIPS AND LANDINGS

1. From Crystal Springs Preserve to Hillsborough River State Park, 6.5 miles. Crystal Springs is located north of Tampa in the town of Zephyrhills. From I-4 east of Tampa, take US-301 north. Go past Hillsborough River State Park. As you approach Zephyrhills, turn right onto Crystal Springs Road and proceed south. The preserve is not open to the public, but arrangements to paddle can be made through Canoe Escape (see Appendix A).

2. From Hillsborough River State Park to Dead River Recreation Area, 2.6 miles. The state park is located north of Tampa on the west side of US-301. US-301 is an exit of I-4. The state park rents canoes but you cannot take them out of the park.

3. From Dead River Recreation Area to Sargents Park, 4.2 miles. Dead River Recreation Area is south of Hillsborough River State Park on the west side of US-301 north of Tampa.

4. From Sargeants Park to Morris Bridge

Above: Paddlers near the rapids in Hillsborough River State Park.

Wilderness Park, 4.5 miles. Sargeants Park is on the west side of US-301 south of Dead River Recreation Area and north of Tampa.

5. From Morris Bridge Wilderness Park to Trout Creek, 4 miles. Morris Bridge Park/Wilderness Park is on Morris Bridge Avenue. Exit I-75 north of Tampa on Fletcher Avenue east. In a short distance, Fletcher becomes Morris Bridge. The landing is on the northwest side of the road just before the Hillsborough River.

6. From Trout Creek to Fowler Avenue, 5.9 miles. Trout Creek is on the northwest side of Morris Bridge less than a half mile from I-75. This is the Fletcher Avenue exit, but Fletcher becomes Morris Bridge going east.

7. Fowler Avenue to Riverhills Park, 6.2 miles. Rotary Park lies on Fowler Avenue. Exit I-75 west on Fowler Avenue and the park is on the north side just before the river.

8. From Riverhills Park to Rowlett Park, 4 miles. Riverhills Park is in southern Temple Terrace. Exit I-75 on Fowler Avenue and go west to 56th Street, then turn south. Pass through the town of Temple Terrace, and just before the Hillsborough Reservoir, turn east at the traffic light for Riverhills South. At the

THE WILDERNESS NORTH OF TAMPA

A first clue that this will be no ordinary canoe journey is a sign reading "Abandon Hope All Who Enter Here." No one knows who placed it at the beginning of the Seventeen-Runs, but everyone appreciates the humor.

Seventeen-Runs on the Hillsborough River are difficult, and become more so as water level falls. In low water, there may well be 40 or more considerable obstacles. In high water, there may be problems finding the way but very few obstacles. It can be tough, but the natural beauty in Seventeen-Runs is blinding. The Seventeen-Runs allegedly take their name from the many potential forks in the river.

To appreciate this beauty during low water, the trip may involve turning over, falling down trying to climb over a log, hauling the boat ashore and around, knocking spiders off your arms and out of your hair, and clambering over many logs. This is a piece of work suitable for the Gonzos out there, but not for everyone. Non-Gonzos should make sure there is ample water by consulting with the outfitter.

As of this writing, the trail through the Seventeen-Runs is marked with white, diamond-shaped trail markers.

Above: The rapids on the Hillsborough River. These rapids can be seen at the end of a short hiking trail within the state park.

stop sign, turn south and follow the bending road to the landing.

9. Rowlett Park. From US-41 in Tampa, turn east on Waters Avenue. When Waters Avenue dead-ends, there are three options: right, hard turn left, and soft left. Take the soft left and Rowlett Park will soon appear on the south side of the road. This is, unfortunately, probably not a safe place to leave a car.

CAMPING

Hillsborough River State Park offers a variety of camping options.

Map. Hillsborough River State Recreational Canoe Trail, Office of Greenways and Trails. The state-designated canoe trail continues to Rowlett Park and starts north of Hillsborough River State Park.

HOMOSASSA RIVER
(Citrus County)

The river flows from first-magnitude Homosassa Springs into coastal saltmarsh. At its headwaters is Homosassa Wildlife State Park, where visitors may see a manatee up close through a submerged viewing station, or visit recuperating injured wildlife. There is no paddling in the park, however.

North of the river, the paddler can pass through Shivers Bay, and the way leads into Greenleaf Bay and St. Martins River, a confusing area of saltmarsh. Exiting the river onto the Gulf, a series of islands, St. Martins Keys, are slightly to the north and west. South through the saltmarsh is Porpoise Bay, and farther south the mouth of the Chassahowitzka River. In such a confusing area, local charts are very helpful, and can be obtained from local marinas.

The outfitter has a landing, and there is a public ramp in Old Homosassa on Cherokee Way. Exit US-19 west on Yulee Road in Homosassa, and turn northwest onto Cherokee Way. Go to the dead end.

A Nature Coast Canoe Trail has been established between Chassahowitzka and Crystal rivers. This new trail has a separate account in this section. The Homosassa River is, of course, between the two and connected on the trail.

Right: A paddler in the Homosassa River pauses to observe the manatees. These mammals are often seen in the nearby Crystal River and also, to a lesser degree, in the Chassahowitzka.

COLLA/SEAPICS.COM

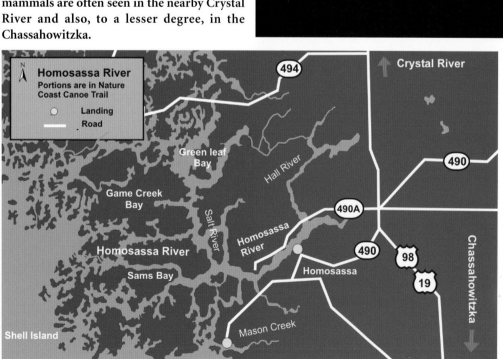

HONEYMOON ISLAND
(Pinellas County)

Honeymoon Island is connected to Dunedin by a causeway and bridge. The causeway provides excellent launching for kayaks. Many small islands dot the area, while to the south lies Caladesi, another favorite kayak area. Honeymoon Island is a state park. This is suntan country, with gorgeous beaches. The island is located south of Tarpon Springs and north of Dunedin, accessed from Alternate US-19 by going west on SR-586.

THE PHOSPHATE INDUSTRY EYES HORSE CREEK

Horse Creek waters are exceptionally pure and used for drinking water by the region, particularly Sarasota and Manatee counties. These waters are of higher quality in fact than the waters of the Peace River into which Horse Creek flows. The Peace has a heavy history of phosphate industry accidents and consequent devastation and pollution. It also has cattle ranches along it.

Several phosphate companies are seeking permits to mine over 100 square miles of land along the creek above SR-72. Another company has been operating at Horse Creek headwaters for many years. The mining spokesmen say they will reclaim all the mined land and mining will have no significant impact to area streams. Downstream counties and environmentalists argue the destruction will never be reversed and the by-products will remain a long-term problem. Opponents along Horse Creek worry about potential breeches in clay settling areas and changes in the hydrology. Charlotte County worries about changes in the quality and timing of freshwater reaching Charlotte Harbor, one of the state's richest estuaries.

Jobs are at stake in some areas of economically disadvantaged Florida. Profits are at stake for corporations. Charlotte Harbor, a rich estuary, is on the receiving end of whatever happens to these rivers.

HORSE CREEK
(DeSoto, Hardee, Hendry, Hillsborough, Manatee, and Polk counties)

Horse Creek, a major tributary of the Peace River, begins in the so-called "four corners" where Hillsborough, Manatee, Polk, and Hardee counties meet, and flows south for 40 miles. It enters the Peace River 12 miles above Charlotte County in southwest DeSoto County. The creek is crossed by three state roads (SR-64, SR-70, and SR-72) and several county roads (CR-665, CR-761, CR-769). The northern half of the creek (above SR-70) is often too shallow during the winter and is difficult to access since it is bordered by phosphate mines and ranches.

Because Horse Creek is relatively underdeveloped, its waters are the cleanest in the Peace River Drainage, a factor in locating the potable water intake pipes just below the mouth of the creek. This splendid creek may in the future be surrounding by phosphate mining.

One can always paddle up it from the Peace River, but putting-in or taking-out at any of the crossing roads should be double checked before proceeding. Cattle interests often erect wire fences across the river, present at SR-64 when last visited.

Like with many Florida rivers, water level is everything. Upper reaches can be impossible if levels are low. Some areas on the upper reaches also have wire fences across them, because at low water, cattle can wander into the river and migrate from one ranch to another.

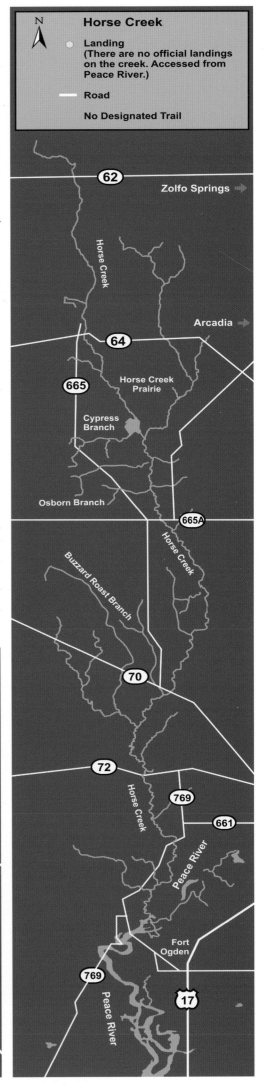

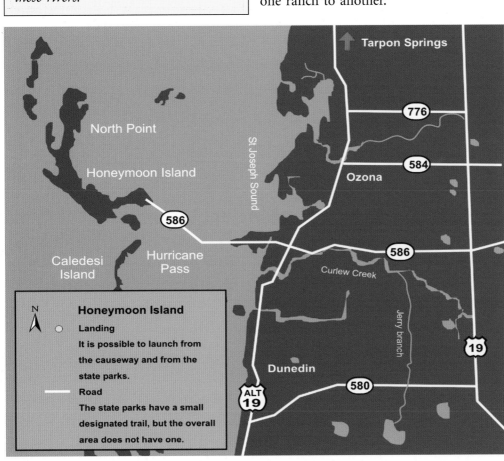

Above: Fall colors at Hillsborough River State Park.

At SR-72 there is an "unofficial" launch. There is no place to leave a car, however, and it might be taken for a broken-down vehicle or hauled away as a safety hazard, if it remained unscathed. This is also true for SR-64 and SR-70. All three are east exits from I-75 from Bradenton and Sarasota.

Farther south, CR-761 (a south turn off of SR-72) crosses Horse Creek, where there is yet another "unofficial" landing.

CR-761 crosses the Peace River after Horse Creek has merged with it. Perhaps the next best take-out on the Peace would be at Lettuce Lake. To reach it, exit I-75 at Kings Highway north of the Peace River, then turn right (or southeasterly) on CR-761. A sign on the west side of the road announces the turn to Lettuce Lake.

INDIAN RIVER LAGOON
(Brevard, St. Lucie and Volusia counties)

This lagoon is south of Mosquito Lagoon and sheltered from the sea by lands of Canaveral National Seashore and Merritt Island National Wildlife Refuge. It is a prime kayaking location and part of the Intracoastal Waterway.

From I-95, take SR-44 east toward New Smyrna Beach and turn south on US-1 in town, and take National Seashore and Kennedy Parkway onto Merritt Island National Wildlife Refuge, the west boundary of the lagoon. There are several landings along the way south. US-1, meanwhile, continues along the mainland. There are also two launches to the west along the lagoon in Turnbull Hammock. Those landings can be found by turning west from numerous roads to East Coast and traveling north and south.

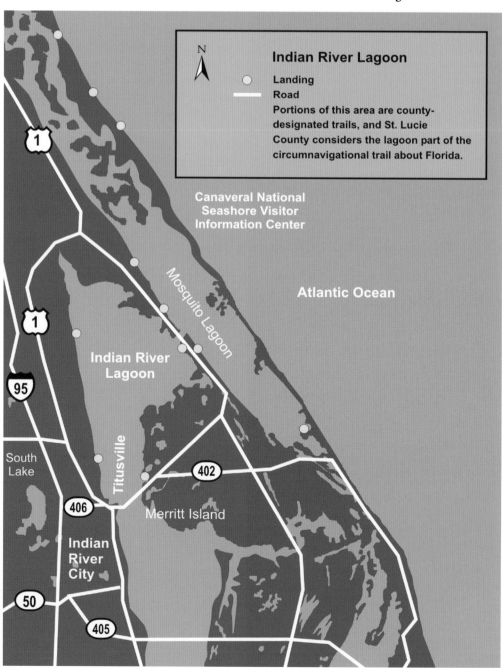

108

KISSIMMEE RIVER
(Glades, Highland, Osceola, Okeechobee, and Polk counties)

The Kissimmee River stretches from Central into South Florida. With origins above Lake Kissimmee, the river travels southeasterly from Lake Kissimmee to Lake Okeechobee. The water reaching Florida's largest lake comes down the Kissimmee River/Canal. The river length was 134 miles, but 60 miles are impacted by canals, and there are dams (called weirs).

Restoration efforts have been underway a very long time, and 10 miles have thus far been restored. Restoration work will not approach too close to Lake Okeechobee because it would interfere with flood control. Nor will it reach upwards toward Orlando where land costs too much for the restoration budget.

Paddlers will have to work out their own way to explore the river until restoration work is complete. It is probably best to check in advance with South Florida Water Management District on any of the river sections, or to ask one of the marinas on Lake Okeechobee for current information concerning the southern portions. It is necessary to portage around the dams.

At the Osceola/Polk County Line, the river is crossed by SR-60; to the south on both banks are boat landings. Perhaps 10 miles or more southeast of Sebring, the next major highway to cross the river is SR-98. To the north off US-98 is Bluff Hammock Road. There was a landing at the end of Bluff Hammock, but it was eliminated in the restoration work. However, paddlers still go to Bluff Hammock and scout about to put-in. To the southeast of Bluff Hammock on US-98 is a boat landing at Istokpoga Creek, which connects Lake Istokpoga to the Kissimmee River.

SR-70 also crosses the river west of the city of Okeechobee, where there is landing. Between US-98 and SR-70 is Nine Mile Grade with a landing at the end of Boat Ramp Road, an east turn. Highway 599 is a north turn from SR-70 on the east side of the river; this road leads to a launch almost directly across from the above launch.

A landing at SR-78 would be the take-out. It is at the Okee-Tantee Recreation Area, a large campground with marina and restaurant.

Primitive camping is allowed at present at only one location: Oak Creek. This is before the C-38 canal and southeast of Bluff Hammock Road.

Where the river begins, Lake Kissimmee State Park overlooks Florida's third largest lake. From the landing there, a practical paddle would be down Tiger Creek to the south into Tiger Lake. It also is possible to

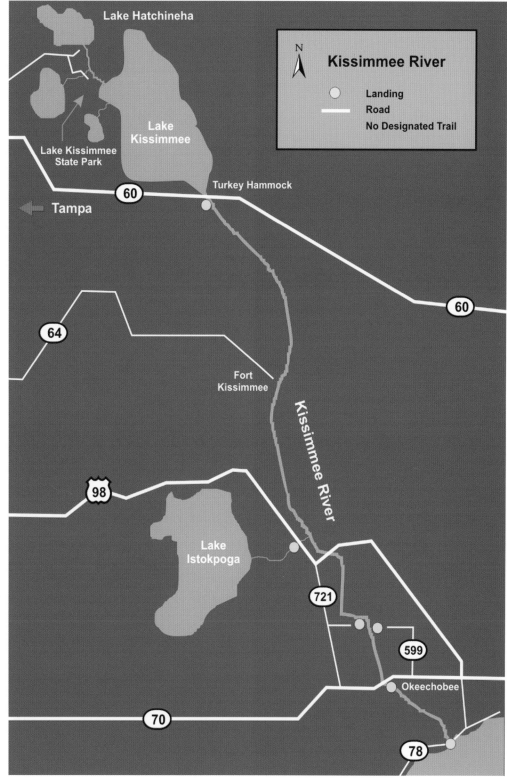

paddle into Tiger Lake from Lake Kissimmee, then into Lake Rosalie to the north, then South into Lake Weohyakapka; this paddle would probably take two days.

Lake Kissimmee itself is broad and forms whitecaps during storms, so it is not recommended for paddling. There are canoe rentals at the park. The state park is reached by going east of Lake Wales on SR-60 and turning north on Boy Scout/Camp Mack Road. When the road comes to a stop sign, turn east and proceed 4 miles.

Paddlers will not want for places to put-in on the Kissimmee River. There are over 30 fishing camps and 27 public access points on the river.

PLUMBING SOUTH FLORIDA

The person who changed the plumbing of South Florida forever was Hamilton (Ham) Disston. The eldest son of a successful immigrant who worked his way up to owning the world's largest sawmill in Philidelphia, Disston bought 4 million acres of South Florida in the 1890s from the state for 25 cents per acre. Soon thereafter, he connected the Chain of Lakes to the Kissimmee River by dredging and Lake Okeechobee to the Gulf by destroying the original Caloosahatchee River. Disston's intent was no less than to create a statewide steamship canal and to drain the Everglades for human use.

LEMON BAY
(Charlotte and Sarasota counties)

Lemon Bay stretches from south of Venice to Don Pedro Island near Placida Harbor. The bay is sheltered primarily by Manasota Key, from which kayakers launch, and other smaller islands. From US-41 in Port Charlotte, turn west on Highway 776 and follow it to Englewood Beach Road which leads to the bridge over Lemon Bay to Manasota Key.

LIDO CANOE TRAIL
(Sarasota County)

Lido, a barrier island west of Sarasota, has a loop trail from the South Lido Nature Center, at the corner of Taft and Boulevard of the Presidents. In the mangroves and shallow lagoons, bird life can be plentiful. The trail can be traveled in a leisurely hour or two. From I-75 in Sarasota, exit west on Fruitville Road and proceed across Ringling Causeway to Lido Key.

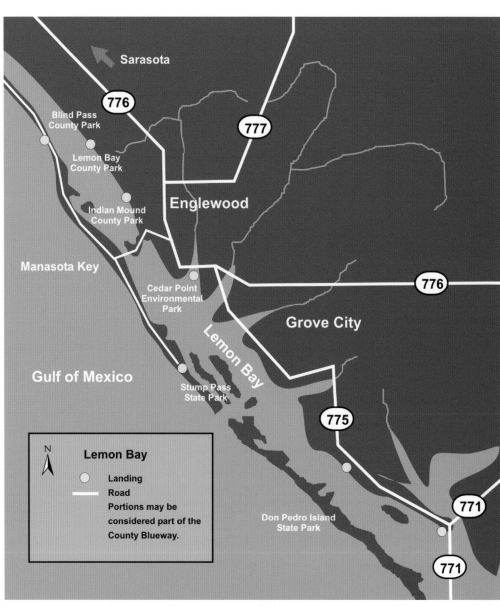

Above: South Lido Canoe Trail.

Above: Sea kayaking off South Lido Beach.

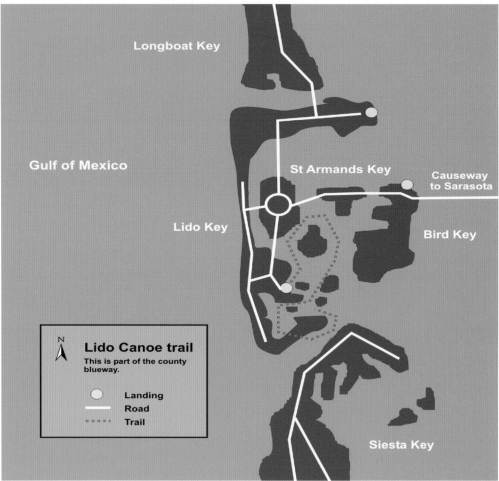

110

Above: Easy kayaking on the Little Manatee River

LITTLE MANATEE RIVER
(Hillsborough and Manatee counties)

The 5-mile, state-designated trail on this blackwater river is from Canoe Outpost to Little Manatee River State Park (formerly designated a recreation area), a delightful paddle. It is possible to paddle beyond the state park to Cockroach Bay, where one can paddle trails in mangroves.

Although the river can be paddled from Leonard Lee Road (east of Wimauma) to Little Manatee River State Park, it is often too shallow on the upper portions for more than wading. On the other hand, immediately after heavy rains, it may be dangerous to canoe the upper portions because of extended branches and on-rushing current. The upper portions must be just right, not only between Leonard Lee Road and CR-579, but also between CR-579 and Canoe Outpost. Thus, as always, checking with the outfitter in advance is wise. The local outfitter may be very handy for another reason; the "landings" and security are close to non-existent at both Leonard Lee Road and CR-579.

A small set of limestone shoals in the segment from Leonard Lee Road to CR-579 will add a little excitement to the narrow, twisty turns.

POSSIBLE TRIPS AND LANDINGS

1. From Leonard Lee Road to CR-579, 7 miles. From I-75, turn east on SR-674. Go through Sun City and Wimauma. A few miles east of Wimauma, turn south on Leonard Lee Road. Go to the end and look for the sign reading Little Manatee River Preserve.

2. From CR-579 to Canoe Outpost (US-301), 9 miles. From I-75, turn east on SR-674. Go through Sun City and turn south on US-301. Just before the Little Manatee River, turn east on Saffold Road. At the stop sign, turn south on CR-579. The river is not at the first bridge, but the second.

3. From Canoe Outpost to Little Manatee River State Park, 5 miles. From I-75, turn east on SR-674. Go through Sun City and turn south on US-301. Canoe Outpost is on the west side of the road after crossing the river. Sometimes Canoe Outpost uses an alternative take-out.
(**Note.** There is an alternate take-out at the end of 24th Street. For this landing, from I-75 go west on SR-674, and turn south on 24th Street. Go to the end. Unfortunately, the landing was found to be locked on several occasion during hours it was supposed to be open. Check with the outfitter.)

4. From Little Manatee River State Park to Cockroach Bay, 13 miles. From I-75, exit east on SR-674, go through Sun City, turn south on US-301, and follow the prominent signs. The park is on the north side. This section is wide river.

5. Cockroach Bay (see separate account, this section).

Above: Sandy bottom and banks along the Little Manatee River.

CAMPING

Little Manatee River State Park offers camping options.

Map. Little Manatee River Canoe Trail, Office of Greenway and Trails.

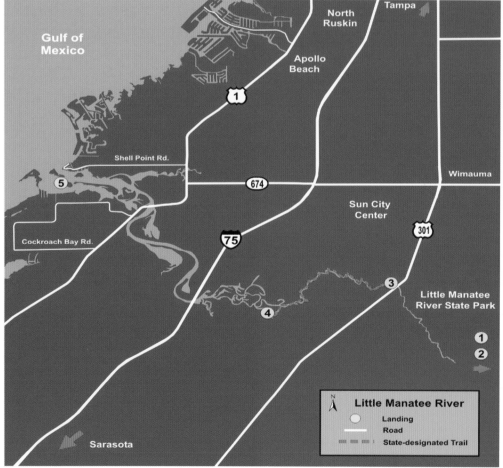

Climbing astor along Little Manatee River.

Above: Little Wekiva River.

LITTLE WEKIVA RIVER
(Lake and Seminole counties).

The Little Wekiva is one tributary to the Wekiva River System, and its waters drain into the St. Johns. The other rivers are: Blackwater Creek, Rock Springs Run, and the Wekiva River. The Little Wekiva attracts a notable number of green herons.

There are no public landings on the Little Wekiva so the paddler has the choice of either going upstream 3 to 4 miles on the Wekiva, depending on water level, or using the services of Katie's Landing. That outfitter has a private launch on the Little Wekiva where they put-in paddlers.

There are obstacles, particularly in low water periods. The way is sometimes split, but by following the water flow, it is difficult to get lost.

Katie's Landing is west of I-4 on SR-46 near Sanford. A few miles after leaving the interstate, there is a large billboard advertising Katie's Landing on the north side of the road announcing the turn.

N

Little Wekiva River

○ Landing
  (Private Landing)
— Road
  No Designated Trail

46A

Markham Road

Little Wekiva River

Wekiva River

4

Wekiva River Road

434

Lake Brantley

Orlando

PC

MANATEE COUNTY BLUEWAY
(Manatee County)

Above: A sunset paddle.

Below: Terra Ceia through the mangroves.

The "Blueway" is a concept, like the Florida Trail. Only instead of being a hiking trail around Florida, it is a sea kayaking route. The Blueway concept is driven by grass roots and supported by national, state, county, and municipal agencies. The Florida Legislature created a circumnavigation trail around Florida in Chapter 260 of The Florida Statutes, with the first official trail the Big Bend Trail. This was spurred by efforts of David Gluckman who has written a book, *Sea Kayaking in Florida*. Inspired by this concept, a number of county Blueways have sprung up, some connected to other counties. These various Blueways are in differing stages of development.

With support from the National Park Service, and a grant from Florida Department of Community Affairs, Manatee County has developed its own Blueways, complete with markers and maps. The Blueways proceed north from Tampa Bay and south into Sarasota Bay. These trails include paddles on the Manatee and Braden rivers, in Terra Ceia and Palma Sola bays, and in Bishop Harbor. In addition to these well-known paddles, the Manatee County Blueway holds some mysteries to be explored, such as Frog Creek and Mosses Holes. All in all, this is 75 miles of great paddling.

There are numerous put-ins and take-outs. Information is available on the internet, by mail, and phone, including maps and an excellent brochure. See Manatee County, Appendix B. Areas included in the Blueway have separate accounts and maps within this section.

TO

MANATEE RIVER
(Manatee County)

The 5-mile, state-designated canoe trail on the Manatee River begins in the east at the Rye Wilderness Park Launch at Rye Road Bridge. It officially ends at a landing that used to be the Aquatel Lodge, which became Lakewood Ranch River Resorts. This segment of the river is identified as the Upper Manatee River Canoe Trial and is but a tiny portion of the river's 60-mile length.

Some paddle the river west, wide and windy, as far as Emerson Point Park on the Gulf. This is part of Manatee County's Blueway.

Those who wish to paddle east from Lake Manatee will need to launch from Lake Manatee Fish Camp at the junction of SR-64 and CR-675. Wind can be a major obstacle wherever the water is wide.

Water is released from time-to-time from the dam at Lake Manatee, which can hold as much as seven billion gallons. Manatee Dam is 30 feet wide at its crown, 50 feet high, and 4,500 feet long. Usually, releases are minor. Major releases could cause paddlers problems and usually occur during the rainy summer months. The outfitters on the Manatee are all notified before major releases, but independent paddlers could put-in at the Rye Road landing and be unaware of a large discharge. A horn is supposed to signal whenever the dam is opened even briefly, but the horn has been broken several times in the past.

Because of the dam, the normal run-off plus the tidal influence make for no or slow flow. Thus, it is possible to paddle up from outfitters, as well as down river.

However, there is a strong tidal influence on the river. Paddling above Rye River Road to the dam is made difficult at low tide by fallen trees. This is a lovely section, passing through Rye Wilderness Park, where high, sandy banks and twisting river make grand natural settings.

The dam has also caused some unusual changes in the river, in particular a lot of silting and the creation of sandbars. When water is released, it obviously moves with great force and causes some flooding far down the river.

Gamble Creek enters the Manatee River from the north just beyond the end of the state-designated canoe trail. It is possible to paddle several miles north on this creek, particularly at high tide. The Braden River flows into the Manatee some distance beyond this point.

In general, one cannot get lost on the river. However, there is one confusing area approximately 1 mile below the Rye Landing. There, it appears there is a small cut to the left, the river in the middle, and a incoming waterway to the right. The correct path lies to the right.

POSSIBLE TRIPS AND LANDINGS
1. East of Lake Manatee. From Lake Manatee Fish Camp, the mileage is problematical. In Bradenton, exit I-75 east at SR-64, and turn north on CR-675. The landing and fish camp are immediately on the west side of the road.
2. From Rye Road to the Dam, 3 miles. Exit I-75 on SR-64 and go east to Rye Road. Turn north and take the south turn onto Upper Manatee River Road just before the bridge. The landing will be obvious.
3. From Rye Road to Ray's Canoe Hideaway, 2.3 miles.
4. From Ray's Canoe Hideaway to Mill Creek Road, 2.5 miles. Exit I-75 east on SR-64. After 2 miles, turn north on Upper Manatee River Road. At the second canoe launch sign, turn north on Hagle Park Road.
5. From Mill Creek Road to Emerson Point Park, about 10 miles. Exit I-75 east on SR-64. In 2 miles, turn north on Upper Manatee River Road. At the first canoe launch sign, turn north on Mill Creek Road. The water becomes very wide in this section.
6. Emerson Point Park is located between the mouth of the Manatee River and beautiful Terra Ceia Bay. From Business US-41 in Palmetto, go west on 10th Street.

CAMPING
Ray's Canoe Hideaway has primitive camping spots on the river. Lake Manatee State Park offers camping options. A separate nearby river, the Little Manatee, has a state park that is very popular for camping. Manatee County's Rye Wilderness Park also offers primitive camping.

Map, Upper Manatee River Canoe Trail, Office of Greenway and Trails.

MERRITT ISLAND NATIONAL WILDLIFE REFUGE
(Brevard and Volusia counties)

Between Canaveral National Seashore on the Atlantic Ocean and Merritt Island National Wildlife Refuge is Mosquito Lagoon which has its own account in this section. Paddlers should note that many of the islands within the refuge are closed. If in doubt, check with the refuge in advance. High winds can be a factor in paddling here, sometimes causing fair-sized waves. While canoes and kayaks are allowed, a kayak would likely be the best choice for most.

There are four popular areas to explore. One area within the refuge leads from the Haulover Canal into the lagoon; Fish and Wildfire Service personnel consider this route to be the best. Some paddlers go west through Haulover Canal to kayak the Indian River, an area with only a few islands and more open area. A manatee sanctuary exists

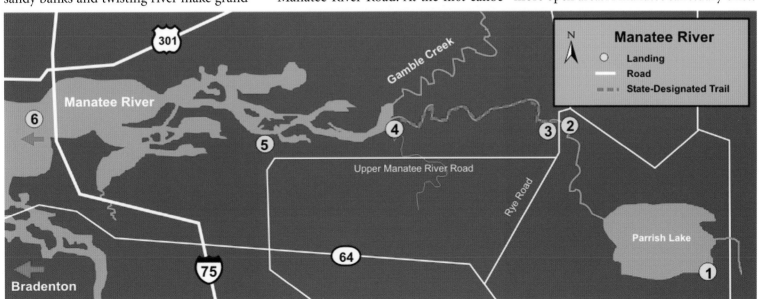

MOSQUITO LAGOON
(Brevard and Volusia counties)

Between Merritt Island National Wildlife Refuge and Canaveral National Seashore, lies Mosquito Lagoon, part of the Intracoastal Waterway. It provides an excellent opportunity for kayaking in an estuary. Charts and a good sense of direction may be helpful. While surf kayakers wait for the right wave during periods when the surf is up along the national seashore, Mosquito Lagoon is usually more tranquil. There are landings along A1A south of New Smyrna Beach. There are also landings on the shore side of the lagoon, somewhat harder to find. From I-95, exit on SR-44 and proceed east to A1A, then turn south.

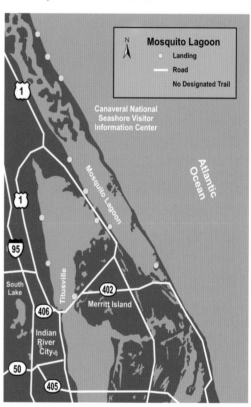

MOSQUITO PROHIBITION

While it might be very easy to guess how Mosquito Lagoon got its name, at first some of the places on the map might seem a little baffling.

Whiskey Point, for example, gets its name from smugglers during the social experiment called Prohibition, when whiskey was illegal and smugglers used the lagoon to stash liquor from Bimini and Cuba.

Bottle Island does not get its name from its shape. Rather, the name has something to do with liquor also, but not what most people would think. Locals call it Battle Island also. Apparently, some fellows having a drink got into a fight there.

Fishing within the Lagoon is said to be awesome.

in the southern portion of the refuge in the Banana River. Motorized boats are forbidden in the sanctuary. Paddlers also put-in from Dummitt Cove to paddle along the impoundments.

A map of the refuge can be obtained during or in advance of visits. For the refuge, exit I-95 on Garden Street (SR-406). Cross the Indian River Lagoon, and follow the signs to the Visitors Center, 4 miles north of the bridge.

Above: Paddlers on the Maykka River.

MYAKKA RIVER
(Charlotte, Manatee, and Sarasota counties)

North of Myakka City, this river forms from a number of seepage streams, flows into Lake Myakka, passes through Myakka River State Park, and into Lower Myakka Lake, before going by Snook Haven and later reaching Charlotte Harbor. The river is 69-miles long, defined as a blackwater river, but has two remarkable springs. In dry months, it exists as almost a trickle in the north, yet approaches a mile wide at its mouth.

Both the National Park Service and the State of Florida have designations of "Wild and Scenic Rivers." The Myakka has been state-designated as a "Wild and Scenic" River. The National Park Service has not so designated the river.

Cypress are noticeable by their absence. Where have all the cypress gone? The flooding cycle, fire frequency, and soil may all have combined to negatively impact cypress. The few cypress seen are likely planted or introduced, but curiously these thrive. Myakka is still a lovely river without the cypress, thanks to many oaks, palms, and willows. Near US-41, mangroves appear.

Humungous alligators and large otters are often seen, and swallow-tail kites are

sighted majestically flying across the river. The alligators on the Myakka deserve the description "behemoth," and (with frequent human traffic by boat, canoe, and kayak) they may not have the normal fear of humans, thus caution, as always, is the order of the day. Alligator phobic paddlers may wish to avoid Lower Myakka Lake.

Passing by populous Sarasota, the river is visited daily by paddlers and boaters. They are rewarded with great natural views, although there are a few houses along the banks - some palatial, some shanties.

At various times, the river has been called Mayaca, Mayaco, Miaco, and Miakka. No one knows the meaning of the word for sure, but its origin is Native American, bestowed perhaps by visiting Choctaws.

Although it is possible with some difficulty to access the river from SR-64 to the north, this stretch is frequently too shallow to paddle and not cleared of overhangs or obstacles. Even Upper Myakka Lake and Myakka State Park may be a difficult or impossible passage during drought.

Most paddlers either explore the state park, where canoes can be rented, or make the run from SR-72 to Snook Haven with their own canoe or kayak. Below Snook Haven, the river widens near US-41. Not too many paddlers try the wide stretch from US-41 to Charlotte Harbor. There are

various landings and marinas in Charlotte Harbor.

A new landing is in progress at Rocky Ford and sure to be open to the public by the first publication date of this book. Rocky Ford lies between the state park and Snook Haven, closer to Snook Haven than the park, and near Carleton Reserve, a Sarasota County conservation land. This landing is located on a bridge reached by exiting east on Jacaranda Boulevard from I-75 south of Sarasota, then turning north at the first stop sign.

There are two dams on the river. The dam on Upper Myakka Lake is not an obstacle. It was created originally for recreational purposes. A dam between the state park and Snook Haven may not be seen in high water but will require a drag-around in low water (often in the company of alligators).

Snook Haven, a rustic and folksy fish camp and restaurant, can be counted on to provide local conditions on the river. The excellent outfitters in Sarasota are not on the river and may not have an up to minute report. Snook Haven will know the current conditions.

In Charlotte Harbor, Myakka Cutoff lies behind Hog Island. Paddles there can lead to some lakes. The Blackburn Canal above Snook Haven connects to estuary and also provides some additional paddling. It

Above: Alligators along the Myakka River.

connects to Curry Creek which connects to Robert's Bay.

POSSIBLE TRIPS AND LANDINGS

1. From Myakka State Park into Upper Myakka Lake, variable.
2. From Myakka State Park to Snook Haven, 15.5 miles. This large state park lies east of Sarasota and I-75 on SR-72 and is prominently announced by signs
3. From Snook Haven to US-41, 7 miles. From I-75 south of Sarasota, exit apparent west (actually south because of the bend of I-75) on River Road. The entrance to Snook Haven, a private campgrounds with restaurant, is made clear by a large billboard on the apparent south (but actually east) side of the road.
4. From US-41 to Charlotte Harbor, 15-20 miles, depending on take-out. From I-75 south of Sarasota, exit apparent west on River Road. Proceed 7 miles to US-41. Turn south on US-41 and the landing is at the bridge.
5. Charlotte Harbor. There are many boat ramps and marinas on Charlotte Harbor.

CAMPING

Myakka River State Park offers a wide range of camping options.

NATURE COAST CANOE TRAIL
(Citrus County)

The Nature Coast Canoe Trail connects Chassahowitzka to both Homosassa and Crystal rivers to the north. The trail is marked with numbered signs bearing crossed paddles; the signs are sometimes torn down by thoughtless pranksters. Kiosks at launch points have printed information. This trail is a valuable contribution to paddling since the wild areas offer plentiful wildlife viewing and spectacular scenery.

The trail is usually paddled in two segments, about a day each. Primitive camping sites have been designated in St. Martins Marsh Aquatic Preserve. It would be wise to contact the preserve or Chassahowitza National Wildlife Refuge to avoid straying onto private property. The section between Homosassa and Crystal River is the easier portion of the trail.

For the section between Chassahowitzka and Homosassa, cautions are necessary. This is an extensive saltmarsh with seemingly endless, twisting pathways before reaching the sea. On the Gulf, the water is shallow with a limestone bottom that may scrape when waves are significant. It is hard to find the way back from the Gulf and through the twisty saltmarsh. Be sure before departing to have good navigational aids or someone confident of the way. Charts are available from local marinas. This a gorgeous area to visit, but many get lost.

It is a straight-line distance of more than 10 miles between Chassahowitzka and

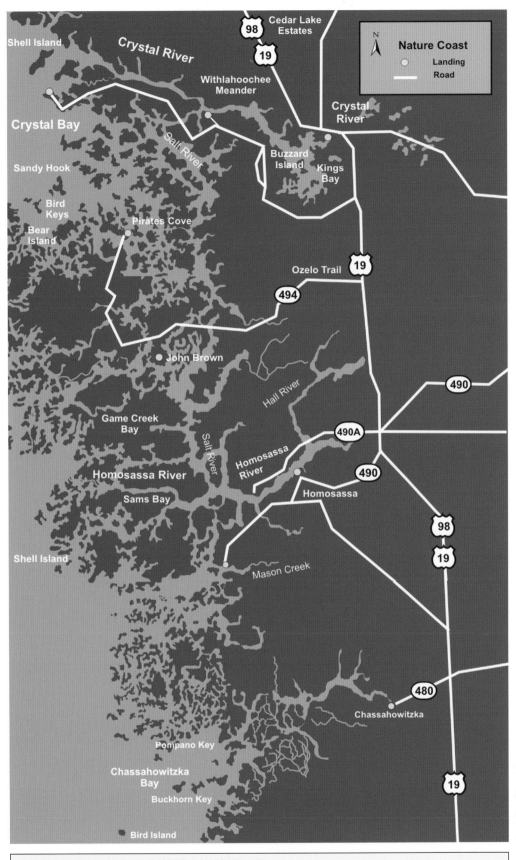

Crystal River, but nothing here can be traveled in a straight line except US-19. The trail is 17-18 miles, but exploring nooks and crannies in the rivers may add significantly to this.

At present, the best map for the area is in the "Boating and Angling Guide to Citrus County" which was prepared by a grant from Florida Fish and Wildlife Conservation Commission. A copy can be requested from the commission, Chassahowitzka National Wildlife Refuge, or St. Martin's Marsh Aquatic Preserve.

Internet resource: www.visitcitrus.com/canoetrail.html. Another internet reference is LeaveNoTrace at http/www.int.org.

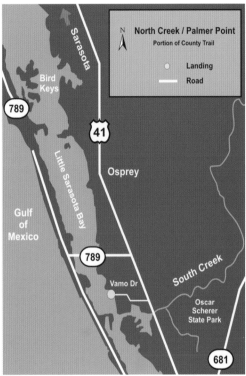

NORTH CREEK/ PALMER POINT
(Sarasota County)

North Point Park is the name of the old Midnight Pass area behind the Jim Neville Preserve in Little Sarasota Bay. The American Littoral Society has been restoring this park since 1993, removing invasive exotic vegetation, and replanting with appropriate native plants. North Creek is located just to the north of Spanish Point, an historical park. The creek has been impacted by condominium development.

Midnight Pass is not an open avenue to the sea. It has been closed-off, creating a 14-mile stretch of sheltered, Intracoastal Waterway. Very controversial proposals to reopen Midnight Pass are being studied.

Access is from a boat launch at a lagoon on Turtle Beach at the south end of Siesta Key. From I-75, go west on Clark Road which turns into Stickney Point Road and leads to Siesta Key. Turn left onto Midnight Pass Road. The park is on the right.

WARM MINERAL SPRINGS

The rarest of all springs in Florida is a warm spring. There are only two, both associated with the Myakka River: Warm Mineral Springs and Little Salt Springs.

Warm Mineral Springs flows into the Myakka River just before the river passes into Charlotte Harbor. About 9 million gallons a day flow from Warm Mineral Springs, where a private health resort and spa has been built.

Visitors come from all around the world to bathe in its waters for their reputed healing powers. Health club literature reports the spring as having the richest mineral content in the world, with more than 50 minerals found. Enthusiasts claim relief from a variety of ailments. The water is sold and taken as a laxative, not a thirst quencher.

The general public can enjoy the springs by paying an entrance charge. The spring is north of US-41 in the town of Warm Mineral Springs, south of Sarasota and north of Charlotte Harbor.

PALMA SOLA BAY
(Manatee County)

A 5.25-mile Palma Sola Bay Trail is part of Manatee County's Blueway. The bay has two exits: a pass facing Anna Maria Island to the west and narrower Perico Bayou to the north. Both are alongside and helping to encircle Perico Island, and the loop trail is around that island.

Palma Sola lies between Sarasota Bay to the south and the Manatee River to the north. From I-75, exit west on SR-64 which becomes Manatee Avenue. It is possible to launch from any point on the causeway. On a map, it looks like one should put in at Anna Maria Island and paddle almost directly across to Perico, but this is a bad idea due to boat traffic which does not stick to the marked channel.

LITTLE SALT SPRINGS

While Warm Mineral Springs is open to the public, Little Salt Springs is a research area. Little Salt Springs is near Warm Mineral Springs. The Sarasota County Blueway announced in 2003 may give the paddler access to it as the paddle includes the Myakkahatchee River on which the spring is located. The remains of more than 200 Paleo-Indians have been removed from the springs. Many of these early Native Americans may have lived there over 10,000 years ago. Also plucked from the spring was the carapace of a giant, ancient tortoise with a spear still impaling it.

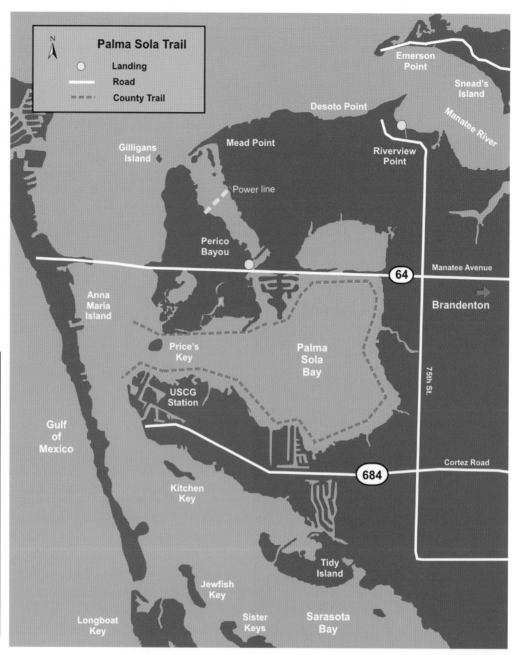

PEACE RIVER
(Charlotte, DeSoto, Hardee, and Polk counties)

The Peace is a gorgeous paddle, and many describe paddling the entire river as a treasured experience. During periods of low water, the Upper Peace may become a chore, as you walk on the sand under two inches of water. Usually the river has passable levels, yet it is wise to check with the canoe liveries concerning conditions before embarking. Portions of the river have limestone runs unless the water is very high. There are plentiful alligators, majestic swallow-tail kites, and large gar to startle the paddler who has been lulled by the peace of the Peace.

A blackwater river with some springs, the Peace is 106 miles long. Historic headwaters were in the area known as the Green Swamp. The Peace starts south of Bartow. SR-60 crosses it when the river is usually a trickle, and meets the Gulf at Charlotte Harbor near Punta Gorda. Along the way, it gradually widens and deepens.

Above: Paddlers pass a small waterfall along the Peace River.

Mangroves appear near Charlotte Harbor. The river generally flows south with a westerly bent.

The 67-mile, state-designated canoe trail starts at the US-98 bridge east of Ft. Meade and ends at SR-70 west of Arcadia. It is often too shallow to paddle north of Ft. Meade, sometimes too shallow to paddle north of Wauchula (check with the outfitters). In the south, it is possible to paddle beyond SR-70 a considerable distance, including into Charlotte Harbor, if one likes broad water paddling.

OTHER LANDINGS

Only one Bowling Green Landing has been used in the trips below, but there are two. Mt. Pisgah Bridge Landing (CR-657), listed as a landing in Greenways information and other guides, was intentionally left out as a landing because of doubtful security and a serious trash problem of major proportions. Hopefully, someone will clean up Mt. Pisgah Landing, as during flood stage, all the decaying debris is touched by the river.

Two new landings may have been built since the area was last visited. One is east of the small community of Homeland at CR-640. The other is south of Fort Meade where Bowlegs Creek runs into the Peace.

POSSIBLE TRIPS AND LANDINGS.

1. From US-98 Bridge to Bowling Green, 11 miles. From US-17 in Ft. Meade, turn east on US-98 and proceed to the bridge.

2. From Bowling Green to Wauchula, 8 miles. To reach CR-664A Bridge, take US-17 into Bowling Green and turn east on CR-664A. Proceed to the river.

3. From Wauchula to Zolfo Springs, 4.5 miles. In Wauchula when CR-64A crosses US-17, it becomes CR-636. Take CR-636 to Crews Park. The concrete landing is on the northwest bank.

4. From Zolfo Springs to Gardner Ramp, 19 miles. From US-17 in Zolfo Springs, turn west on SR-64. On the northwest corner is Pioneer Park where there is a concrete landing.

5. From Gardner Ramp to SR-70, 13.5 miles. From US-17 in Gardner, a sign announces a west turn to the public boat ramp.

6. SR-70. There is a prominent outfitter, a campground, and a county park on the south bank of the Peace River at different locations on SR-70 west of Arcadia. The campground and park are prominently announced, and a sign directs the north turn to the outfitter.

7. Beyond SR-70. After the end of the state-designated canoe trail, the river flows a considerable distance south of SR-70 to reach Charlotte Harbor. As it does, it widens considerably and is tidal influenced. There are four landings before Charlotte Harbor on CR-760, one near Nocatee, and a cluster of three between CR-761 and CR-776 in lower DeSoto County. There are numerous landings in Port Charlotte, for those who insist on traveling rivers to their ends.

Above: Along the Peace River.

CAMPING

Pioneer Park in Zolfo Springs has a campground. There are few sandbars, even at low water levels.

Map. Peace River Canoe Trail, Office of Greenways and Trails.

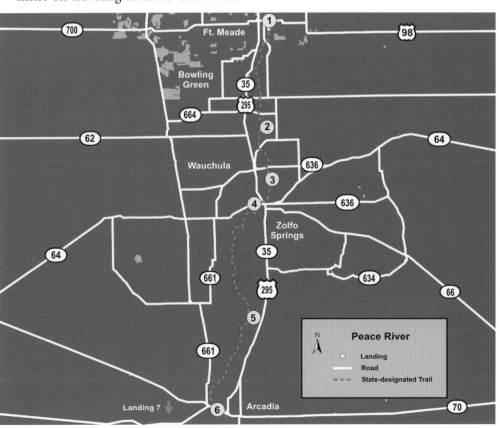

121

PITHLACHASCOTEE RIVER
(Pasco County)

This river's tongue-twisting name is frequently shortened to the "Cotee." If one was traveling over it forty years ago, on a two-lane bridge over US-19, there were beckoning vistas to the east. Only a few homes were to be found along the shore, some allegedly owned by silver and silent screen actors and their progeny. Today looking east from the six-lane concrete bridge, the allure is gone, replaced with housing developments and sufficient concrete to render a portion of the river a canal. Fortunately, there still remains one incredibly spectacular section inland, but it requires work to reach it. There is also gorgeous saltwater paddling in mangroves.

A portion of the river is a 5-mile, state-designated canoe trail. This trail is between Rowan Road Bridge and Francis Avenue City Park on Louisiana Avenue. Undoubtedly when the trail was established, there was a landing at the bridge on Rowan Road. There was none when visited. Paddlers had to climb down the slope on the southwest corner, adjacent to a Marine Corps League building.

This river can now be thought of as four separate and quite different sections. These sections begin east of Port Richey and end in salt water.

1. A stretch from Rowan Road to a campground/fish camp, probably 2 miles, has many fallen logs. The river is tidal influenced, and this section can best be traveled at high tide. Even then there will be dead falls.
2. Beyond the camp, fishermen keep the channel open. Just west of this camp, the river is beautiful, and natural like the river once was in its entire length. It twists and turns, with several attractive backwaters, through about 2 miles of natural banks.
3. Before the take-out is reached for the state-designated trail at Francis Avenue City Park, the last mile or so of the designated trail is dominated by homes, fishermen, boats, and sea walls. Habitation continues unabated to and beyond US-19.
4. Once the salt water is reached, it is possible to paddle north into Boggy Bay and south into Rocky Creek and Oyster Creek, where the paddle is by gorgeous mangroves. The mangroves can be best navigated with the high or incoming tide.

The outfitter also takes twilight tours due west to a spoil island. For tidal conditions and progress on clearing the upper river, check with the outfitter in Appendix A. There are stilt homes still standing in the bay, referred to on nautical charts as Shacks.

Port Richey lies north of New Port Richey, and both lie between Tarpon Springs to the south and Hudson to the north, along US-19 in Pasco County.

From SR-54, between Tampa and New Port Richey, turn north on Rowan Road. Proceed to the bridge which was not identified in any way when visited. SR-54 runs between US-19 and I-75.

For Francis Avenue City Park, go east from US-19 in Port Richey. Find Main Street, then go south on Madison, and east on Louisiana Avenue to the park entrance.

There is also a landing at Nicks Park to the west of US-19 as the river opens up.

Map. Pithlachascotee River Canoe Trail, Office of Greenways and Trails.

REEDY CREEK
(Osceola County)

Shallow, narrow, with vegetation logjams and some log obstacles, Reedy Creek is so gorgeous that these impediments will be overlooked. In times of low water, upper sections in particular may become impassable. The creek is paddled in either direction from US-17/92 at a bridge in Intercession City, located east of Kissimmee and south of Orlando. The distance one can paddle in either direction has been said by some to reach as much as 8 miles. There has never been sufficient water to test this hypothesis when visited.

ROCK SPRINGS RUN/ WEKIVA RIVER
(Orange County)

Many consider Rock Springs Run their favorite trip because of its natural splendor. The river is lush with grasses, water plants, and wildlife. The Wekiva System is bear territory, despite the human population not far from the banks. The elusive mammals (bear, not humans) are rarely seen.

Rock Springs Run flows 9 miles into the Wekiva River System, which in turn flows into the St. Johns. The run serves as the boundary between Rock Springs Run State Reserve and Wekiwa Springs State Park. It is a popular paddle on weekends. It is sand bottomed and very narrow in places.

It is approximately 7 miles from the springs at an Orange County park (Kelley Park) to the primitive camp at Wekiwa Springs State Park. It is approximately 2 miles from there to the confluence with the Wekiva River. Shortly after meeting Wekiva River, there is a marina on the southeast bank. Or push on to Katie's Wekiva Landing.

Why is it sometimes Wekiva and other times Wekiwa? Not for very good reasons. See the account for the Wekiva River.

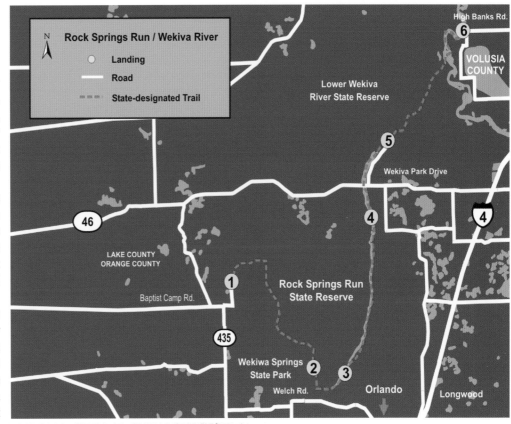

POSSIBLE TRIPS AND LANDINGS

1. From Kelly Park to Wekiwa Springs State Park, 9 miles. From US-441 west of Longwood, go north on Rock Springs Road, and turn east on Kelly Park Road to Rock Springs.
2. From Wekiwa Springs State Park to Katie's Landing, 9.25 miles. From I-4 at Longwood, go west on SR-434 for 1 mile. Turn north on Wekiva Springs Road and follow the signs.
3. Katie's Landing. Exit I-4 west on SR-46 near Sanford. After a few miles, there is a large billboard advertising Katie's Landing announcing the turn north.

Additional Landing. There is a launch at Wekiva Marina. It is possible to stop the trip after Wekiwa Springs State Park by taking-out at the Marina. The Marina is located at the end of Miami Springs Road, a north turn from Wekiva Springs Road. To reach Wekiva Springs Road, exit I-4 west on CR-434, and proceed for 1 mile. Signs will indicate Wekiwa Springs State Park, but the turn is before the park is reached.

CAMPING

Wekiwa Springs State Park provides a wide range of camping options.

Map. Wekiva River and Rock Springs Run Canoe Trail, Office of Greenways and Trails. The 27-mile, state-designated trail runs from the headwaters of Rock Springs Run through the Wekiva River and onto the St. Johns River.

Above: Along Rock Springs Run.

SARASOTA BLUEWAY
(Sarasota County)

Kayaking is a popular recreational activity in Sarasota Bay and along Sarasota's Gulf beaches. On most weekends, many kayaks can be sighted traveling on bay waters. It is possible to paddle quite some distance from the mouth of Sarasota Bay at Big Pass, north between the mainland and barrier island Long Boat Key, passing New Pass and Longboat Pass, then north as far as Anna Maria Island, and east into Palma Sola Bay.

The Sarasota Bay National Estuary Program publishes a guide called the "Sarasota Bay Blueways." This map extends from south of Englewood to Tampa Bay, including Lemon Bay, Little Sarasota Bay, and Sarasota Bay. Many Sarasota landings are shown. Local kayak guides report all these areas to be excellent. This map should not be confused with the Blueway for paddlers.

A Blueway guide is available for Sarasotta County that includes sixteen trails. Some of these paddles have already been mentioned in this book, like the Lido Paddling Trail and two on the Myakka River, but others will be new. The title of their trails are:

Above: Launching a kayak from a dock for a leisurely cruise on Sarasota Bay.

Sarasota Bay, Lido, Phillippi Creek, Neville Marine Preserve, South Creek, Dona Bay, Four Bays, Casperson, Forked Creek, Lemon Bay, Myakka River/Carlton, Myakka River (South), Myakkahatchee Creek, North Metrok Park, and Celery Fields Trail.

Information is available from Sarasota County Parks and Recreation. (Appendix B)

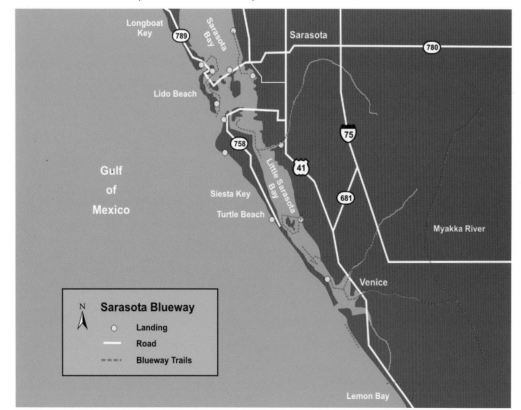

RIVER WALK

In times of low water, canoes and kayaks sometimes grind to a halt in sand or on limestone. At such times, it is necessary to walk one's boat. This is why a line tied to the bow is always a handy idea.

Bottoms vary greatly in Florida. Sandy bottom streams generally provide good footing and are easy to walk in. Limestone, however, has jagged edges and is porous (has holes). Some wear water sandals, others sneakers.

Perhaps the most unpleasant of bottoms are muck bottoms. There you may slide in quite deep, sometimes to your ankles, sometimes to your waist. Before leaving the boat, test the bottom with a paddle.

Walking in the river can cool you off in summer. In fact, if you get really hot and are suffering, it is helpful. If the water is too deep to walk, and you want to cool down, try taking off your shoes and socks and letting one leg dangle from each side in cooling waters.

SEBASTIAN CREEK
(Brevard and Indian River counties)

Creek or river? Saint or sinner? The St. Johns Water Management District maps refer to this as Sebastian River. The Gazetteer refers to it as St. Sebastian River. At least two paddling guides call it St. Sebastian Creek. It is all the same and a wonderful place to paddle.

Sebastian Creek/River flows into the Indian River, a waterway between the mainland and barrier islands. The creek is paddled up each of two prongs and back. The North Prong is perhaps 7 miles, while South Prong is 9. Both are usually relatively easy paddling, with little flow, and few if any obstacles.

North Prong passes the C-54 canal and leads to St. Sebastian River Buffers Preserve. This is a large tract of conservation land of the St. Johns Water Management District, and home to a scrub-jay population.

The North Prong and the South Prong are usually paddled upstream from either of two parks: Dale Wimbrow and Donald MacDonald parks. The North Prong does have a launch in St. Sebastian River Preserve north of Sebastian Point. CR-512 also crosses the South Prong, where a put-in is said to be in progress. Both prongs could be accessed by paddling in from a landing on US-1, but the water is broad at that point, subject to wind and boating. In fact, reaching the North Prong from either of the two parks requires a little wide water paddling.

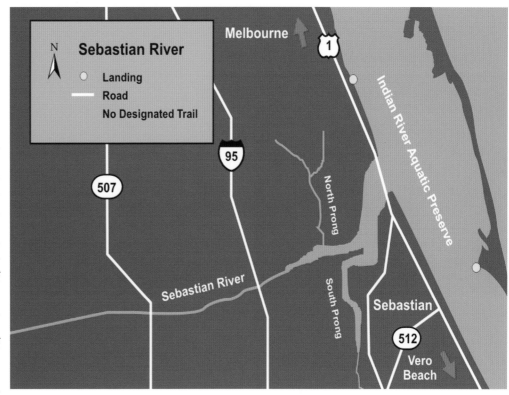

Both parks are in the town of Sebastian. For Donald MacDonald Park, go west on CR-505 from US-1. For Dale Wimbrow Park, continue farther west on CR-505. A camping option is Sebastian Inlet State Park.

OUTSTANDING FLORIDA WATERWAYS

The Florida Department of Environmental Protection has designated the Sarasota Bay Estuarine System as an Outstanding Florida Waterway. This designation helps protect waterways from degradation. Most waterways in state and federally managed lands receive this designation. Others so designated include: the Apalachicola River, Aucilla River, Black Creek (North Fork), Blackwater River, Butler Chain of Lakes, Chassahowitzka River, Clermont Chain of Lakes, Crooked River, Cross Creek, Crystal River, Econlockhatchee River, Estero Bay Tributaries, Florida Keys, Hillsborough River, Homosassa River, Kingsley Lake, Lake Powell, Lemon Bay, Little Manatee River, Lochloosa Lake, portions of the Myakka River, Ochlockonee River, Ocklawaha River, Orange Lake, Rainbow River, River Styx, St. Marks River, Sante Fe River, Shoal River, Silver River, Spruce Creek, Suwannee River, Tomoka River, Wacissa River, Wakulla River, Wiggins Pass Estuarine System, and Withlacoochee Riverine and Lake System.

SOUTH CREEK

South Creek is a small, pretty creek in Oscar Scherer State Park, Access is available inside the park, which is located south of Sarasota on US-41. A sign on I-75 south of Sarasota announces the turn west at the Laurel/Nokomis exit. Turn south on US-41 and proceed to the park on the east side of the road.

TO

ST. LUCIE RIVER
(St. Lucie County)

This relatively small river drains into an enormous tidal bay still considered the St. Lucie River. This "river" continues on into St. Lucie Inlet and the Atlantic Ocean. The following information was provided by Linda Leeds, who paddles the area frequently.

"It's a pretty, little creek, a great spot for beginners. It's wide at the beginning, then narrows down a bit, and by then, novices have hopefully figured it out. It's gently tidal.

"The paddle is an up-and-back trip, perhaps 1 hour and 30 minutes each way. There is a great little landing and picnic area at the usual turnaround, on the right as you approach from downstream. The picnic area is also a trailhead for a short Florida Trail Association trail, a nice walk after lunch, and with permission of the South Florida Water Management District, one can also camp there." Thanks, Linda, for this account of South Fork.

Exit I-95 at Stuart on SR-76 east to the second signal, Cove Road. Turn right and then immediately turn right again on Gaines. Hobart Park is a couple of blocks down on the right.

TAMPA BAY
(Hillsborough, Manatee, and Pinellas counties)

At almost 400 square miles, Tampa Bay is one of Florida's largest bays. Tidal waters reach almost 35 miles inland, and most of the bay is 5 to 10 miles wide. While the average depth is 13 feet, there is one deep, 89-foot hole in Egmont Channel. Forty-two nautical miles have been dredged into a shipping channel averaging 40 feet deep, to the benefit of commerce, but to the detriment of the bay. Four major rivers feed the bay: Alafia, Hillsborough, Little Manatee, and Manatee. Each river is a terrific paddle in itself, and all have accounts within this section.

Shipping and boating may present problems for paddlers, especially in some southern portions of the bay. All areas of the bay are boated, but the section to the north of SR-60 (Courtney Campbell Causeway) has no shipping, just too many jet skis and powerboats.

As can be expected of such a large body of water, there are many opportunities for exploration. Canoe opportunities, including some designated trails, are treated separately; they pass primarily through mangroves, including Cockroach Bay and Weedon Island.

The mouth of Tampa Bay between St. Petersburg and Bradenton is spanned north

Opposite page: Bent and broken palms on Egmont Key. This key is located in the mouth of Tampa Bay and has served as a military fort, a home for harbor pilots, and a premier destination for Florida's sea kayakers.

Right: The skyline of the city of Tampa as seen from Tampa Bay.

to south by the Sunshine Skyway Bridge. Four bridges span Tampa Bay from east to west. Courtney Campbell Causeway (SR-60), between Tampa and Clearwater, is a length of dredged land that offers many places to launch. The same is true at both ends of the Gandy Bridge, especially on the Pinellas side. Another interesting place to launch in the northwest portion of the bay is Upper Tampa Bay County Park. It is located on SR-580 (Hillsborough Avenue out of Tampa) near Oldsmar, and is mostly a meandering mangrove area. Adjacent to it is Double Branch Creek, a small winding waterway sometimes paddled up from the park, or down from the Town and Country area of Tampa.

On balmy days, anyone with a board that will float can travel the bay. However, when the wind is up, serious whitecaps and currents make this a place most should avoid. Remarkably, due to the causeway, it is not surprising to see whitecaps on one side of the Courtney Campbell and flat water on the other.

Attempting to cross Tampa Bay to Bradenton is for those with the best of open sea kayaking skills, including navigation. Currents can be strong, waves can be high, and winds can be a powerful deterrent. This crossing is part of some concepts about a trail to kayak around the state, but it is not for novices. More than one experienced local kayak guide feels that kayaking across the bay beneath the Skyway is like having a death wish.

On the Manatee County side, the area between the Skyway and Joe Island is especially treacherous when the tide is changing, almost to the point of requiring a white water kayak. Paddling in small, placid areas is one thing, but putting into such a large area with strong currents requires preparation.

There are numerous places around the bay where nautical charts can be purchased, including dozens of marinas and bait shops.

SAVING TAMPA BAY

An estimated 80% of the seagrasses and 50% of the mangroves in Tampa Bay have been lost over the last 100 years due to dredging, clearing, and enrichment of the water. The Tampa Bay Estuary Program is an effort to help the bay. This group stages volunteer days. Contact www.tbep.org.

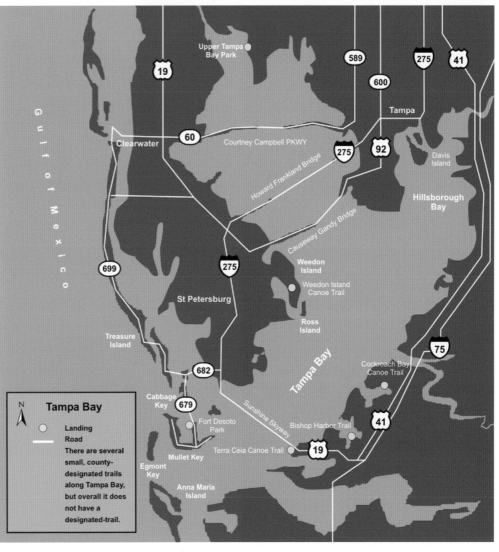

TERRA CEIA BAY
(Manatee County)

Above: Paddling on Terra Ceia Bay with the Sunshine Skyway in the background.

Enclosed by the mainland, keys, and barrier islands, Terra Ceia, located to the west of Palmetto and south of the Sunshine Skyway Bridge, is considered part of Tampa Bay. It is a rich area for nature observation.

Rich sea grasses (manatee, shoal, turtle, and widgeon grasses) attract manatees to its shallows. 29,000 acres is protected within the Terra Ceia Aquatic and Buffer Preserves; of that, 27,000 is in the water, while the remainder is largely mangroves.

Bird Key (Nina Griffith Washburn Sanctuary) has 16 species of nesting birds, including up to 3,000 breeding pairs. It sits in the west of Terra Ceia Bay near Rattlesnake Key and Sister Keys. At times, up to 3000 pairs of nesting birds of 16 species can be found there, including reddish egrets and roseate spoonbills.

Terra Ceia Trail is part of Manatee County's Blueways. Their information urges caution at the pass and near US-19 where Terra Ceia Bay is separated from Terra Ceia Bayou and strong currents sometimes occur.

Perhaps the best recommended launch is from the kiosk on I-275 before reaching the Skyway from the Manatee County side. This launch is on the way north and on the east side of the road. You must pay a toll to get to this area, but you do not have to go over the Skyway to Pinellas County as there is a turnaround.

Paddlers often put-in at an "unofficial" launch next to the Crab Shack on US-19. Paddlers advise avoiding going under the US-19 Bridge during tide changes.

From Emerson Point Park in Palmetto,

it is possible to launch east beside beautiful mangroves. Some of the black mangroves are said to be 140 years old. For this first-class park, turn west from Business US-41 in Palmetto on 10th Street and follow the signs.

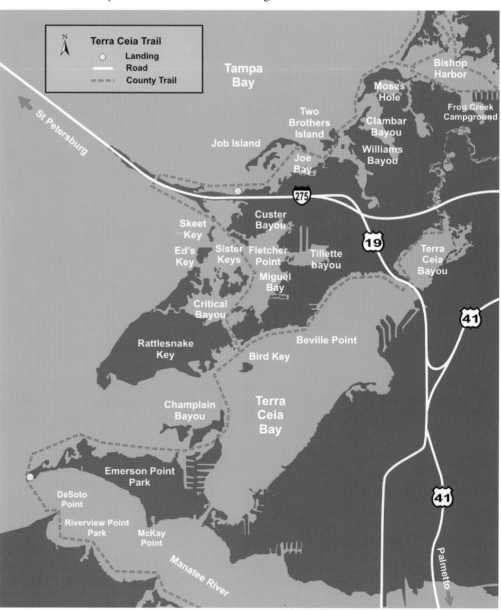

Above: Mangrove shoreline at Emerson Point, Palmetto.

WEEDON ISLAND TRAIL
(Pinellas County)

This is a delightful, 4-mile trail in and out of mangroves along Tampa Bay. Another shorter trail built by boy scouts is part of the preserve.

The 1,500-acre Weedon Island Preserve is roughly at the southwest end of the Gandy Bridge (US-92) in St. Petersburg. On the St. Petersburg side, look for San Martin Boulevard and follow it south to the end.

TURKEY CREEK
(Brevard County)

Turkey Creek flows from Turkey Creek Sanctuary to the Intracoastal Waterway. It is canoed down and back for a total of 4 miles. Along the way it, passes some surprising bluffs. From I-95 in Palm Bay, exit east on Palm Bay Road, then south on Babcock Street, and go east on Port Malabar Boulevard. It is less than 2 miles to the entrance.

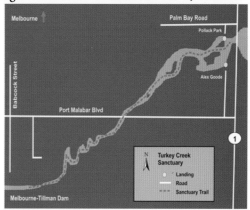

Left: The canoe trail on Weedon Island.

Above: Fishing from a small boat in one of Central Florida's many scenic rivers.

WEEKI WACHEE RIVER
(Hernando County)

North of New Port Richey (and south of Chassahowitzka) lies the Weeki Wachee attraction known for the "mermaids" diving in a clear spring with steep walls. From the comfort of a glassed-in, underwater amphitheater, many tourists have witnessed "mermaids" descending into this first-magnitude spring. The Weeki Wachee River runs from the spring, a traditional summer tubing experience.

Manatees are prevalent on this river, especially during the cooler months. At least one Weeki Wachee manatee has surfaced under a canoe, lifting it up and giving the word "spill" a new meaning.

Traditionally, this river has been paddled upstream against the current. However, there is hope. First, there is a canoe livery that will put paddlers in and allow them to paddle down to the park at the end of the river. Second, in 2001 the commercial attraction was acquired as public lands. It is hoped that paddling will be allowed from the springs down river. The following landings are for paddling upriver.

Weeki Wachee is also sometimes spelled as one word: Weekiwachee.

TWO LANDINGS
1. From Bayport Boat Ramp to SR-595, 2

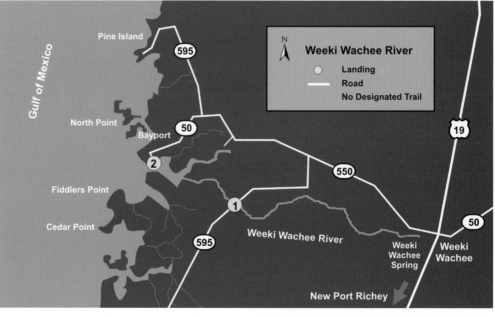

miles. From US-19 in New Port Richey, go north to SR-50. Turn west on SR-50 and go to Bayport. Proceed to the launch.
2. From SR-595 to Weeki Wachee Springs and back, 12 miles. From US-19, turn west on SR-50 and proceed to SR-595. Turn south and proceed to the bridge.

CREEKS, RIVERS, SYSTEMS, DRAINAGE
Technically, a creek is a small river. However, this description is not very uniform in application. To scientists, rivers often flow into river systems, so that there are four rivers in the Wekiva River System. The Wekiva flows into the St. Johns and becomes part of the St. Johns River Drainage. A drainage is an area of land from which water drains into a river or river system.

WEKIVA RIVER
(Lake, Orange, and Seminole counties)

The Wekiva pours out of Wekiwa Springs in the state park, joins Rock Springs Run first, then the Little Wekiva, and finally Blackwater Creek. The Wekiva River System flows north and east to enter the St. Johns River.

What people usually mean when they describe the Wekiva River trip is the paddle between Katie's Wekiva Landing and the St. Johns River. This stretch of Wekiva River is wide with a good northerly flow. However, it also can become shallow during periods of low water, to the point of occasional canoe walking. With good flow, this is not hard paddling, and there are many alligators, birds, and turtles to watch. Before the St. Johns, Blackwater Creek flows in from the west.

Paddlers on the Little Wekiva or Rock Springs Run, come onto the Wekiva River south of Katie's Landing. The Wekiva joins Rock Springs Run within Wekiwa Springs State Park boundaries, and the next take-out is at a marina, then Katie's Landing. The Wekiva Marina is located about 1 mile down river from the confluence of Rock Springs Run with the Wekiva River. The Little Wekiva joins farther north (remember that the flow is north) and the next take-out is Katie's Wekiva Landing.

THE NAME OF THE RIVER

"You say Wekiva. I say Wekiwa." Despite assertions otherwise, linguists believe these are corruption of the same Seminole word meaning spring. However, others believe that Wekiwa means "bubbling waters" and Wekiva means "flowing waters." While some even attempt to pronounced them differently by emphasizing the w or the v, if these words are made interchangeable, no one will ever have a problem.

Wekiva River is one of only two "Wild and Scenic Rivers" designated by the National Park Service in Florida (the other is the Loxahatchee River). Such designations derive from the Wild and Scenic Rivers Act passed by the US Congress in October 1968, which provides some degree of protection for the rivers.

Katie's Wekiva Landing is located near Sanford. Go west on SR-46 from I-4. Within a few miles, a billboard advertising Katie's Wekiva Landing announces the northerly turn to Katie's, a campground with cabins, and a long-time canoe rental and livery service. The St. Johns take-out is at High Banks Marina at the end of High Banks Road, a westerly turn from US-17/92 in DeBary, north of Katie's.

WITHLACOOCHEE RIVER (SOUTH)
(Citrus, Hernando, Marion, Pasco, and Sumter counties)

Both blackwater and spring-fed, 83 of its 100 plus miles are a state-designated canoe trail. Its headwaters are in the boundaries of the historic Green Swamp. In its beginnings, it is not too wide, except in time of flood, when its bank stretch off into the forest.

The Green Swamp once exceeded a half-million acres. It was bounded by four ridges: Brooksville, Lakeland, Lake Wales, and Winter Haven ridges. Four rivers drained from it: the Hillsborough, Ocklawaha, Peace, and Withlacoochee. The Withlacoochee flows to the north-northwest, then bends sharply west toward the Gulf.

Large portions through public lands pass by gorgeous tall trees. In summer, the banks are a shimmering green wall of trees, especially cypress, gum, and maple, while in winter the banks are brown-gray. Airboat traffic on the river is an annoyance to paddlers, and air-boating is controversial around some public lands, such as Potts Preserve, where an impressive Florida trail segment over boardwalk was apparently deliberately destroyed.

Dependent on rainfall, these headwaters (and portions of the river extending into Withlacoochee State Forest) become puddles. Thus, it is a good idea to be aware of local conditions, and your best source is local outfitters.

While there are a number of small tributaries, like Gum Slough, the Rainbow River surges into the Withlacoochee from Rainbow Springs. This is a major contribution to the river. Just beyond the Rainbow River confluence, at a landing on US-41, is the end of the state-designated canoe trail which began at Lacoochee Park in Withlacoochee State Forest. This is referred to as Coulter Hammock Recreation Area, a proper designation, but one that will not help you find the launch.

The river flows west into the Gulf at Inglis near Yankeetown. Before it does so, to the east of Dunnellon it passes through Lake Rousseau, where there are flooded backwaters. The waters of Lake Rousseau are contained by a dam originally built for power generation in the early 1900s. This lake is famed for bass fishing. The dam is no longer used to generate electricity. Lake Rousseau is full of stumps, usually submerged below paddlers.

POSSIBLE TRIPS AND LANDINGS

Additional Trip. The water level in the area above Lacoochee Park is frequently too

Above: The Hillsborough River as seen from Wilderness Park, near Tampa.

low to paddle. However, when the water level is up, a beautiful paddle exists from Withlacoochee River Park, a Southwest Florida Water Management District Land managed by Pasco County. The trip between this park and Lacoochee Park is 13 miles. From US-301 in Dade City, go east 3 miles on River Road, then south a short distance on Anton Road to the entrance of the park.

1. From Lacoochee Park (Coulter Hammock Recreation Area) to SR-50 Bridge, 12 miles. Lacoochee Park is part of Richloam Tract in Withlacoochee State Forest. Lacoochee is east of Brooksville and north of Tampa. Exit I-75 west on SR-50, and turn south on US-301. In Lacoochee, go east on SR-575 to Durden Road and turn south. Go to Coit Road and turn east. Take the first dirt road to the left, and then take the second next road to the right. Proceed to the river. The road is sandy, and in times of rain might be best to have a four-wheel drive vehicle. Otherwise, standard drive is fine.

2. From SR-50 Bridge to Silver Lake, 7 miles. SR-50 is an east-west exit of I-75 north of Tampa. Turn east from the interstate and go to the river. There is no official landing here, and it would probably not be wise to park a car off on the side of the road. The river can be accessed on both the southwest corner of the bridge and the northeast corner behind a fire station.

3. From Silver Lake to CR-476 Bridge, 9 miles. Silver Lake is located in Withlacoochee State Forest. From I-75, go east on SR-50, and turn north into the first forest entrance.

4. From CR-476 Bridge to CR-48 Bridge, 9 miles. From Brooksville, go north on US-41 and turn east on CR-476. Proceed to the bridge. A popular outfitter, Nobleton Canoes, is located on the northwest corner.

5. From SR-48 Bridge to CR-44 Bridge, 15 miles. From I-75 in Bushnell, turn west on CR-48 and proceed to the bridge. Greenways and Trails lists this as SR-48 as do many maps. The signs on the road itself say CR. From the interstate, the signs say SR.

6. From SR-44 Bridge to SR-200 Bridge, 16 miles. From I-75 at the Wildwood/Inverness exit, turn west on SR-44 and proceed to the bridge. There is a campground on the southeast bank which charges a small fee.

7. From SR-200 Bridge to US-41 Ramp, 15 miles. In Inverness, go north on US-41. SR-200 is a north fork to the right just after passing the county line. Fork right and continue toward the bridge. Just before the bridge, turn apparent north on the first road, and proceed to the park on the river bank.

8. US-41. US-41 meets the Withlacoochee River in the town of Dunnellon before Lake Rouseau.

Additional Trips. Usually, paddlers stop at US-41 Ramp. However, it is possible to push west into Lake Rousseau, a backwater created by a dam. There is a public boat launch off CR-40 (the extension of SR-40 from Dunnellon) which is reached by a south turn on 115th Avenue. There are also many fish camps on the lake since bass fishing is exceptional in the backwaters. From US-19 north of Inglis, it is possible to put-in and paddle east upstream, or west to the Gulf where there is a landing at the end of SR/CR-40. The barge canal cuts across the river to the west of the Inglis Lock and Dam, which was non-operational when visited in 2002. Water coming over the last of these series of dams can be turbulent.

Above: The Withlacoochee River.

CAMPING

Southwest Florida Water Management District has an excellent primitive campground at Potts Preserve near Dunnellon. Withlacoochee State Forest offers camping options.

Map. Withlacoochee River (South), Office of Greenways and Trails.

PC

Above: The Withlacoochee River pictured here is at flood stage. The river channel cannot be seen because the river is so high it has slipped off into the trees lining both banks.

AN APPROPRIATE NAME

The name Withlacoochee apparently means "little big water" in the language of the Native American Creeks in Georgia and Seminoles in Florida. In the case of the southern Withlacoochee River, this is particularly appropriate. In normal times and periods of drought, the river is a narrow, twisting, uplands stream for most of the state-designated trail. With heavy rains, particularly in summer or during unusual winter rain events, the river may flood so badly that the main path would be lost if not for the trees lining the banks.

Flooding usually occurs wherever there is a river and heavy rains. Central Florida, however, has a number of streams which can become dangerous with high water. These include the Alafia, Econlockhatchee, Little Manatee, Peace, and many others. At such times, bridges become obstacles which canoes cannot pass under. Branches can reach out to snag paddlers or their craft. It is always a good idea to check local conditions on these rivers. High, powerful water may be fun for expert paddlers, but can be dangerous for those with lesser skills.

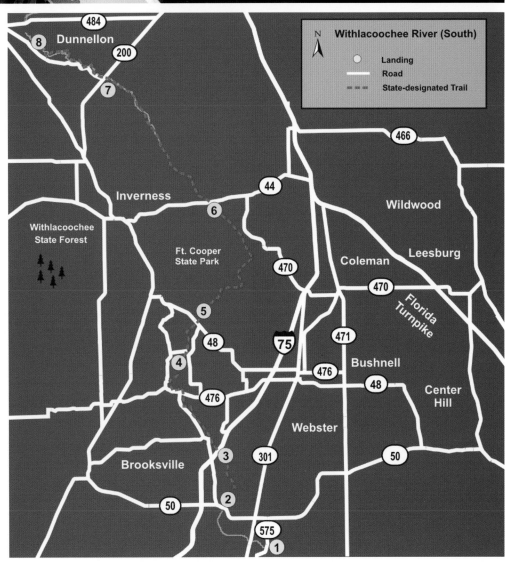

133

ARTHUR R. MARSHALL LOXAHATCHEE NATIONAL WILDLIFE REFUGE
(Broward and Palm Beach counties)

A 5.5-mile loop trail within this national wildlife refuge has a significance far beyond the enjoyment of paddling it. It is arguably the trail passing through areas most like the historic Everglades central marsh system. This is a fine place to remind the old and educate the young about the value of the remaining Everglades.

This is a sawgrass paddle with great variety. Sloughs and wet prairies (a form of marsh) encircle tree islands dominated by coastal plains willow, with cocoplum and wax myrtle. Among the other trees and shrubs, primrose willow and dahoon holly are found. Wild flowers present a pageant as they each take their turn in the sun. Many ferns, including leather and Boston fern, grow in untamed profusion. In every season you visit, whatever the water level, there is beautiful, colorful plant life.

The refuge is famous for its birding. Over two-hundred species of bird life are found at various seasons. Great blue herons, tricolor herons, ibis, and great egrets are commonplace. Snail kites (Everglade kites) nest in the refuge. Wood storks, limpkins, glossy ibis...this is a wonderful place to observe bird life and add to life lists.

Plentiful wildlife is not limited to the flying kind. Otters are seen by quiet paddlers; actually they are sometimes seen at the boardwalk behind the visitors center too. Deer splash across open vistas. Heavy alligator populations are seen particularly well during lower waters. During high water, the alligators may be more noticeable by their wake or the cloud of rising bubbles as they submerge. Bass have jumped into the boats of children on paddling tours, to the delight of everyone. During a recent visit, the author witnessed a primordial battle between a shrike and a pygmy rattlesnake.

The Arthur R. Marshall Loxahatchee National Wildlife Refuge is a 147,392-acre refuge protecting the last remaining portion of the northern Everglades. It is named for Art Marshall, a passionate defender of wilderness and wild things. This is appropriate because the staff and volunteers are justifiably passionate about their wild place.

A paddling trail has been carved through the sawgrass using a machine. Volunteers and dedicated staff keep the trail open. In addition to a splendid trail, there are interpretive signs at several locations. At about the midway point, there is a floating dock with a Port-o-let. Mile markers and directional arrows keep the paddler informed and on the trail. Paddling off the trail is not a very good idea since the way is often hard to find in a vast landscape of visually similar tree islands.

When the water level is right, guided tours at times depart from the loop to cross an area of wet prairie. A wet prairie is a marsh that is flooded 50 to 150 days a year and has a peat bottom. Because of the flooding interval, wet prairies are rich in grasses, sedges, and flowers.

Perhaps the best way to experience this trail is to savor it. Somewhere between mile two and three, stop paddling, close your eyes, and feel the sun beating down while the wildlife around the boat begins to ignore you and goes about the business of living. Do this and you will experience how the Everglades feels and sounds. This is indeed the Everglades, at least as close to the original as we are likely to come.

Additional paddling is possible on L-40, a canal of over 50 miles about the refuge. While wide and boated, the canal offers additional wildlife viewing. It is too long, however, to take in with a single day paddle, and there is no camping along the trail.

There are plans to expand the current trail with a second loop, and perhaps add overnight camping options.

During low water, the trail may be closed. It is always best to check in advance of a visit. Sun block, water, and a hat are good precautions. There is a short deer fly season, but in the summer months this area lacks the infamous saltwater mosquitos found in Everglades National Park. But it still has a few pesky natives.

The entrance is on US-441, 2 miles south of the junction of SR-804 (BoyntonBeach Boulevard). Check with the refuge concerning hours prior to a visit. There is an admission fee. In this area, US-441 parallels I-95 and the Florida Turnpike. The refuge should not be confused with the Loxahatchee River which is farther north.

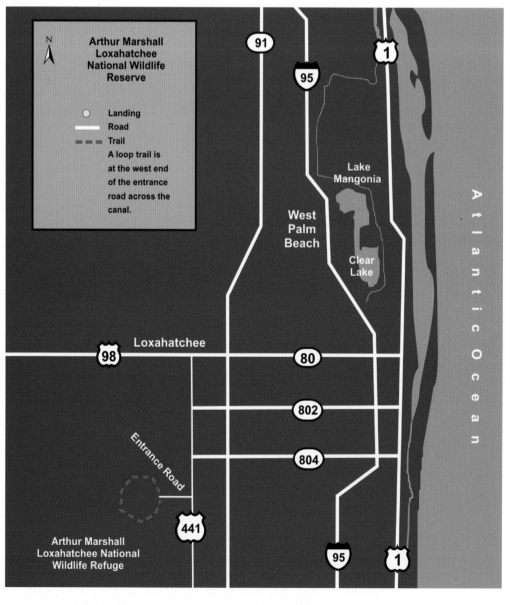

Above: Wildlife refuge trail.

Below: A great egret stalks through a South Florida swamp.

WK

Above: Paddlers at Fort Jefferson in the Dry Tortugas, 70 miles west of Key West.

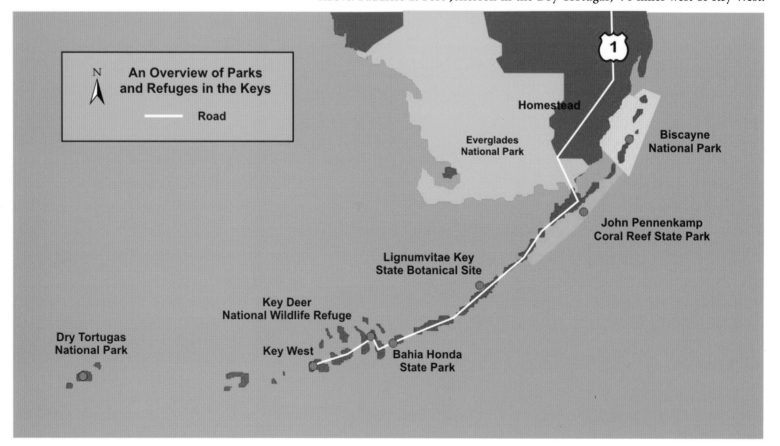

An Overview of Parks
and Refuges in the Keys

N

—— Road

Homestead

Everglades
National Park

Biscayne
National Park

John Pennenkamp
Coral Reef State Park

Lignumvitae Key
State Botanical Site

Key Deer
National Wildlife Refuge

Dry Tortugas
National Park

Key West

Bahia Honda
State Park

PADDLING IN THE KEYS

Bahia Honda is the first of several areas paddlers will want to visit in the Keys. They are presented in alphabetical order within this book. The Keys, from the Spanish word Cayo, are a string of about 40 islands connected by the Overseas Highway, running a length variously estimated at 135 to 150 miles depending on what is included and what is left-out. This is a big area, perhaps 300 miles of coast, with numerous islands on the Florida Bay-Gulf side, and a lesser number along the Atlantic. Most paddling trips described are either along the highway or out from it to the islands.

Such a vast area cannot be covered in this book. There are in fact several books dealing strictly with paddling the Keys. Kathleen Patton has written Paddling the Keys, University Press of Florida, and Bruce Wachob authored Sea Kayaking in the Florida Keys.

Photographer Bill Keogh, whose wonderful photos appear in this book, is the author of The Florida Keys Paddling Guide (Backcountry Guides, 2003). Bill is the owner of Big Pine Kayak Adventures,

lives in the Keys, and leads tours.

Keys' waters, often described as azure, are usually clear, and in many places around islands and Florida Bay/Gulf side there are shallows where the bottom is revealed. Thus it is easy to catch glimpses of many large fishes, such as tarpon, stingrays, and sharks, as well as small colorful fish. Keys scenery is naturally beautiful, thus there are many visual rewards for paddling in the Keys.

Kayakers in the Keys should accurately judge their abilities. Some paddles can be quite long, and distances are hard to judge at sea. The wise paddler going far to sea will not only carry provisions, like water and food, but will obtain nautical charts and tidal information, especially for shallow areas. Flares should be considered an essential, like sun block and insect repellent. Tides around the bridges and passes can be quite strong. When taking-out or putting-in, look for areas without shells to step on which might be sharp and which might scrape a kayak.

Key trips definitely have a season. Almost no one paddles in the hot mosquito plagued summers. In the cooler months of fall and

winter, accommodations can be hard to get, and staying at a state park with camping options may require reservations a year in advance.

Boating is a popular activity in the Keys. Kayakers should use caution when crossing or otherwise using boating channels.

Public lands along and on the Keys include: Bahia Honda State Park, Coupon Bight Aquatic Preserve, Crocodile Lake National Wildlife Refuge, Curry Hammock State Park, Dagny Johnson Key Largo Hammocks State Park, Fort Zachary Taylor Historic State Park, Indian Key Historic State Park, Key Largo National Marine Sanctuary, Key West National Wildlife Refuge, Lignumvitae Key Botanical State Park, Looe Key National Marine Sanctuary, Long Key State Park, National Key Deer Refuge, San Pedro Underwater Archaeological Preserve State Park, White Heron National Wildlife Refuge, and Windley Key Fossil Reef Geological State Park. Dry Tortugas National Park is approximately 70 miles west of Key West and accessed by sea or air shuttle.

WK

BAHIA HONDA STATE PARK
(Monroe County)

Kayakers will experience Bahia Honda one of three ways: paddling around it, making the trip along the Seven-Mile Bridge, or as part of the Florida Blueway, a trail about the Sunshine State which is every day becoming more of a reality. However they experience Bahia Honda, it is a place well-worth visiting for the natural beauty of a gorgeous Keys' beach.

"Bahia Honda is the only significant, undeveloped beach in the Keys," says *Florida's Fabulous Natural Places*, 1999. It is also home to the endangered and rarely seen Florida Keys mole skink, which might be glimpsed along the short nature trail.

Pronunciation tells everyone whether you are stranger or an old Keys hand. The traditional Spanish tongue has been twisted into *Bay-ah* when saying Bahia Honda. The words mean deep bay and, yes, Bahia Honda served as a deep bay in days of yore.

Although camping is possible at Bahia Honda, one cannot just paddle-up and pitch a tent. In fact, that will get paddlers in serious trouble. Camping is by reservation and reservations are difficult to

obtain. Park personnel say it is best to make reservations eleven months in advance. Fortunately, there are private options nearby. Kayaks can be rented at the park.

A lagoon at Bahia Honda beckons from the map. The lagoon is surrounded by mangroves and has been mentioned as a potential paddle in another guide book. Despite it lacking depth, the author of this book actually went into it and found it to

Above: Bahia Honda State Park.

be a beautiful place. However, park personnel report not only is it too shallow but the way is blocked by fallen vegetation.

Canoes and kayaks can be rented at the park, and there is a store where provisions can be purchased. The state park is located on Overseas Highway between Mile Markers 36 and 37, 12 miles south of Marathon.

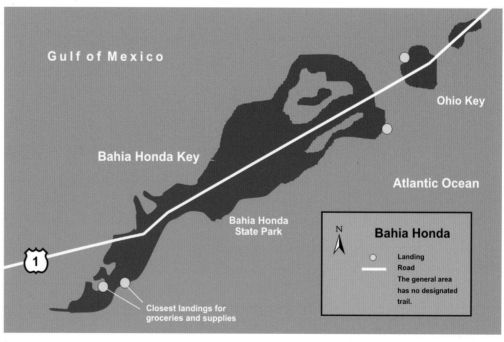

Gulf of Mexico

Bahia Honda Key

Ohio Key

Atlantic Ocean

Bahia Honda State Park

1

Closest landings for groceries and supplies

N

Bahia Honda

○ Landing
— Road
The general area has no designated trail.

Above: Kayaking at sunset near Big Pine Key.

Below: The beach at Gasparilla Island, Boca Grande.

Vertical text along left edge: DOUG PERRINE/INNERSPACE VISIONS

Above: Cape Florida lighthouse at Key Biscayne.

BISCAYNE BAY/BISCAYNE NATIONAL PARK
(Dade County)

Between Miami and Miami Beach lies Biscayne Bay, a very large bay, which is crossed by at least six bridges and accessed from many points, including Oleta State Park in the north, Bill Bags Cape Florida State Park, numerous county parks along the beach, and Biscayne National Park. Such a large area deserves a book of its own, and this can only be a thumbnail sketch.

Biscayne National Park is one of Florida's natural treasures, with 37 island destinations, including Boca Chita and Elliott keys. It is, of course, managed by the National Park Service. From US-1 in Homestead, take SW 320th Street east to the national park headquarters. Canoes and kayaks are rented by the park concessionaire. Regulations and charts are available at the visitor center. There are camping options. The 173,000 acres in the park stretch to the Keys.

Paddling from Biscayne National Park to Elliott Key is approximately 8 miles one way. It is also possible to travel to the Key on a concession boat and paddle once there around Elliot Key and Boca Chita Key to the north, saving 16 miles of open water. To the south of Elliott Key, lie Old Rhodes Key and Swan Key, and if one paddles around them and turns west then north, Totten Key lies toward the mainland, and Adams Key lies to the north. Arrangements should be made in advance if possible for the concession boat ride and camping. Conditions should be thoroughly checked, and in addition to weather, mosquito conditions merit questioning. Information on tidal conditions and charts are very helpful and should be obtained.

Cape Florida State Park faces Biscayne Bay to the west and the Atlantic Ocean to the east. The beach there was selected by the Laboratory on Coastal Research as among the top ten in the entire 50 states. From US-1, take the Rickenbacker Causeway east. Turn south and go south on the beach.

Oleta River State Park lies to the south of the Oleta River and includes a small peninsula along the mainland with mangrove areas. When last visited, there was a concession renting canoes and kayaks, and cabins were available for rent. From I-95, exit east on SR-826 (163d Street) and turn south before reaching the Sunny Isle Causeway.

Local Miami outfitters also specialize in moonlight kayaking to nearby islands.

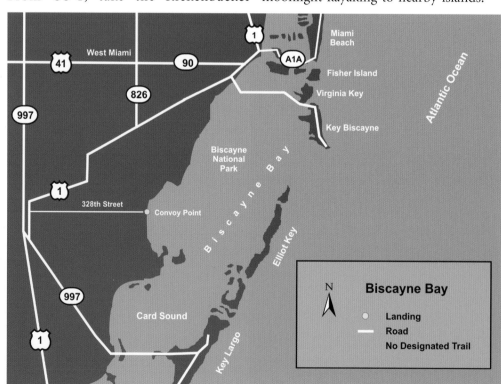

Map labels: West Miami · Miami Beach · Fisher Island · Virginia Key · Key Biscayne · Biscayne National Park · Biscayne Bay · Atlantic Ocean · 328th Street · Convoy Point · Elliot Key · Card Sound · Key Largo · 41 · 90 · 826 · 997 · 1 · A1A

Biscayne Bay
N
● Landing
— Road
No Designated Trail

BLACKWATER RIVER/ROYAL PALM HAMMOCK/COLLIER SEMINOLE STATE PARK
(Collier County)

The 13-mile loop of the state-designated canoe trail is through mangroves and along tidal creeks leading from Collier-Seminole State Park. One clump of mangroves looks much like another, so paddlers sometimes become confused and lost. It is thus a very good idea and a requirement to file a float plan with park rangers before departing. Except during the cold months (and maybe even then), another excellent idea is to take plenty of repellent. Mosquitoes in this area are legendary for inflicting near-terminal itchiness. Sand flies, or no-see-ums, are the monarchs of the mangrove anywhere in Florida.

There is an excellent concession boat ride available through the mangrove tunnels. This mangrove estuary is a favorite kayak paddle. One reason is it is an exceptionally rich and natural ecosystem with plentiful fish and bird life, mangrove water snakes, alligators, raccoons, and even American crocodiles.

Collier-Seminole offers a wide variety of camping options. It is located 18 miles south of Naples on US-41. There is a primitive campsite along the canoe trail, and it is necessary to register prior to arriving by calling the number listed in Appendix B.

Map. Blackwater River/Royal Palm Hammock Creek Canoe Trail, Office of Greenways and Trails.

MANGROVES

South and Central Florida have four types of mangroves. Paddlers will likely encounter all four of these woody trees which have adapted to life in salty conditions. The most common species is the red mangrove with its distinctive root pattern, which may help both in support and the processing of salt. Where black mangrove appears, it is likely to be on relatively higher ground behind the red mangroves. Black mangrove and white mangrove are both named for the color of their bark. Buttonwood, a fourth mangrove, is usually found on sandy areas, not in mangrove thickets, and takes its name from the shape of its flowers. Mangroves are among the most productive ecosystems. In Florida, mangroves are found in estuaries where they provide habitat for such popular fish as mullet, redfish, and snook. Mangroves are also home to mosquitoes and no-see-ums. For this reason, mangrove paddles are usually more enjoyable during cool weather.

Above: Kayaking at the southern edge of Biscayne National Park.

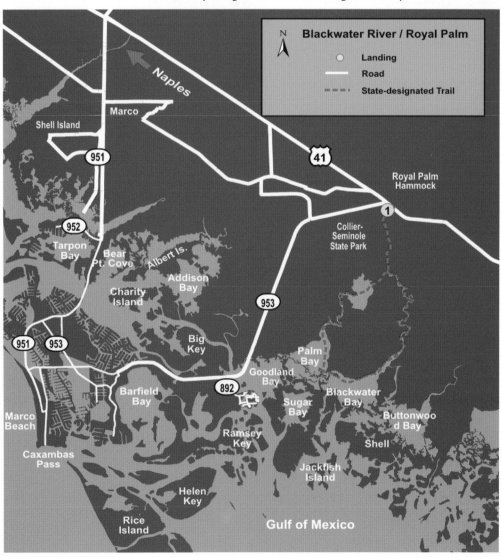

Above: A derelict sailboat in a Caloosahatchee oxbow.

CALOOSAHATCHEE RIVER
(Glades, Hendry, and Lee counties)

A 76.6-mile long river, the Caloosahatchee stretches from Lake Okeechobee to the Gulf of Mexico, where it flows into San Carlos Bay. It is connected to Okeechobee by a canal that enters and exits a smaller lake, Hicpochee.

The connection of the river to Florida's largest lake, Okeechobee, was not part of the Corps of Engineers project that enclosed Lake Okeechobee for flood control. Rather, it was accomplished before 1900 through the efforts of Hamilton Disston as part of a larger effort to drain land for agriculture. Disston was a developer said to have saved the State of Florida from bankruptcy when he purchased 6,250 square miles around Lake Okeechobee.

Paddlers have mixed feelings about the river for several reasons. It is wide with buildings and agricultural along its banks. It is heavily boated. The river is classified as a canal by scientists, but it is a long canal, with many nooks and crannies, much wildlife, and precious side trips, like Hickey's Creek and Orange River. The channel has also created backwaters, called oxbows locally. Within a 10 mile stretch between North Ft. Myers and LaBelle, there are 35 such oxbows and little-known Telegraph Creek.

From LaBelle east to Moore Haven, the river is of little value to paddlers. The river is wide with spoil banks on both sides reaching up to 14 feet high. Large motorboats, speed boats, jet skiers, and cruising ships roar down the river.

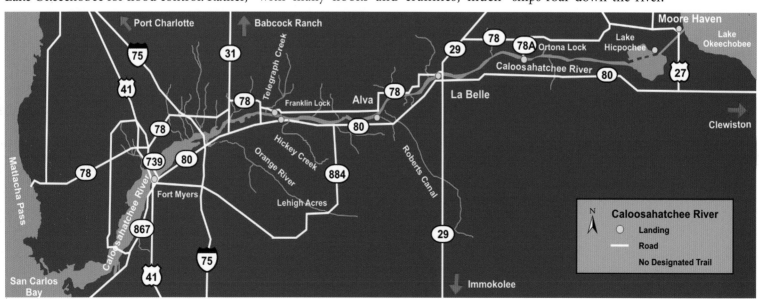

Above: A path through mangroves.

Franklin Lock and Caloosahatchee Regional Park will be the locations of most value to paddlers. Both are used to reach Hickey's Creek, and Franklin Lock is the nearest location to Telegraph Creek. While 35 oxbows lie between Franklin Lock and LaBelle, this is 17 miles of river full of speeding craft and large wakes.

THE ORIGINAL CALOOSAHATCHEE RIVER

Disston's canal replaced the original Caloosahatchee River and went inland far beyond it to connect Lake Okeechobee to the Gulf. Before Disston built his canal with a dredge in the early 1890s, the river started at Flirt Lake (or Lake Flirt, take your pick). The lake was named for a supply boat to Fort Thompson, one of several forts still functioning in Florida during the Civil and Seminole wars. Out of Lake Flirt, the river poured over a substantial waterfall, which Disston dynamited out of existence. The river was incredibly serpentine, with one curve, known as the Rope Bend, which could only be negotiated by attaching a rope to a tree and pulling the boat around it. Another difficult curve was called the Devil's Ebow.

CAYO COSTA
(Lee County)

Cayo Costa, a large barrier island, is at the northwest of Pine Island Sound, as well as the expansive mouth of Charlotte Harbor. It is the northernmost of a chain of islands beginning at Sanibel, continuing to Captiva, and North Captiva. There are miles of potential kayaking between these and Pine Island, and also many of the smaller islands. This area is included in the Lee County Paddling Trail.

One favorite paddle is from Bokeelia Island to Cayo Costa, a distance of perhaps 5 miles over water that is surprisingly shallow in spots. Bokeelia Island is at the north end of Pine Island. From US-41 in North Ft. Myers, turn west on SR-78 and north on CR-767.

SR-78 runs through Matlacha (pronounced Matt-la-shay) and over Matlacha Pass. The pass is an aquatic preserve with mangrove fringes, another of many areas worthy of exploration by avid kayakers. The town itself is famous for its seafood and has several seafood restaurants.

A state park is located on Cayo Costa with camping options. Cabbage Key to the south has for years provided boat docking, good eating in the restaurant, and quarters for the night.

Among the many waterbirds seen in this area are white pelicans and migratory loons.

Charts are necessary as there are busy channels to be avoided. Many of the passes in this area are swift and therefore treacherous. Checking with local marinas and outfitters is thus a prime idea. The Intracoastal Waterway runs north-south through the sound.

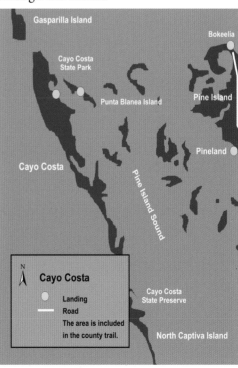

Gasparilla Island

Bokeelia

Cayo Costa State Park

Punta Blanea Island

Pine Island

Pineland

Cayo Costa

Pine Island Sound

N

Cayo Costa

○ Landing

— Road

The area is included in the county trail.

Cayo Costa State Preserve

North Captiva Island

CHARLOTTE COUNTY BLUEWAY
(Charlotte County)

In March 2003, paddlers were pleasantly stunned when the long-awaited Charlotte County Blueway was revealed. An astonishing 212 miles of paddling exists in 53 separate trails. A complete guide to these trails can be requested from Charlotte County Parks and Recreation whose address can be found in Appendix B. Included in the guide is an aerial map, directions to 53 put-ins, lengths of the paddles, and ratings on difficulty and scenery. So much paddling in all the various seasons could in itself provide many treasured memories of a lifetime.

CHARLOTTE HARBOR
(Charlotte and Lee counties)

Charlotte Harbor, at 350 square miles is the second largest estuary in Florida and widely reported as the most productive. It is surrounded by a wide band of protected islands and mangroves, and it is separated from the Gulf of Mexico by a string of beautiful barrier islands.

Pine Island cradles the south side of the harbor and separates Matlacha (*Matt-la-shay*) Pass from Pine Island Sound to the west. Cape Haze is on the north side of the harbor and boasts some of the nation's oldest settlements in North America, Calusa shell mounds dating to 6,500 BC.

At 5-7 miles wide and 20 miles long, and with an average depth of 8 feet, the Harbor is capable of rough sea-like conditions during summer storms and winter fronts. Most of the harbor can be circumscribed behind mangrove islands and tidal creeks.

Bokeelia and Cayo Costa are to the south of the Harbor. Cayo Costa is treated separately within this section.

Cape Haze Aquatic Preserve and Gasparilla Sound are other areas of interest to paddlers. Gasparilla Sound lies just south of Placida between Gasparilla Island and the mainland. Cape Haze is south of Turtle Bay and Island Bay National Wildlife Refuge and Wilderness.

Freshwater, essential for a rich estuarine environment, enters primarily from the Myakka and Peace rivers. Those two rivers travel through Central Florida into the harbor. Myakka enters from the northwest and the Peace flows in from the southeast. Myakka's waters arrive largely unspoiled, although some want to divert a portion of the freshwater for drinking supplies. Waters from the Peace have been harmed by the phosphate industry. One tributary of the

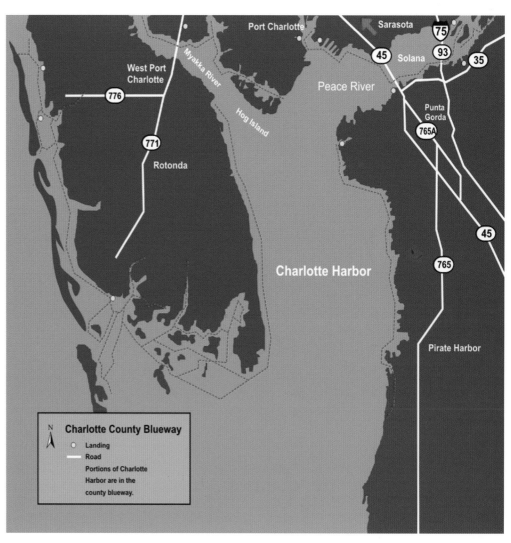

Peace, Horse Creek, improves the Peace water quality before it gets to Charlotte Harbor, but the phosphate industry would like to do more mining in the vicinity of Horse Creek too. At time of first publications, two mines are operating along Horse Creek, one at the headwaters.

Preparations including water, sun block, and charts are a very good idea. Local marinas can help with directions. For putting-in, there are many marinas, boat launches, and piers in Port Charlotte and Punta Gorda, cities to the west of I-75. Charlotte County Blueway includes trips on the north side of the harbor with access

points at El Jobean, Placida, and Gasparilla Island, best reached south of Sarasota on a number of county roads leading from US-41. The south side of the harbor can be accessed from Matlacha, Bokeelia, and Captiva; these towns are west and to the north of Ft. Myers, generally to the west of I-75 following Pine Island Road.

PROTECTING OUR ESTUARIES

Many of Florida's estuaries are in greatly diminished condition. This problem has occured because of development, clearing, dredging, runoff, pollution, and enrichment from fertilizers. The goal of the National Estuary Program is the improvment of the estuaries. Once a program is established for an estuary, a comprehensive plan is developed including programs which can help maintain or improve the health of a waterway. Those who wish to know about the efforts underway, learn what they can do, or even volunteer their time can contact Florida's three Gulf and one Atlantic estuary program through the following contacts.

Charlotte Harbor Estuary Program
4980 Bayline Drive, 4th Floor
North Fort Myers FL 33917
239-995-1777
www.charlotteharbornep.org
Indian River Lagoon Estuary Program
St. Johns River Water Management District
525 Community College Parkway SE
Palm Bay FL 32909
www.sfwmd.gov
Sarasota Bay Estuary Program
111 South Orange Ave, Suite 200W
Sarasota FL
941-951-3650
www.sarasotabay.org
Tampa Bay Estuary Program
100-8th Avenue SE
St Petersburg FL 33701
727-893-2765
www.tbep.org

Above: A river scene near Punta Gorda.

Above: A great egret building a nest in the mangroves.

145

PC

"DING" DARLING NATIONAL WILDLIFE REFUGE
(Lee County)

There are two popular paddling trails within "Ding" Darling: Buck Key and Commodore Loop, adjoining Tarpon Bay. Tarpon Bay Recreation has rentals and guided tours in this area. Buck Key has a private outfitter. In addition, there is extraordinary paddling in Sanibel Bayou, which can be accessed from Wildlife Drive.

On nautical maps, the entire area of mangroves adjoining and extending beyond the refuge is known as Sanibel Bayou. A housing development in the area has taken its name from the nautical charts. Within the mangrove system are a number of smaller bayous and creeks. Some of the names of these smaller systems include Clam Bayou and Hardworking Bayou.

This refuge is named for the famous cartoonist and creator of the Federal Duck Stamp. The refuge staff is assisted by a number of dedicated volunteers.

Buck Key Loop Trail

This 4-mile loop trail takes the kayaker through mangroves and out onto Pine Island Sound. About 600 feet across Roosevelt Channel from Captiva lies Buck

Key, a mangrove island. The channel leads into Pine Island Sound Aquatic Preserve.

On guided tours, or with proper information, it is possible to get out on Buck Key and visit an old settler home, the US Champion largest Jamaican dogwood, and Native American burial mounds.

"Ding" Darling National Wildlife Refuge is widely known for its bird congregations. In this area, manatees appear from time-to-time and dolphins, including sometimes a mother with calf taking shelter in the shallow estuary.

From I-75, exit west on Daniels Parkway. Turn left on Summerlin Avenue and proceed to Sanibel over the toll bridge. On Sanibel, turn right on Periwinkle. Turn right on Tarpon Bay road. At the next stop sign, turn left on Sanibel-Captiva Road. Continue to Captiva Road and Captiva Island. There is an outfitter with both kayaks and canoes at the bay-end of Andy Rosse Lane, a right hand turn.

Tarpon Bay

From Tarpon Bay, there is an easy, marked, 2-mile loop trail through mangroves and into Mullet Lake. This trail is the Commodore Creek Canoe Trail.

Above: Paddling past mangroves at Tarpon Bay.

Mullet Lake is an opening in the mangroves where mullet jump and boil the water with their wakes.

Canoes and kayaks are rented at Tarpon Bay Recreation. There are also guided tours, including a longer, unmarked trek. Sunset paddles go to a rookery island in Tarpon Bay.

Tarpon Bay Recreation is located on Sanibel Island at 900 Tarpon Bay Road.

Sanibel Bayou

Sanibel Bayou is an extensive mangrove habitat alongside Sanibel Island. It can be accessed off Wildlife Drive in "Ding" Darling. To the south of Wildlife Drive is an impoundment originally built for mosquito control and to create a freshwater lake that might attract ducks; paddling is not allowed in this area. To the north lies access to Sanibel Bayou.

Paddlers are advised to be cautious in this area since the way through mangroves is twisty. It is difficult to tell one similar-looking mangrove cluster from another. "Tunnels" or "caves" through the mangroves are uncharted. A few rash turns without too much thought and the paddler will be lost.

....But lost in paradise. Among a small portion of the birds to be encountered are: roseate spoonbills, white pelicans, wood storks, kingfishers, ibis, great blue herons, great egrets, and tricolor herons. However, plentiful raccoons who love bird eggs keep the birds from nesting in the area.

A guided-tour in the mangroves while the sun sets and the moon rises can be unbelievably beautiful. Birds will swoop in to congregate on a mangrove island for the night, arriving in the hundreds to roost on mangrove branches. As the sun sets, mullet seem to be jumping everywhere. The streaking fishes darting just below the surface are redfish.

Follow the directions given for Buck Loop, but turn at the entrance to "Ding" Darling long before reaching Captiva. It is best to make reservations for the guided-tours which can take place twice a day.

CURRENTS

One of the reasons to check with a local outfitter is to be forewarned about areas with powerful currents or significant boating. Buck Key Loop itself is a leisurely trip mostly in the mangrove shallows.

Some paddlers naturally want to branch out onto the sound.

Exiting Pine Island Sound, however, there are passes where the tidal rip is significant. Redfish Pass and Captiva Pass require advanced kayaking skills. These are deep passes.

When tarpon are running, another thrill to paddling across the passes can be hammerheads bumping the kayak when mistaking it for a tarpon snack.

The trip from Boca Grande to Cayo Costa is far from routine. It is part of the paddle along the entire Gulf Coast or circumnavigating the state as well as part of the Blueway concept. Many kayakers go across. But be warned that this is a very deep channel, perhaps running to 90 feet or more. The waters in this area can be very violent even without stormy con-ditions. Local outfitters caution even experienced sea kayakers away from this pass. Kayakers who have crossed call the trip grueling.

Spray skirts are worn around the cockpits of kayaks at sea, particularly in rough waters. When literature about a paddle mentions a skirt is required, this is often a signal the paddle is not routine. This is a paddle where a skirt may often be necessary, as well as stamina, strength, skills, and good weather.

Above: Along the Estero River.

ESTERO RIVER CANOE TRAIL/ESTERO BAY
(Lee County)

From US-41 to Lovers Key State Park, paddlers pass through Koreshan State Historic Site and experience a 7-mile, state-designated canoe trail. There is a population of exotic squirrel monkeys in this area.

The river is bordered by lush South Florida vegetation. This includes large leather ferns and several types of palms. Once the river enters Estero Bay, it is estuary and mangroves. Estero is the Spanish word for estuary.

Between Koreshan and Lovers Key is Mound Key, located in Estero Bay Aquatic Preserve. Mound Key is now a state park, where paddlers may pause, stretch their legs, or explore 125 acres of island once inhabited by Calusa. There are two large mounds, one reaching 50 feet in height. The aquatic preserve reaches north into wild recesses.

Koreshan State Historic Site is an interesting place for the history of the would-be saintly Yankees who migrated there in the 19th Century. The founder of Koreshanity, Dr. Cyrus Reed Teed of Chicago, believed he was immortal, that the earth was concave, and that inside the earth was a hollow sphere. With his followers, he established a commune in 1894. When Teed died in the early 1900s, as unfortunately all living things must, the Koreshan movement died-out.

If paddlers wish to linger at lazy

mangrove paddling, the bay-side of Lovers Key is also a fine place. The recreation area concession rents kayaks. With its fine beaches, Lovers Key State Park is a busy place during suntan season, and a great place with or without humans.

POSSIBLE TRIPS AND LANDINGS

1. From US-41 to Koreshan State Historic Site, 1 mile. From I-75 south of Fort Myers, exit east on Corkscrew Road. Then go north on US-41 to the bridge.
2. From Koreshan State Historic Site to Estero Bay and Return, 7.5 miles. From I-75, exit east on Corkscrew Road and keep going across US-41. The site will be on your right, or the north side.
3. From Koreshan State Historic Site to Lovers Key State Park, 7 miles. The state park is south of Ft. Myers Beach.

CAMPING

Koreshan State Historic Site offers camping options.

Map. Estero River Canoe Trail, Office of Greenways and Trails.

AMERICAN CROCODILES

Florida is host to the nation's small population of American crocodiles. Some are found in Estero Bay. The largest population is found in wetlands bordering Florida Bay, Barnes Sound, Card Sound, and Biscayne Bay.

There have been no recorded attacks on humans by these giant reptiles in Florida. Still give them a wide berth if encountered because they are potentially dangerous.

In contrast to alligators, crocodiles have long, narrow snouts, and the fourth tooth of the lower jaw is exposed when the mouth is closed. Florida crocs are thought not to grow longer than 15 feet.

MANGROVE WATER SNAKES

Guide Mark Westall describes gently stroking mangrove water snakes on the back, then stroking them under the chin. The snakes usually lick Mark's hand to get a sense of him. Why are these snakes so docile? Mark thinks it is because their life in the mangroves rarely exposes them to humans.

Do not try this. Leave that to experts like Mark. Why? Because mangrove water snakes, although variable in color, are usually dark gray to black. This is almost the same as the mature Florida cottonmouth (water moccasin), a venomous snake. And other water snakes are known to have a mean (but non-venomous) bite too.

Above: Ranger in Everglades National Park demonstrates handling of "dug-out canoe" replica.

Above: Canoeists camping in Everglades National Park.

EVERGLADES NATIONAL PARK
(Collier, Dade, and Monroe counties)

The sights of the Everglades are truly Floridian. There is no better way to come to a personal understanding of the Everglades than to experience them in person.

Paddling trails begin on the road to Flamingo. They travel primarily through mangroves.

Its vast central marsh system is unique to the world, historically fed by the overflow of Lake Okeechobee. But there are many habitats within the national park besides marsh dominated by vistas of sawgrass and tree islands. Driving to Flamingo leads through rocklands, cypress swamp, marsh, hammocks, and mangroves.

There is a large visitors center at the main park entrance where there is information on paddling trails. A map of the Everglades is essential for finding the way, and it is available at park headquarters, Shark Valley, and Flamingo. Tidal charts are recommended for any coastal paddle, and can be obtained at the marina in Flamingo.

It is best to check in advance before proceeding on any of the trails because of changing conditions. A permit is needed for camping. Charts and information are available at the marinas in Flamingo and Everglades City.

The National Park Service divides the trails in the park into three areas: Flamingo Area Canoe Trails, Gulf Coast Area Canoe Routes, and Wilderness Waterway, a long primitive trail beloved by kayakers and scouts.

Once the Everglades was vast - 4,000 square miles. Its size is now greatly diminished. In current times, the historic Everglades is divided into three parts, only one of which is Everglades National Park. The two public areas are the national park south of US-41 and a water conservation

Below: Low tide.

area mostly north of US-41. Various paddles are possible also in the water conservation area. Agriculture uses the remaining 1/3 of the historic Everglades.

Shark Valley on US-41 in the middle of Miccosukee country is a wonderful experience and should not be missed, but for paddling go to the Flamingo entrance. The road to Main Park Road is SR-9336, which goes west from Florida City, turns 90 degrees south, then bends westerly again into the park.

Entire books have been devoted to Glades paddling: *A Paddler's Guide to Everglades National Park* by Johnny Malloy, University Press of Florida is one. Another smaller, nifty book is *Boat and Canoe Camping in the Everglades Backcounty and Ten Thousand Island Region*, Dennis Kalma, Florida Flair Books.

FLAMINGO AREA CANOE TRAILS

Bear Lake Canal. Few paddles in the Everglades are short. It is 1.6 miles to Bear Lake through a canal, then 11.5 miles one way to Cape Sable. Bear Lake Canal may be impassable early in the dry season.

Florida Bay. Pick your distance. Camping is allowed on Carl Ross Key. One young librarian described this as the adventure of a lifetime. Her kayak was bumped by sharks on the way out. Florida Bay camping on Carl Ross Key requires a permit which can be obtained at the Flamingo or Gulf Coast visitor centers within 24 hours of departure. The fee depends upon trip duration and the number of paddlers.

Hells Bay Trail. "Hell to get into and hell to get out of." This slogan may give many paddlers pause. During low water, portions may be impassable. The paddler may feel he is paddling in mud. The trail is marked at more than 160 places as it passes through mangroves, lakes, and ponds.

Mud Lake Loop. This 6.8-mile loop trail proceeds from Coot Bay Pond north of Flamingo. It meets Bear Lake Canoe Trail and also connects to Buttonwood Canal and Mud Lake.

Nine Mile Pond Loop. This 5.2-mile loop travels through mangroves and sawgrass. It is located 11 miles north of Flamingo and is blazed with white poles. In the dry season, the trail may be impassable.

Noble Hammock Trail. At 2 miles, this is the only short trail in the bunch. It passes through mangroves and ponds, but is often impassable during low water.

West Lake Trail. It is slightly more than 7.5 miles to Alligator Creek, then the same distance to return, making the paddle over 15 miles. The trail passes through mangroves, open areas, creeks, and ponds.

Above: A ranger takes some inner-city children on a canoeing adventure in the Everglades.

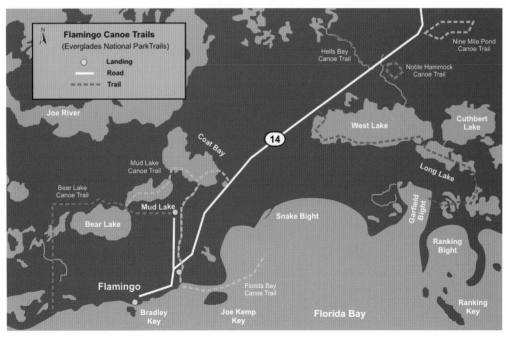

MOSQUITO SEASON

There is definitely a time to paddle the Everglades and a time to stay away. For those arriving in August, for example, this is the likely scenario of events.

You show up at the marina and ask about paddling. They tell you no one has paddled there in months and offer to sell you a head to toe mosquito suit.

When you pull up to the famous Flamingo Lodge, you are pursued and bitten on exposed portions of your body by mosquitos - despite jogging from your car. It takes you three trips to unload your car, running back and forth to your room, during which you are bitten, and your trunk stands open. In the morning, when you open that trunk again, a cloud of mosquitos will float out like smoke from the barrel of a recently fired shotgun.

Inside your room, you will kill all the mosquitos you can see with your rolled newspaper. You open the drapes and kill all the mosquitos that fly up against the clear glass. You turn on the light in the bathroom, and kill all the mosquitoes that show up. Your newspaper is now covered in blood.

Before you go to bed, the air-conditioner has been set on high. You have swatted and killed everything buzzing by you. You spray insect repellent on, sleep in a long sleeve shirt, and try to sleep under the covers. When you wake, unfortunately you find the mosquitos have eaten your face.

Rather than paddling, you flee to your car in the morning. After killing a couple of thousand more mosquitos inside your car, you drive out of Everglades National Park without paddling.

Come in the cool months when there are fewer mosquitos, and the paddling is gorgeous.

Above: Hoseshoe crabs lay eggs on the beach at Cape Sable.

THE UN-ENDANGERED MANATEE

A manatee mother skillfully keeps herself between the kayak and her calf. She makes turns that would impress a ballerina. Once the kayaker sits still long enough, the reward may be a view of gently breathing manatees coming to the surface. These are the kinds of sights paddlers witness often on Florida waters. Manatees are one thing paddlers can't find in North Carolina or in the Pacific river gorges.

As recent censuses have resulted in increased manatee counts, there have been efforts to delist the manatee as an endangered species, making it a threatened species instead. Support for this change often comes from boaters who do not like those pesky manatee zones which force them to slow down. A lot of boaters are not real keen on those troublesome kayakers either.

Some scientists are skeptical about the increased numbers, feeling that there are now more census takers, and that conditions for the recent census were optimum.

A few thousand is not a large population of any species. What if there were only three thousand humans left in Florida? Three thousand is not anywhere close to historical levels, nor enough to fend off any type of cataclysm. Certainly such a population is not large enough to guarantee continuation in local waters. Manatee reproduction goes slowly, one offspring at a time, with long calf-raising periods.

It is hard for paddlers, who often witness these graceful animals in the wild, to be sympathetic to changing the status for the manatee. Doing so may be a symbolic win for boaters and a defeat for those defending the manatee. What's to gain? Rewarding boating interests? Is zipping and roaring over the waves at full throttle worth even one of these gentle fellow mammals?

GULF COST AREA
CANOE ROUTES

Halfway Creek and Turner River Loop. This loop proceeds from Gulf Coast Visitors Center to Turner Lake and returns. The distance is not given in park literature, instead it is described as a 4-hour trip

Turner River. This trip has its own account in this section.

Sandfly Island Trip. This trail is perhaps a mile across Chokoloskee Bay to a mangrove island and a 1-mile return, although more distance can be added paddling about the mangroves.

There is a 1-mile hike on the island for those who wish to take it. Sand fly is another and more proper name for "no-see-um," a nearly-invisible, small biting fly.

WILDERNESS WATERWAY

This is perhaps the premier paddling trip in the Everglades. It is an epiphany for scout troops and naturalists. It winds around 99 miles of mangroves and islands, enters Whitewater Bay, and reaches Florida Bay. It can take as long as two weeks with a "back country permit" for camping. Some of the camping is on stilt platforms. Tidal information is critical to successful paddling on the Wilderness Waterway.

FISHEATING CREEK
(Glades and Highland counties)

Dense, lush vegetation borders many portions of Fisheating Creek. There is only one notable public launch. Paddles stretch east and west from it into some very wild country. Panthers are not unknown in this area, although rarely seen.

For years, the campground and launching site were open to the public and a popular site for paddling, camping, and fishing. It is easy to see why. The natural beauty and wildness is spellbinding. Then a business blocked the entrance to the river, despite the fact that the public used it, and a dispute ensued in which the business insisted it owned the river bottom. Fortunately, public interest prevailed over private. The land has been acquired by the state and is now a wildlife management area open to all.

Fisheating Creek Campground is at the entrance to the wildlife management area. In addition to camping, it has a general store and bathrooms. The launch is at the campground.

From SR-80 west of Ft. Myers, turn north in LaBelle on US-29. Turn north on US-27. The entrance is on the west side in less than 2 miles. Or, if traveling on US-27 south or north, the entrance is on the west side of US-27 just south of the small community of Palmdale.

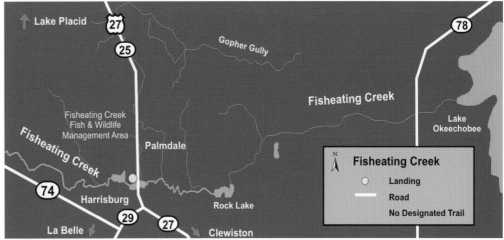

Below: Canoeists on Fisheating Creek.

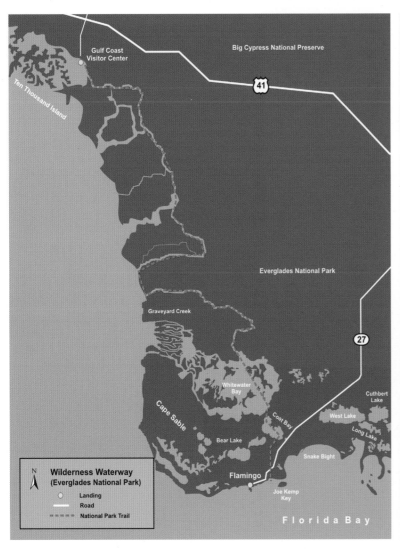

FLORIDA BAY
(Dade and Monroe counties)

While approximately 850 square miles, the average depth in Florida Bay is only three feet. It is a wild area of mangroves, islands, and estuary, fed by freshwater entering from Big Cypress and the Everglades. It stretches across south Florida to the Keys.

Many guides lead trips into Florida Bay. They offer half-day, full-day, and camping trips. Most of these services are associated with the Keys to the east and the Everglades to the north. One trip that has been highly recommend by several outfitters is North Nest Key, a 15-mile round-trip with beautiful sunsets, manatees, dolphins and birds.

Florida Bay includes hallowed fishing grounds and many boaters. From Everglades National Park, the launch is at Flamingo. See Everglades account for directions. There is a launch on US-1 south of the mainland at Little Blackwater Sound. It is also possible to put-in from many

Top: Kayaker searching for mating nurse sharks on sponge flats.

locations in the Keys.

Controlling the flow of the Everglades has altered the amount of freshwater entering the bay. The salinity has increased, which is believed to have damaged the sea grasses. Sea grasses are a valuable and intrinsic part of the ecosystem for many creatures, including manatees.

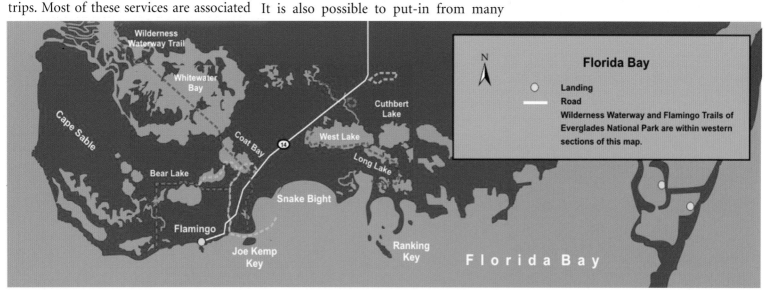

HICKEY CREEK
(Lee County)

Above: Telegraph Creek and Hickey Creek are both located along the Caloosahatchee River and are similar in appearance. This photo shows a view of Telegraph Creek.

Locally, this stream is called Hickey's Creek. This trail is off the Caloosahatchee River east of I-75 and Ft. Myers. The only practical way to go onto Hickey Creek is from the Caloosahatchee. From Caloosahatchee Regional Park, it is 2.5 miles east to Hickey Creek, 2 miles up the creek, 2 miles back down, and 2.5 back to the park, a total of about 9 miles, some say more. This effort is rewarded by the scenes of subtropical splendor along the creek.

Caloosahatchee Regional Park is east from I-75 at the North Ft. Myers exit. Go east from I-75 on SR-78 to the stop sign at SR-31 (at times this is a dangerous intersection, with no light and fast cars approaching from both directions at times of heavy traffic, so use care). Turn north and proceed 1 mile to River Road. Turn east and go 7 miles. The regional park offers a variety of camping options.

It is also possible to enter the Caloosahatchee River from Franklin Lock where there is a campground. See also the account for the Caloosahatchee River.

Map. Office of Greenways and Trails.

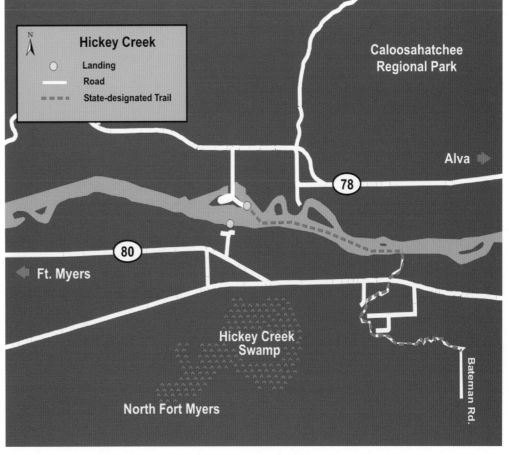

Hickey Creek
- ○ Landing
- ── Road
- ╌╌╌ State-designated Trail

Caloosahatchee Regional Park

Alva

78

80

Ft. Myers

Hickey Creek Swamp

Bateman Rd.

North Fort Myers

IMPERIAL RIVER
(Lee County)

The Imperial River flows into Estero Bay and could provide an alternative paddle north and west to Lovers Key State Park or the Estero River. It is about 2 miles to the bay from the launch on US-41 in Bonita Springs, a town south of Ft. Myers. The river is an enjoyable paddle inland also, and many local paddlers prefer this to the longer journey to Lovers Key. See account for Estero River.

INDIAN KEY HISTORIC STATE PARK
(Monroe County)

Indian Key and the area about it present many interesting sights plus a slice or two of equally fascinating history. South of it lies Alligator Reef Lighthouse, one of 13 reef lighthouses in Florida, named for the USS Alligator which battled pirates in the early 1800s. Alligator Reef Lighthouse personnel withstood 200 mile per hour winds and 50 feet seas during a the Category 5 Labor Day Hurricane of 1935. Indian Keys' history includes salvers and wreckers, and an attack on settlers by Seminoles on August 7, 1840, in which several settlers were killed.

To the west about a mile lies the wreck of the San Pedro, a Spanish vessel which sunk in 1733. The state park sits south of Islamorada in the midst of Lower Matecumbe Key to the southwest, Upper Matecumbe Key to the northeast, and Lignumvitae Key to the west. While Indian Key takes it name from the Seminole attack, Upper and Lower Metecumbe keys actually served as home to Calusas long before the

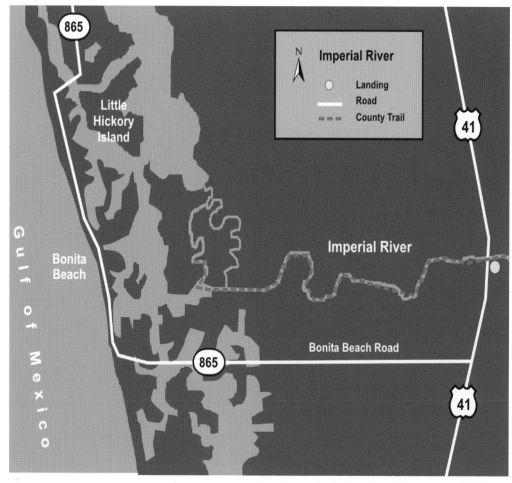

Spanish arrived.

The park closes at sundown and opens at 8:00 AM. There are ranger-guided tours twice daily. There are at least four landings in the immediate area. Maps show two on the west side of Upper Matacumbe Key, paddler guides describe one on the Atlantic side of the same key, and there is one at the state park.

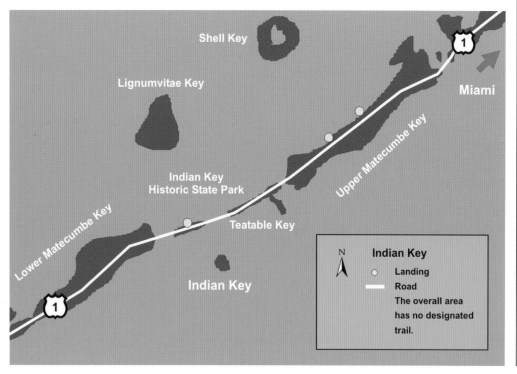

A LITTLE KNOWN STREAM

Along the Caloosahatchee River lies not only Hickey Creek, a state-designated canoe trail, but also Telegraph Creek, perhaps equally beautiful and seldom paddled. Both creeks are fed from rainfall and surface waters which make their way into the Caloosahatchee River.

Both creeks are accessed from Franklin Lock, which is along both SR-78 on the north bank and SR-80 on the south bank, east of I-75 and the city of Fort Myers. For Hickey Creek, it is necessary to paddle from Franklin Lock to the south bank. For Telegraph Creek, one must paddle west of the lock to the north bank. In both cases, the river is wide, thus subject to wind and big wakes from power-boats.

Civilization is arriving at formerly rural Hickey Creek in the form of housing. The newly created Hickey Creek Mitigation Park, run by Lee County, lies along SR-80. It has a canoe dolly, and could be used to put-in and out. It may save some of this land from development.

Telegraph Creek is largely natural or agricultural, with less homes. How far up it one can travel depends on water levels. When explored in winter 2004, it was possible to paddle at least a mile. Many local residents consider Telegraph Creek a better trip than Hickey Creek.

Manatee Park on SR-80 rents kayaks and Caloosahatchee Regional Park on SR-78 presently rents canoes.

JOHN PENNEKAMP CORAL REEF STATE PARK
(Monroe County)

John Pennekamp was an environmental hero and an associate editor of the Miami Herald. He brought to public attention the plight of coral reefs diminished by run-off and human carelessness. His efforts helped create the state park which has been named in recognition of his efforts.

Most people come to Pennekamp for the coral reefs. Reefs provide rich aquatic habitats and when destroyed take many human lifetimes to recover, if they can recover at all. The coral reefs off Pennekamp are a natural treasure to be cherished and protected. They attract diving enthusiasts from around the world.

Kayakers going to the reefs must travel 3 to 5 miles over open sea. There are mooring buoys near the dive locations. There is also a 2.5-mile, interpretive paddling trail with markers. Of course, Pennekamp can be considered a stop along the Florida Blueway. A saltwater aquarium and exhibits provide vital educational information to visitors. Pennekamp offers camping options, but reservations must be made almost a year in advance. Kayaks are available for rental.

The state park is in Key Largo off US-1.

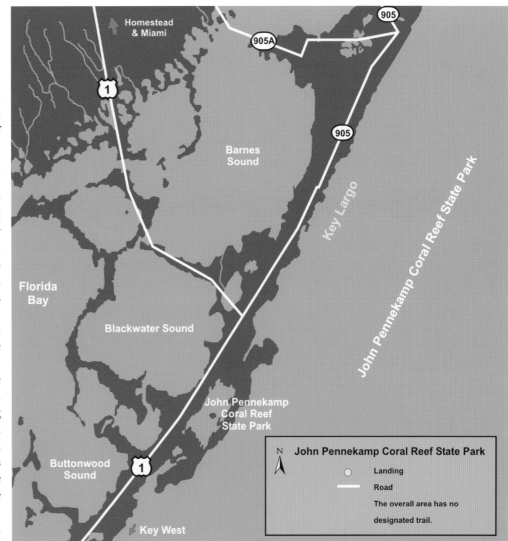

Homestead & Miami

905

905A

1

Barnes Sound

905

Key Largo

John Pennekamp Coral Reef State Park

Florida Bay

Blackwater Sound

John Pennekamp Coral Reef State Park

Buttonwood Sound

1

Key West

N

John Pennekamp Coral Reef State Park

○ Landing

— Road

The overall area has no designated trail.

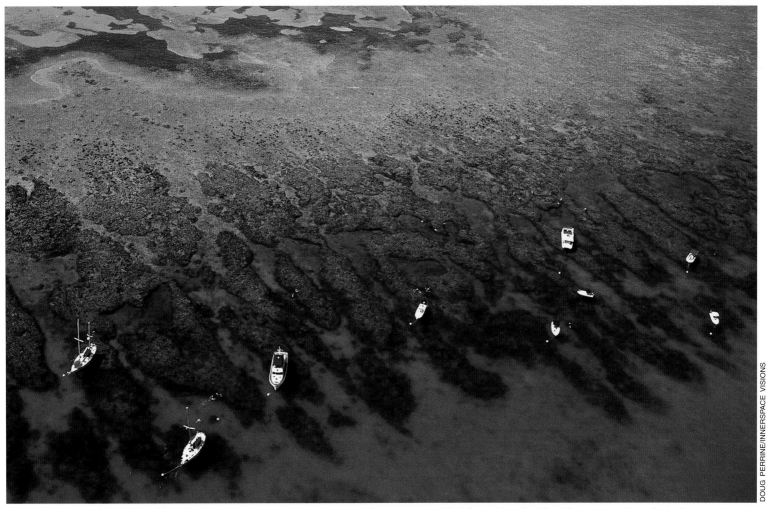

DOUG PERRINE/INNERSPACE VISIONS

Above: Looe Key Reef shows the spur-and-groove coral formations of bank reef in the Florida Keys National Marine Sanctuary.

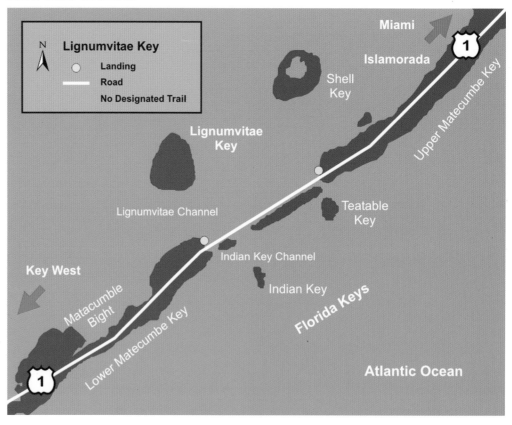

LIGNUMVITAE KEY STATE BOTANICAL SITE
(Monroe County)

Distances along the Keys sole north-south road are described in mile markers (MM). Lignumvitae is roughly west from MM 77.5 and MM 78.5. The highest MM number is to the north. MM 1 is in Key West.

On Lignumvitae is a remarkable variety of trees, including the understory tree for which the key is named. While so much of the Keys has been cleared for humans, or changed in one way or the other, this island is essentially the same as it has existed for hundreds of years, with some minor exceptions. "Stepping back in time" is not a trite phrase here, rather it is a reality. The tropical hammock on this island should be experienced by anyone who wants an appreciation of what the untouched Keys must have been like.

It is only possible to tour the island with a ranger. These tours occur at present Thursday through Sunday at 10:00 am and 2:00 pm. This is a fine tour, unfortunately usually plagued by hordes of mosquitos. In the past, repellent was available at the ranger office.

The journey to the island is basically open water. Depending on where you put-out and the wind, the paddle may take an hour or more. It may be 1 mile to the island and 2 miles around it.

Above: Fishing on the flats off Saddlebunch Key.

Miami

Islamorada

Lignumvitae Key
○ Landing
— Road
No Designated Trail

Shell Key

Lignumvitae Key

Upper Matecumbe Key

Lignumvitae Channel

Teatable Key

Key West

Indian Key Channel

Indian Key

Matacumbe Bight

Lower Matecumbe Key

Florida Keys

Atlantic Ocean

1

LEE ISLAND COAST CANOE/KAYAK TRAIL
(Lee County).

Currently this is a work in progress, but it should be really something when it is finished. This is Lee County's Blueway and involves several paddles described within this section of the book.

The first phase of this trail was begun in 2001 and expanded in 2005. The trail begins in the south at the Imperial River in Bonita Springs, proceeds north through Estero Bay, and may be joined from the Estero River. In Estero Bay, it passes by Mound Key, Lovers Key, and Ft. Myers Beach, ending at Bunche Beach.

The trail passes Cayo Costa and ends at Boca Grande. (Crossing to Boca Grande is usually a mean paddle, sometimes dangerous, always physically challenging.)

This trail is a project of the Lee Island Coast Visitor and Convention Bureau. They may be contacted at 2180 West First Street, Suite 100, Ft. Myers FL 33901, phone 941-338-3500, fax 941-334-1106. www/LeeIslandCoast.com. Maps are available over the phone and through the website www.TheGreatCalusaBlueway.com.

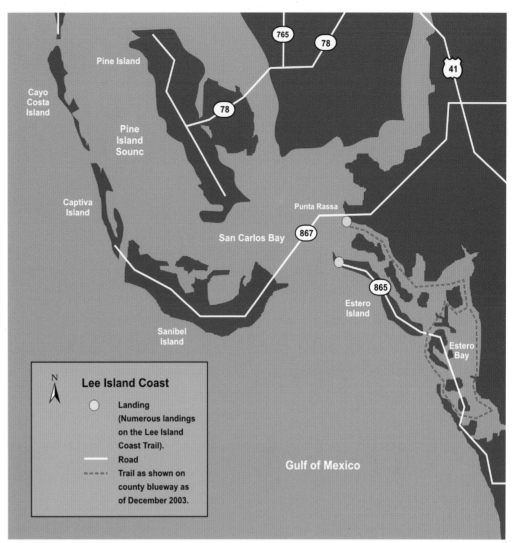

Lee Island Coast
- ○ Landing (Numerous landings on the Lee Island Coast Trail).
- ——— Road
- - - - - Trail as shown on county blueway as of December 2003.

ROLLING A KAYAK

Most kayakers learn to do Eskimo rolls as a way of righting their boat in a spill. Rolls are done with a movement of the hips. This technique should be taught by an instructor, because it is a disconcerting feeling for the inexperienced kayaker to be upside down in a kayak underwater.

A "new" trend in kayaking for Americans is Greenland style. It is considered "new" here, but native Innuits were rolling their kayaks before there was a USA.

Greenland kayakers have a longer paddle with smaller scoops. This makes for some graceful kayaking.

Greenlanders also practice a number of distinctive 360 degree rolls based on where the paddle and body are located. They can paddle upside down. They practice a tug with a walrus with one end of a rope held by men on shore and one end held by the paddler. One Greenlander exercise is rolling with an eighteen pound rock. That will separate the weekend paddlers from the truly serious.

In the US, Greenland-style is a sort of Zen for those who do it. However, to native Greenlanders hunting in Arctic waters, leaving one's boat means death, so learning how to roll, even while holding a weight, was traditionally a matter of survival.

Orlando's Greg Stammer competes in the Greenland International Championship and also teaches Greenland-style sea-kayaking. In the photo above, Joshua Broer performs a Greenland-style roll.

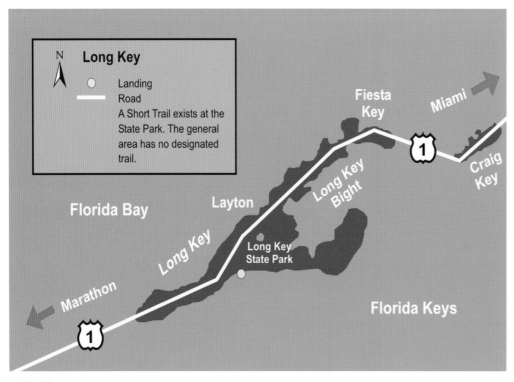

LONG KEY STATE PARK
(Monroe County)

To the Spanish, this was *Cayo Vivora* - Rattlesnake Key. The Spanish saw in its shape on a map the open mouth of a pit viper. This might be a more appropriate name for the island, since there are many longer islands. Long Key was not a lucky place for the Spaniards. Spain suffered the tremendous loss of 19 sailing vessels and many sailors between Long Key and Key Largo in a 1733 hurricane.

Long Key Fishing Camp brought many notables, include the western writer Zane Gray, to the area for feats of fishing lore. A creek is named for him. Zane Gray was prolific. He produced a pile of westerns which are beloved by those who read the genre. The fishing camp washed, blew, and was pounded away with the Labor Day Hurricane of 1935, a category 5 storm with winds of 200 miles per hour.

The state park has its own 1.25-mile paddling trail, serves as a launch point for other locations, and is a pleasant stop along the Florida Blueway. On the Atlantic side is a lagoon with the designated trail. A map of this trail is available at the park. The trail includes interpretative stops marked by posts.

Curry Hammock State Park is managed by Long Key State Park. Curry Hammock is the smaller park at 260 acres compared to Long Keys 965.

Long Key lies to the southwest of Islamorada and to the northeast of the Conch Keys at MM 67.5. Curry Hammock lies farther southwest at MM 56.

LOXAHATCHEE RIVER
(Martin and Palm Beach counties)

Loxahatchee was the first Wild and Scenic River designated in Florida by the National Park Service. Only two rivers in Florida have this special designation which affords some protection. More deserve the designation. The other river so designated is the Wekiva in Central Florida. Interestingly, both rivers flow northward. The special designation is well deserved as there is nothing else in Florida quite like the Loxahatchee River.

The trail is roughly divided in half by Trapper Nelson's homestead. This is an historic site within Jonathan Dickinson State Park, which is named after an unfortunate shipwrecked Quaker, whose exploits hundreds of years ago can still be read in his journal, which can be purchased at the concession in the park.

An immigrant, Trapper Nelson made his living trapping on the river. Allegedly he read *The Wall Street Journal* every day and prospered as an investor as well as a trapper. He died under mysterious circumstances.

The 4 miles above Trapper Nelson's are twisty and subtropical. With substantial flow, it requires good skills to make all the turns and not slam into a cypress tree or cypress knees. Below the cypress are lush ferns. Growing up the cypress and palm trunks, are vines. In the trees are grassy airplants and bromeliads. Native orchids can be found in this area.

There are also two dams (Masten and Lainhart dams) within the first mile or so of the paddle. The first dam is often paddled over, paddled to the left, while the second dam is only run in high water, then to the

right. Care should be used if one decides to ride over the dams as this is potentially dangerous. Also, paddlers will gain speed going over the dam and have to watch out for collisions on the other side with trees or logs. There are excellent, wooden, constructed drag-over ramps for those who are not adventuresome (or foolish, depending on how you look at it).

In normal to low water, this first half of the river has some drag-overs, pull-overs, and blocked logs to stand on while pulling the canoe over. In these cases, and most other times, a good sense of balance is a fine thing to possess.

Beyond Trapper Nelson's, the river opens up. It is a wide paddle for 4 miles. Two creeks flow in from the west: Cypress and Kitching creeks. The vegetation also makes a dramatic change. Mangroves appear, especially extensive red mangroves. Mangrove and cypress grow side by side. Palms and pines mix in with the mangroves and cypress. This is very unusual within remaining mangrove areas in Florida. There are even a few, towering royal palms.

In the first half of the river, barred owls hoot from the trees and pileated woodpeckers peck away in the floodplain. Belted kingfishers swoop in front of paddlers. As the river widens, large great blue herons appear and many other waterbirds. In season, however, the birds most associated with this wide part of the river may be the ospreys, perched high in dead cypress branches in the wider second half of the river. Away from the river, scrub-jays may be seen among the sand pines.

Alligators are plentiful along the whole run of the river. Some are quite large. Many paddlers travel this trail so the gators may be habituated to humans. Care should be used. Manatees are also seen frequently enough that paddlers comment on their presence.

Loxahatchee River should not be confused with the canoe trail in Loxahatchee National Wildlife Refuge. The two are separated by a great deal of distance and are different kinds of paddles through differing kinds of habitat. In fact, two areas with the same first name could not be more different. Loxahatchee River is first dominated by beautiful cypress then mangroves as it becomes tidal, while the national wildlife refuge is essentially Everglades with tree islands and sawgrass.

The river flows north so the 8-mile state-designated trail begins at Riverbend Park, 1.5 miles west on SR-706 from the Florida Turnpike. This trail ends within Jonathan Dickinson State Park. The park entrance is located on US-1 near Hobe Sound.

One can continue another 8 miles beyond the state park to a bridge at US-1.

Above: The Loxahatchee River.

There the river becomes Intracoastal Waterway in both directions.

Amazingly for a "wild river," the trail passes within the first quarter mile under a county road with zipping traffic Later paddlers go under the Florida Turnpike and I-95. At that point, the two interstates are almost joined. This brief blare of noise from zooming trucks and cars will soon disappear, replaced by the more tranquil sounds of wildlife and running water.

Map. Loxahatchee River Canoe Trail, Office of Greenways and Trails.

PC

Above: The Loxahatchee River, one of Florida's two designated Wild and Scenic Rivers, passes through portions of Jonathan Dickinson State Park.

MYRTLE CREEK
(Charlotte County)

Myrtle Creek flows north into Shell Creek. It has been the favorite kayak trip of a Director of Natural Resources for the county, a fact that should recommend it.

Washington Loop (CR-764) encircles the area and crosses Myrtle Creek, Prairie Creek, and Shell Creek. There are "unofficial" landings on CR-764. How much distance can be accomplished is a matter of water level and how cleared the river. To reach CR-764, exit from I-75 east on US-17 and turn onto CR-764.

On DeLorme Atlas maps this is called Myrtle Slough and Myrtle Creek appears elsewhere on the same page.

DOUG PERRINE/INNERSPACE VISIONS

Above: A Key deer.

NATIONAL KEY DEER REFUGE
(Monroe County)

At a time when most conservation efforts, like that of the Florida panther, sputter along, the success for the Key deer is phenomenal. If only panthers could make the astonishing come-back made by Key deer.

Before the establishment of the refuge, this diminutive subspecies of Virginia white-tailed deer was almost hunted to extinction. It is widely reported that the population got down to less than 50 - some accounts say there were just 25 individuals in the 1950s. Today there are several hundred Key deer, a small vegetarian about the size of a German shepherd and with an even more docile temperament.

Key deer don't bark, but like some dogs, they don't mix well with cars. Drivers should obey the speed laws within this area. The life they save may be their own, but it could also be the life of a Key deer.

A local hero in the preservation of the animals was Jack Watson. His efforts are largely credited with establishing the refuge. J. N. "Ding" Darling's cartoons had a role in alerting the public to the deer's plight. The refuge was established in 1957. Hunting was stopped. It is hard to imagine any thrill in hunting these brown-eyed, gentle creatures.

Big Pine Key is a substantial, fairly well-populated key with dozens of surrounding islands on all sides. Those islands include Howe Key, Annette Key, Little Pine Key, No Name Key, the Torch Keys, and many others.

Big Pine Key lies just southwest across the bridge from Bahia Honda State Park. There are at least a dozen landings given on maps of the area.

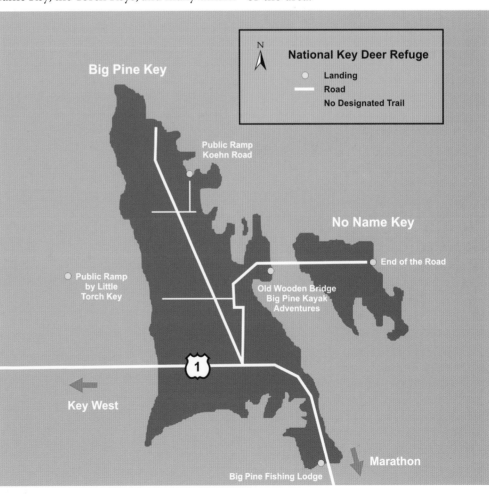

Above: Kayaking over sand flats.

ORANGE RIVER
(Lee County)

The Orange River is accessed from Manatee Park on SR-80, an east exit from I-75 in Ft. Myers. The county park rents kayaks. The nearby marina at various times has rented canoes and kayaks, but as of 2004, it is not offering either. Both locations are just a short drive east from the interstate.

The Orange River is a meandering and pleasant offshoot of the Caloosahatchee River. The river trails-off perhaps 7 miles (towards the community of Buckingham) and is twisty and shallow. How far one can go depends on water level.

Lee County's Manatee Park is built along a small canal from a power company that runs into the Orange River. In the winter months, spectacular congregations of manatees take haven there. Watching can be thrilling on cold days.

N

Orange River

○ Landing
— Road

The county park has a paddle which could be considered a short trail. The river itself has no designated trail.

PLACIDA HARBOR
(Charlotte County)

South of Lemon Bay and north of Gasparilla Sound lies Placida Harbor, a destination for at least two kayak guide services operating from Sarasota County. From US-41 in Port Charlotte, turn south on CR-776. Take CR-771, a left fork, and proceed to a landing between Placida and Gasparilla Island.

PRAIRIE CREEK
(Charlotte County)

Prairie Creek flows into Shell Creek above a dam. See the account for Shell Creek concerning the safety warning. Prairie Creek is a little-used stream, twisty and winding, and in very good natural condition, with only a few homes.

There are two ways to visit Prairie Creek. From a very good landing on CR-764 (Washington Loop Road), paddle downstream to the reservoir and then up Shell Creek some distance. It is possible to paddle upstream on Shell Creek to Prairie Creek from Hathaway Park.

From I-75 on the south bank of the Peace River, exit east on US-17. To reach Hathaway Park, make the soft right on the first of two CR-764 (Washington Loop) turns. The park will be on the north side of the road. For the "unofficial" landing, continue on US-17 to the second CR-764 turn and go east until you come to the bridge. The good, "unofficial" landing is on the north side of the road.

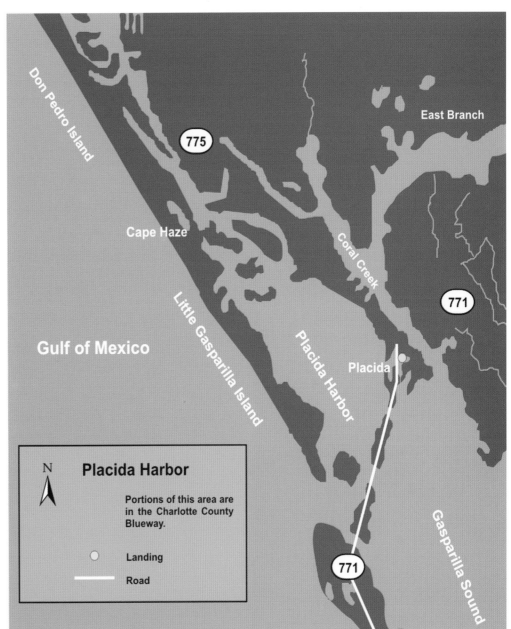

Placida Harbor

Portions of this area are in the Charlotte County Blueway.

○ Landing

— Road

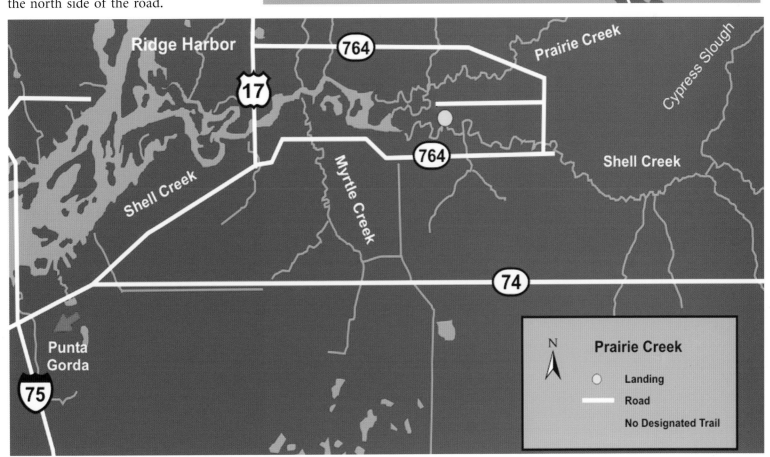

Prairie Creek

○ Landing

— Road

No Designated Trail

Above: Small red mangrove trees.

SHELL CREEK
(Charlotte County)

This remarkable creek is in excellent natural condition and not well-known except to locals. It is a wonderful paddle that can stretch as long as 20 miles, if the water is high, but much less if the water is low.

Interestingly, the creek has hickory trees along it despite being so far south. The banks are a mix of cypress swamp, floodplain, and high, sandy banks with flatwoods.

Prairie Creek runs into Shell Creek below the launch given and above the backwater from a dam. The character of the river is quite different above and below the dam. Above it is a slow-moving, narrow stream, quickly rising with rain, and just as rapidly falling afterwards. Below the dam, the river is mostly saltmarsh and tidal estuary.

There is one official launch above the dam. It is possible to paddle both east and west from there. There is an "unofficial" launch at SR-17 Bridge on the south side of the stream. Other landings include ramps at Tara Lane and Riverside Drive.

Below the dam is saltmarsh. Very quickly this area becomes Peace River on the map, but on the water, this is essentially a bay. A railroad trestle limits boaters, and manatees may be in this area all year long.

The dam creates a major backwater, and at times of very high water, the dam can be dangerous. At least two people have died - maybe more - going accidentally over the dam. The jet may shoot five feet or more beyond the dam with a drop said to be five feet, but looking more like ten. Below is rock. The backwater is not necessarily interesting paddling since it is broad, often windy, and sometimes choked with water hyacinths, so taking-out before the clog is an excellent idea.

The official launch is at Hathaway Park on Washington Loop (CR-764). Take the south exit by the Peace River and go west on US-17. CR-764 (Washington Loop Road) is a soft right, and the park is located about 5 miles farther.

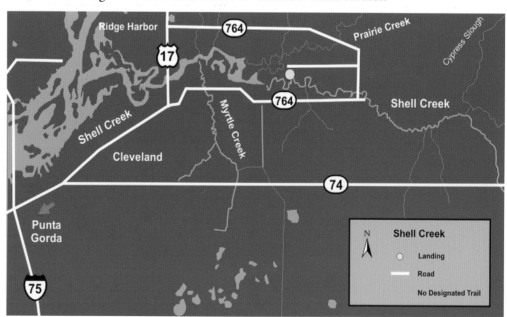

TEN THOUSAND ISLANDS
(Collier and Monroe counties)

South of Naples and above Collier-Seminole State Park, lies Rookery Bay Aquatic Preserve. Below Collier-Seminole lies the beginning of Cape Romano - Ten Thousand Island Aquatic Preserve. This enormous area of mangrove and estuary reaches far south and east. There are not really 10,000 islands, rather there are numerous small clusters of mangroves and vast mangrove forests.

This is a large wilderness, and a place where fisherman like to come with powerboats. This area is best explored in winter. Paddling here is for the self-reliant and confident, and good charts, as well as advice from local marinas and fishermen, are wise precautions.

There are various designated campsites within the wilderness. Perhaps the easiest put-ins from north to south are at: Marco Island to the west of Collier-Seminole State Park, Collier-Seminole State Park on US-41 south of Naples, and Chokoloskee at the south dead-end of SR-29.

TURNER RIVER
(Collier County)

This paddle is between Chokoloskee, an island at the extreme southern end of SR-29, and a roadside park along US-41 in Big Cypress National Preserve. The trip is 9 miles, however, many have pushed on farther in both directions.

Ranger-guided tours take place in the colder months. In part, this is because there are many more tourists in those months. However, the warmer months can bring sometimes intolerable biting flies, mosquitoes, and no-see-ums.

This is uniquely Floridian paddling, in portions dominated by tall cypress covered with bromeliads, sometimes in very large concentrations. In other portions, it is a mangrove paddle. Alligators are plentiful, and this is the land of black bears and Florida panthers.

From I-75 south of Naples, exit south on SR-29, cross US-41, and continue until reaching the island. The island launch is well-marked. The take-out is on US-41 at the Turner Canal where there is a small park. To reach it from SR-29, turn east on US-41. To check on ranger-guided tours, stop at the Visitor Center for Big Cypress National Preserve on US-41.

Wilderness Waterway
(See Everglades National Park)

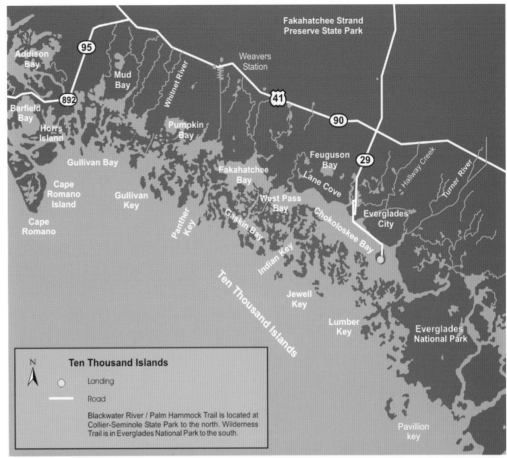

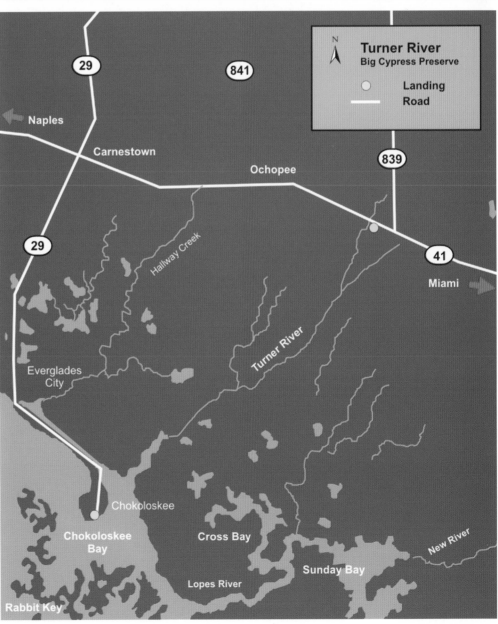

APPENDIX A

Paddling Services by Location. The range of services offered by these private companies varies greatly. Some rent canoes and/or kayaks. Some provide guided tours. Others provide livery. A few have campgrounds. Some offer guided trips. Some offer all these services. Fees vary considerably. Usually, outfitters are closed for one day a week, sometimes closed completely in the off season. An asterisk means the author and/or photographer used their services during the making of this book.

ALAFIA RIVER
Alafia Canoe Rentals*
4419 River Drive
Valrico FL 33594
813-689-8645

Canoe Country Outfitters, Inc.
6493 54th Avenue North
St. Petersburg FL 33709
727-545-4554
www.canoecountryfl.com

ALAPAHA RIVER
Canoe Outpost*
Spirit of the Suwannee Music Park
2461 95th Drive
Live Oak FL 32060
386-364-4991
www.suwanneeoutpost.com

ALEXANDER CREEK
Alexander Springs Concession*
49525 CR-445
Altoona FL 32702
352-669-3522

AMELIA RIVER
Kayak Amelia
13030 Heckscher Dr.
Jacksonville FL 32226
904-251-0016
www.kayakamelia.com

ANCLOTE KEY
Adventure Kayak Centers*
5446 Baylea Avenue
Port Richey FL 34668
727-848-8099
727-784-6357 (Palm Harbor)
www.ospreybay.com

ARBUCKLE CREEK
Kayaks, Etc.
2626 US-1
Vero Beach FL 32960
561-794-9900

AUCILLA RIVER
The Canoe Shop
1115 West Orange Avenue #B
Tallahassee FL 32310
850-576-5335
www.paddlenorthflorida.com

BISCAYNE BAY
Florida Bay Outfitters
104050 Overseas Highway
Key Largo FL 33037
305-451-3018
305-451-9340 (fax)
www.kayakfloridakeys.com
kayak@terranova.com

Kayak Influence*
1771 Sunset Harbor Drive
Miami Beach FL 33139
305-535-1227
305-674-9488 (fax)
www.sailmiami.com

BLACK CREEK
Outdoor Adventures
13110 Mandarin Road
Jacksonville FL 32223
904-393-9030 (phone and fax)
OutdoorFL@aol.com

Venture Up*
2216 South Mimosa
Middleburg FL 32068
904-291-5991

BLACKWATER RIVER
Action on Blackwater
6293 SR-4 West
PO Box 283
Baker FL 32531
850-537-2997
www.actiononblackwater.com

Adventures Unlimited*
Rt. 5 Box 283
Milton FL 32570
850-623-6197
850-626-3124 (fax)
www.adventuresunlimited.com

Andrew Jackson Canoe Rentals
4516 Water Street
PO Box 666
Bagdad FL 32530
850-623-4884

Blackwater Canoe Rental & Sales
10274 Pond Road
Milton FL 32583
850-623-0235

Bob's Canoe Rentals & Sales
7525 Munson Highway
Milton FL 32570
850-623-5457

BLUE SPRING
Blue Spring Enterprises
2100 West French Avenue
Orange City FL 32763
904-775-6888

BRADEN RIVER*
Jiggs Landing
6106 63d Street East
Bradenton FL 34281
941-748-4501

Kayak Treks*
3667 Bahia Vista Street
Sarasota FL 34232
941-365-3892
kayakgide1@aol.com
www.kayaktreks.com

Linger Lodge*
7205 Linger Lodge Road
Bradenton FL 34202
941-755-2757
941-758-0718 (fax)
www.lingerlodgeresort.com

BUCK KEY
Canoe Adventures, Inc.*
716 Rabbit Road
Sanibel FL 33957
239-472-3184

Captiva Kayak Company*
Wildside Adventures
PO Box 122
11401 Andy Rosse Lane
Captiva FL 33924
239-395-2925
www.captivakayak.com
captivakayak@att.net

Tween Waters
15951 Captiva Drive
Captiva FL 33924
239-472-5161
239-472-0249 (fax)
www.tween-waters.com

BULOW CREEK
Bulow Plantation Ruins
State Historic Site
PO Box 655
Bunnell FL 32110
904-517-2084

CALOOSAHATCHEE RIVER
Coastal Marine Mart/Manatee World
SR-80
North Ft Myers FL 32919
239-694-4042

CEDAR KEYS
Fishbonz
509-3d Street
Cedar Key FL
352-543-9922

CHASSAHOWITZKA RIVER
River Sports Kayak
5297 South Cherokee Way
Homosassa FL 34448
877-660-0929
www.flakayak.com

CHARLOTTE HARBOR
Grande Tours, Inc.
PO Box 281*
Placida FL 33946
941-697-8825
www./grandetours.com

CHIPOLA RIVER
Bear Paw Canoe Trails*
2100 Bear Paw Lane
Marianna FL 32446
850-482-4948
www.bearpawcanoe.com

Florida Caverns State Park
3345 Caverns Road
Marianna FL 32446
850-482-1228

Scott's Ferry General Store and Campgrounds*
Rt 1 Box 63 (SR-71)
Blountstown FL 32424
850-674-2900

CITRUS COUNTY PADDLING TRAIL
River Sports Kayak
5297 South Cherokee Way
Homosassa FL 34448
877-660-0929
www.flakayak.com

COCKROACH BAY AQUATIC PRESERVE
Canoe Outpost, Little Manatee*
18001 US-301 South
Wimauma FL 33598
813-634-2228
www.canoeoutpost.com

COLDWATER CREEK
Adventures Unlimited*
Route 6 Box 283
Milton FL 32570
850-623-6197
850-626-3124 (fax)
www.adventuresunlimited.com

CRYSTAL RIVER
Adventure Outpost
18238 US-441 NW
High Springs FL 32643
386-454-0611
Riverguide2000@yahoo.com
www.adventureoutpost.net

River Sports Kayak
5297 South Cherokee Way
Homosassa FL 34448
877-660-0929
www.flakayak.com

CYPRESS SPRINGS
Cypress Springs Canoe Trail
PO Box 726
Vernon FL 32462
850-535-2960
www.cypressspringsfla.com

DEEP CREEK (Central)
Nav-A-Gator Grill DeSoto Marina
9700 SW Riverview Circle
Arcadia FL 34269
239-627-3474
239-629-2287 (fax)
www.nav-a-gator.com

DELEON SPRINGS
Old Spanish Sugar Mill
PO Box 691
DeLeon Springs FL 32130
904-985-5644

"DING" DARLING NATIONAL WILDLIFE REFUGE
see also, Buck Key
see also, Tarpon Bay
see also, Sanibel

Canoe Adventures, Inc.*
716 Rabbit Road
Sanibel FL 33957
239-472-5218

DUNNS CREEK
Stegebone's Fish Camp
144 Norton Fish Camp Road
Satsuma FL 32189
904-467-2464
www.stegebones.com

ECONFINA CREEK
Econfina Creek Canoe Livery
5641-A Porter Pond Road
Youngstown FL 32466
850-722-9032
www.canoeeconfina.com

ECONLOCKHATCHEE RIVER
Hidden River Canoe Livery
15295 East Colonial Drive
Orlando FL 32826
407-568-5346

Kayaks, Etc.
2626 US-1
Vero Beach FL 32960
561-794-9900

Osprey Outfitters
132 South Dixie Avenue
Titusville FL 32796
407-267-3535
www.nbbd.com/osprey

ESCAMBIA RIVER
Jim's Fish Camp
3100 US-90
Pace FL 32571
850-994-7500

ESTERO RIVER
Estero River Canoe Outfitters
20991 South Tamiami Trail
Estero FL 33928
239-992-4050
www.all-florida.com/swestero.htm

EVERGLADES
Adventure Kayaking
3435 Aviation Boulevard
Vero Beach FL 32960
561-567-0522
www.paddleflorida.com

Everglades National Park Boat Tours
PO Box 119
Everglades City FL 34139
239-695-2591

Florida Bay Outfitters
PO Box 2513
Key Largo FL 33037
305-451-3018
305-451-9340 (fax)
www.kayakfloridakeys.com
kayak@terranova.net

Flamingo Lodge Marina & Outpost Resort
No. 1 Flamingo Lodge Highway
Flamingo FL 33034
239-695-3101

North American Canoe Tours
PO Box 5038
Everglades FL 34139
239-695-4666
www.evergladesadventures.com

Sweetwater Kayaks
13060 Gandy Boulevard
St. Petersburg FL 33702
727-570-4844
727-563-0553 (fax)
www.sweetwaterkayaks.com

FLORIDA BAY
Florida Bay Outfitters
104050 Overseas Highway
Key Largo FL 33037
305-451-3018
305-451-9340 (fax)
www.kayakfloridakeys.com
kayak@terranova.net

FLORIDA KEYS
Adventure Kayaking
3435 Aviation Boulevard
Vero Beach FL 32960
772-567-0522
www.paddleflorida.com

Big Pine Kayak Adventures, Inc.
PO Box 431311
Big Pine Key FL 33043
305-872-7474
www.keyskayaktours.com

Florida Bay Outfitters
104050 Overseas Highway
Key Largo FL 33037
305-451-3018
305-451-9340 (fax)
www.kayakfloridakeys.com
kayak@terranova.net

Marathon Kayak
at Sombrero Resort
19 Sombrero Boulevard
Marathon FL 33050
305-395-0355
www.marathonkayak.com

Mosquito Coast Island Outfitters
1107 Duval Street
Key West FL 33040
305-294-7178

FORT DESOTO PARK
Canoe Country Outfitters, Inc.
6493 54th Avenue North
St. Petersburg FL 33709
727-545-4554
www.canoecountryfl.com

Canoe Outpost*
18001 US-301 South
Wimauma FL 33598
727-864-1991
www.canoeoutpost.com

Sweetwater Kayaks
13060 Gandy Boulevard
St. Petersburg FL 33702
727-570-4844
727-563-0553 (fax)
www.sweetwaterkayaks.com

HALLS RIVER
Riversport Kayaks
2300 South Suncoast Boulevard
Homosassa FL 34448
352-621-4972
www.flakayak.com

HICKEY CREEK
Coastal Marine Mart/Manatee World
SR-80
North Ft. Myers FL 32919
239-694-4042

HILLSBOROUGH RIVER
Canoe Country Outfitters, Inc.
6943 54th Avenue North
St. Petersburg FL 33709
727-545-4554
www.canoecountryfl.com

Canoe Escape*
9335 East Fowler Avenue
Thonotosassa FL 33592
813-986-2067
www.canoeescape.com

Oak Haven River Retreat
12143 Riverhills Drive
Tampa FL 33617
813-988-4580
813-935-6912 (fax)
www.oakhavenriverretreat.com
oakhavenrr@aol.com

Sweetwater Kayaks
13060 Gandy Boulevard
St. Petersburg FL 33702
727-570-4844
727-563-0553 (fax)
www.sweetwaterkayaks.com

HOLMES CREEK
Cypress Spring Canoe Trail
PO Box 72
Vernon FL 32462
850-535-2969

HOMOSSASSA RIVER
River Sports Kayak
5297 South Cherokee Way
Homosassa FL 34448
877-660-0929
www.flakayak.com

Sweetwater Kayaks
13060 Gandy Boulevard
St. Petersburg FL 33702
727-570-4844
727-563-0553 (fax)
www.sweetwaterkayaks.com

ICHETUCKNEE RIVER
Adventure Outpost*
18238 US-441 NW
High Springs FL 32643
386-454-0611
Riverguide2000@yahoo.com
www.adventureoutpost.net

Ichetucknee Family Grocery and Campsites
Rt 1 Box 1576
O'Brien FL 32071
386-497-2150
386-497-3122 (fax)
www.itchetuckneecanoeandcabgins.com

River Run Campground
2739 US-27
Brandford FL 32008
386-935-6557

Sante Fe Canoe Outpost
PO Box 592
High Spring FL 32655
386-454-2050

Steamboat Canoe Outfitters
PO Box 28
Branford FL 32008
386-935-0512

Suwannee Expeditions
PO Box 60
Branford FL 32008
386-935-9299
www.canoeflorida.com

INDIAN RIVER LAGOON
Adventure Kayaking
7647 Aviation Boulevard
Vero Beach FL 32960
772-567-0522
www.paddleflorida.com

Jupiter Outdoor Center
18095 Coastal A1A
Jupiter FL 33477
561-747-9666
www.jupiteroutdoorcenter.com

JOHN PENNEKAMP CORAL REEF STATE PARK
Pennekamp State Park Concessions
MM102.5 Overseas Highway US-1
Key Largo FL 33037
305-451-1621
www.pennekamppark.com

JUNIPER CREEK
See Blackwater River for more listings

JUNIPER SPRINGS RUN
Juniper Springs Canoe
26701 East SR-40
Silver Springs FL 34488
352-625-2808

JUPITER INLET
Jupiter Outdoor Center
1000 North Highway A1A
Jupiter FL 33477
561-747-0063
www.jupiteroutdoorcenter.com

LEE COUNTY BLUEWAY
Estero River Canoe Outfitters
20991 South Tamiami Trail
Estero FL 33928
239-694-4050

Salty Sam's Marina
2500 Main Street
Ft. Myers Beach FL
239-463-7333

LITTLE MANATEE RIVER
Canoe Country Outfitters, Inc.
6493 54th Avenue North
St. Petersburg FL 33709
727-545-4554
www.canoecountryfl.com

Canoe Outpost*
18001 US 301 South
Wimauma FL 33598
813-634-2228
www.canoeoutpost.com

LOXAHATHCEE NATIONAL WILDLIFE REFUGE
Loxahatchee Canoeing
10216 Lee Road
Boynton Beach FL 33437
561-733-0192
www.CanoeTheEverglades.com

LOXAHATCHEE RIVER
Canoe Outfitters of Florida*
9060 West Indiantown Road
Jupiter FL 33478
561-746-7053
www.canoeoutfittersofflorida.com

Kayaks, Etc.
2626 US-1
Vero Beach FL 32960
561-794-9900

Jonathan Dickinson State Park River Tours
16450 SE Federal Highway
Hobe Sound FL 33455
561-746-1466
jdtours@aol.com

MANATEE RIVER
Ray's Canoe Hideaway & Kayak Center*
1289 Hagle Park Road
Bradenton FL 34212
941-747-3909
www.rayscanoehideaway.com

MATANZAS RIVER
Outdoor Adventures
1625 Emerson Street
Jacksonville FL 32207
904-393-9030
OutdoorFL@aol.com

MYAKKA RIVER
Canoe Country Outfitters, Inc.
6493 54th Avenue North
St. Petersburg FL 33709
727-545-4554
www.canoecountryfl.com

Economy Tackle/Dolphin Dive*
6018 South Tamiami Trail
Sarasota FL 34231
941-922-9671
www.floridakayak.com

Kayak Treks*
3667 Bahia Vista Street
Sarasota FL 34232
941-365-3892
kayakgide1@aol.com
www.kayaktreks.com

Snook Haven Restaurant & Fish Camp*
5000 East Venice Avenue
Venice FL 34292
941-485-7221
www.venice-.fla.com/snookhaven

Sweetwater Kayaks
13060 Gandy Boulevard
St. Petersburg FL 33702
727-570-4844
727-563-0553 (fax)
www.sweetwaterkayaks.com

OCHLOCKONEE
The Wilderness Way
3152 Shadeveille Road
Crawfordsville FL 32327
850-877-7200
www.thewildernessway.com

OCKLAWAHA RIVER
Adventure Outpost*
18238 US-441 NW
High Springs FL 32643
386-459-0611
Riverguide2000@yahoo.com
www.adventureoutpost.net

Oklawaha RV Park and Canoe Outpost*
15260 NE 152d Place
Ft. McCoy FL 32134
352-236-4606
http:members.aol.com/ocooutpost/

ORANGE RIVER
Coastal Marine Mart
SR-80
North Ft. Myers, FL 33917
329-693-1434
CaptDLT@aol.com

PEACE RIVER
Canoe Outpost
3020 NW CR-661
Arcadia FL 34266
863-494-7865
www.canoeoutpost.com

Canoe Safari
3020 NW CR-661
Arcadia FL 34266
941-494-7865
www.canoesafari.com

Nav-A-Gator Grill
Desoto Marina
9700 SW Riverview Circle
Arcadia FL 34266
941-625-4907
941-629-2287 (fax)
www.nav-a-gator.com

PERDIDO RIVER
Adventures Unlimited*
160 River Annex Road
Cantonment FL 32533
850-623-6197

PITHLACHASCOTEE RIVER
Adventure Kayak Centers*
5446 Baylea Avenue
Port Richey FL 34668
727-848-8099
727-784-6357 (Palm Harbor)

PLACIDA HARBOR
Economy Tackle/Dolphin Dive*
6018 South Tamiami Trail
Sarasota FL 32431
941-922-9671
www.floridakayak.com

Kayak Treks*
3667 Bahia Vista Street
Sarasota FL 32432
941-365-3892
kayakgide1@aol.com
www.kayaktreks.com

RAINBOW RIVER
Angler's Resort
12189 South Williams Street
Dunnellon FL 34432
352-489-2397

Dragonfly Watersports*
19158 SW 81st Place
Dunnellon FL 34432
352-465-2100
352-489-3046

Sweetwater Kayaks
13060 Gandy Boulevard
St. Petersburg FL 33702
727-570-4844
727-563-0553 (fax)
www.sweetwaterkayaks.com

SALT SPRINGS RUN
Salt Springs Run Marina*
25711 NE 134th Place
Salt Springs FL 32134
352-685-2255

SANIBEL
Canoe Adventures, Inc.*
(Mark Westall)
716 Rabbit Road
Sanibel FL 33957
329-472-5218

Tarpon Bay Explorers
900 Tarpon Bay Rd
Sanibel Island, FL 33957
239 472-8900
EcoErler@aol.com
www.tarponbayexplorers.com

SANTA FE RIVER
Adventure Outpost*
18238 US-441 NW
High Springs FL 32643
386-454-0611
Riverguide2000@yahoo.com
www.adventureoutpost.net

Ginnie Springs
7300 NE Ginnie Springs Road
High Springs FL 32643
386-454-2202

Ichetucknee Family Grocery and Campsites
Rt 1 Box 1576
O'Brien FL 32071
386-497-2150

Sante Fe Canoe Outpost
PO Box 592
High Springs FL 32644
386-454-2050
386-454-2510 (fax)
www.santaferiver.com

Steamboat Canoe Outfitters
PO Box 28
Branford FL 32008
386-935-0512

SEBASTIAN RIVER
Kayaks, Etc.
2628 US-1
Vero Beach FL 32960
727-754-9902

SILVER RIVER
Ocklawaha RV Park & Canoe Outpost*
15260 NE 152d Place
Ft. McCoy FL 32134
352-236-4606
www.members.aol/ocooutpost/

Sweetwater Kayaks
13060 Gandy Boulevard
St. Petersburg FL 33702
727-570-4844
727-563-0553 (fax)
www.sweetwaterkayaks.com

SOPCHOPPY RIVER
Dark Water Kayak Company
PO Box 207
Sopchoppy FL 32358
1-850-962-1000
1-850-962-1012 (fax)
www.levybay.com

Sopchoppy Outfitters
PO Box 99
Sopchoppy FL 32358
850-962-2220

The Wilderness Way
3152 Shadeveille Road
Crawfordsville FL 32327
850-877-7200
www.thewildernessway.com

SPRING GARDEN RUN
Old Spanish Sugar Mill
DeLeon Springs State Park
PO Box 692
DeLeon Springs FL 32130
904-985-5644

ST. GEORGE BAY

Journeys of St. George Island
240 East 3d Street
St. George Island FL 32398
850-927-3259
www.sgislandjourneys.com

ST. JOSEPH BAY

Broke-a-Toe Outdoor*
PO Box 486
Pt. St. Joe FL 32456
850-229-WAVE
www.stvincentislandecotours.com

Happy Ours*
Canoe & Kayak Rentals
775 Cape San Blas Road
Cape San Blas FL 32456
850-229-1991
www.happyourskayak.com

ST. LUCIE RIVER

Kayaks, Etc.
2626 US-1
Vero Beach FL 32960
561-794-9900

ST. MARKS RIVER

The Wilderness Way
3152 Shadeveille Road
Crawfordsville FL 32327
850-877-7200
www.thewildernessway.com

ST. MARYS RIVER

Canoe Country Outpost
2218 Lake Hampton Road
Hilliard FL 32046
904-845-7224
www.canoecountryoutpost.com

ST. VINCENT SOUND

Broke-a-Toe Outdoor*
PO Box 486
Pt. St. Joe FL
850-229-WAVE
www.stvincentislandecotours.com

Happy Ours*
775 Cape San Blas Road
Cape San Blas FL 32456
850-229-1991
www.HappyOurskayak.com

STEINHATCHEE RIVER

Steinhatchee Landing Resort
PO Box 789
Steinhatchee FL 32359
800-584-1709
www.steinhatcheelanding.com

Steinhatchee Outpost*
PO Box 48
Perry FL 32348
800-589-1541
www.steinhatcheeoutpost.com
steinhatchee@perry.gulfnet.com

SUWANNEE RIVER

Adventure Outpost*
18238 US-441 NW
High Springs FL 32643
386-454-0611
Riverguide2000@yahoo.com
www.adventureoutpost.net

American Canoe Adventures
10610 Bridge Street
White Springs FL 32096
386-397-1309
www.acal.com

KOA Campground
PO Box 460
Old Town FL 32680
904-542-7636

Otter Springs RV Resort
6570 SW 80th Avenue
Trenton FL 32693
352-463-0800

Okefenokee Adventures, Inc.
Route 2 Box 3325
Folkston GA 31537
912-496-7156
www.okefenokeeadventures.com

Outdoor Adventures
1625 Emerson Street
Jacksonville FL 32207
904-393-9030

Santa Fe Canoe Outpost
PO Box 592
High Springs FL 32655
386-454-2050

Suwannee Expeditions
Canoe and Kayak
PO Box 60
Branford FL 32008
386-935-9299
www.canoeflorida.com

Twin Rivers Outfitters
4862 NE Belleville Road
Pinetta FL 32350
850-929-4044
www.twinriversoutfitters.com

SWEETWATER CREEK

See Blackwater River

TAMPA BAY

Sweetwater Kayaks
13060 Gandy Boulevard
St. Petersburg FL 33702
727-570-4844
727-563-0553 (fax)
www.sweetwaterkayaks.com

TARPON BAY

Canoe Adventures, Inc.*
(Mark Westall)
716 Rabbit Road
Sanibel FL 33957
329-472-5218

Tarpon Bay Explorers
900 Tarpon Bay Rd
Sanibel Island, FL 33957
239 472-8900
EcoErler@aol.com
www.tarponbayexplorers.com

TERRA CEIA BAY

Canoe Outpost, Little Manatee*
18001 US-301 South
Wimauma FL 33598
813-634-2228

Kayak Trek*
3667 Bahia Vista Street
Sarasota FL 34232
941-365-3892
kayakgide1@aol.com

Sweetwater Kayaks
13060 Gandy Boulevard
St. Petersburg FL 33702
727-570-4844
727-563-0553 (fax)
www.sweetwaterkayaks.com

WACCASASSA RIVER

Adventure Outpost
18238 US-441 NW
High Springs FL 32643
386-454-0611
Riverguide2000@yahoo.com
www.adventureoutpost.net

WACISSA RIVER

The Canoe Shop
1115 West Orange Avenue #B
Tallahassee FL 32310
850-576-5335
www.paddlenorthflorida.com

The Wilderness Way
3152 Shadeveille Road
Crawfordsville FL 32327
850-877-7200
www.thewildernessway.com

WAKULLA RIVER

Riverside Cafe and Recreational Rentals*
69 Riverside Drive
St. Marks FL 32327
850-925-5668

TNT Hideaway*
6527 Coastal Highway
Crawfordville FL 32327
850-925-6412

The Wilderness Way
3152 Shadeveille Road
Crawfordsville FL 32327
850-877-7200
www.thewildernessway.com

WEEDON ISLAND

Canoe Country Outfitters, Inc.
6493 54th Avenue North
St. Petersburg FL 33709
727-545-4554
www.canoecountryoutfitters.com

Sweetwater Kayaks

13060 Gandy Boulevard
St. Petersburg FL 33702
727-570-4844
727-563-0553 (fax)
www.sweetwaterkayaks.com

WEKIVA RIVER

Blue Springs Enterprises
2100 West French Avenue
Orange City FL 32763
904-775-6888

Wekiwa Marina*
1000 Miami Springs Road
Longwood FL 32779
407-862-1500

WITHLACOOCHEE RIVER (North)

Canoe Outpost*
Spirit of the Suwannee Music Park
2461 95th Drive
Live Oak FL 32060
386-364-4991
outpost1@lani.net
www.suwanneeoutpost.com

WITHLACOOCHEE RIVER (South)

Adventure Outpost*
18238 US-441 NW
High Springs FL 32643
386-454-0611
Riverguide2000@yahoo.com
www.adventureoutpost.com

Angler's Resort
12189 South Williams Street
Dunnellon FL 34432
352-489-2397

Canoe Country Outfitters, Inc.
6493 54th Avenue North
St. Petersburg FL 33709
727-545-4554
www.canoecountryfl.com

Dragonfly Watersports*
19158 SW 81st Place
Dunnellon FL 34432
352-465-2100
352-489-3046

Nobleton Canoe Rental
PO Box 265
Nobleton FL 34661
352-796-7176
www.nobletoncanoes.com

Turner's Camp*
3033 Hooty Point
Inverness FL 32650
352-726-0085

Withlacoochee RV
Park & Canoe Rental
PO Box 114
Lacoochee FL 33537
352-583-4778

APPENDIX B

Public Lands, Land Management Agencies, Private Organizations. The following public lands mentioned in the text may have areas to paddle, may offer camping, and in some cases rent canoes and kayaks. They have different hours of operation and varying entrance and use fees. In all cases, it is best to plan a visit in advance and coordinate with the public land to be visited.

Alafia River State Park
Managed by Hillsborough River State Park
www.floridastateparks.org

Amelia Island State Park
Talbot Islands GeoPark
12157 Heckscher Drive
Jacksonville FL 32226
904-251-2320
www.floridastateparks.org

Anastasia State Park
1340A A1A South
St. Augustine FL 32084
904-461-2033
904-461-2006 (fax)
www.floridastateparks.org

Anclote Key State Park
Gulf Islands GeoPark
#1 Causeway Boulevard
Dunedin FL 34698
727-893-2627
www.floridastateparks.org

Apalachicola National Forest
Apalachicola Ranger District
PO Box 579
Bristol FL 32321
850-643-2282
850-643-5246 (fax)
www.fs.fed.us

Apalachicola National Forest
Wakulla Ranger District
1773 Crawfordville Highway
Crawfordville FL 32327
850-926-3561
850-926-1904 (fax)
www.fs.fed.us

Avon Park Bombing Range
Natural Resource Manager
56-CSS-DEN
236 South Boulevard
Avon Park FL 33825
863-452-4254
863-452-4161 (fax)

Bahia Honda State Park
36850 Overseas Highway
Big Pine Key FL 33043
305-872-3897
305-292-6857 (fax)
www.floridastateparks.org

Big Cypress National Preserve
HCR-61
Ochopee FL 34141
239-695-2000
239-695-3493 (fax)

Big Lagoon State Park
12301 Gulf Beach Highway
Pensacola FL 32507
850-492-1595
www.floridastateparks.org

Big Shoals State Park
7620 133d Road
Live Oak FL 32322
904-208-1460
904-208-1465 (fax)
www.floridastateparks.org

Bill Baggs Cape Florida State Park
1200 South Crandon Boulevard
Key Biscayne FL 33149
305-361-5811
www.floridastateparks.org

Biscayne National Park
PO Box 1369
Homestead FL 33090
305-230-7275
305-230-1190 (fax)
www.nps.gov

Blackwater River State Forest
11650 Munson Highway
Milton FL 32570
850-957-6140
850-957-6143 (fax)
www.fl-dof.com/state_forests

Blackwater River State Park
7720 Deaton Bridge Road
Holt FL 32564
850-983-5363
www.floridastateparks.org

Blue Springs State Park
2100 West French Avenue
Orange City FL 32763
904-775-3663
904-775-7794 (fax)
www.floridastateparks.org

Bulow Plantation Historic State Park
PO Box 665
Bunnell FL 32110
904-517-2084
www.floridastateparks.org

Caledesi State Park
Gulf Islands GeoPark
#1 Causeway Boulevard
Dunedin FL 34698
727-469-5942
727-469-5703 (fax)
www.floridastateparks.org

Caloosahatchee Regional Park
239-693-2690
See Lee County Parks
www.floridastateparks.org

Canaveral National Seashore
308 Julia Street
Titusville FL 32796
407-267-1110
407-264-2906 (fax)
www.nps.gov

Cayo Costa State Park
PO Box 1150
Boca Grande FL 33921
239-964-0375
www.floridastateparks.org

Cedar Keys National Wildlife Refuge
16450 NW 31st Place
Chiefland FL 32626
352-493-0238
352-493-1935 (fax)
www.fws.gov/refuges

Charlotte County
Parks and Recreation
2300 El Jobean Road
Port Charlotte FL 33948
941-625-7529
941-235-2196 (fax)
www.charlottecountyfl.com

Chassahowitzka National Wildlife Refuge
Crystal River National Wildlife Refuge
1502 Kings Bay Drive
Crystal River FL 34429
352-563-2088
352-795-7961 (fax)
www.fws.gov/refuges

Collier-Seminole State Park
20200 Tamiami Trail East
Naples FL 34114
239-394-3397
239-394-5113 (fax)
www.floridastateparks.org

Curry Hammock State Park
PO Box 776
Long Key FL 33001
305-664-4815
www.floridastateparks.org

Dead Lakes State Park
510 Gary Rowell Road
Wewahitchka FL 32465
850-639-2702
850-639-3806 (fax)
www.floridastateparks.org

DeLeon Springs State Park
PO Box 1338
DeLeon Springs FL 32130
904-985-4212
www.floridastateparks.org

Department of Environmental Protection
Division of Parks and Recreation
3900 Commonwealth Boulevard
Tallahassee FL 32399
850-488-9872
850-922-4925 (fax)
http://www.dep.state.fl.us/parks

"Ding" Darling National Wildlife Refuge
1 Wildlife Drive
Sanibel FL 33957
239-472-1100
239-472-4061 (fax)
www.fws.gov/refuges

Division of Forestry
Florida Department of Agriculture
3125 Conner Boulevard
Tallahassee FL 32399
850-488-8180
850-921-8305 (fax)
www.fl-dof.com

Econfina River State Park
Tallahassee/St. Marks GeoPark
1022 DeSoto Park Drive
Tallahassee FL 32301
850-922-6007
850-488-0366 (fax)
www.floridastateparks.org

Eglin Air Force Base
Natural Resources
Jackson Guard
107 SR-85 North
Niceville FL 32578
850-882-4164

Egmont Key State Park
Gulf Islands GeoPark
#1 Causeway Boulevard
Dunedin FL 34698
727-893-2627
www.floridastateparks.org

Everglades National Park
40001 SR-9336
Homestead FL 33034
305-242-7700
305-242-7711 (fax)
www.nps.gov

Fanning Springs State Park
Suwannee Basin GeoPark
11650 NW 115th Street
Chiefland FL 32626
352-463-3420
352-493-6089 (fax)
www.floridastateparks.org

Faver-Dykes State Park
1000 Faver-Dykes Road
St. Augustine FL 32086
904-794-0997
www.floridastateparks.org

Florida Caverns State Park
3345 Cavern Road
Marianna FL 32446
850-482-1128
850-482-9114 (fax)
www.floridastateparks.org

Florida Fish and Wildlife Conservation Commission
620 South Meridian Street
Farris Bryant Building
Tallahassee FL 32390-1600
www.state.fl.us/fwc

Florida Keys National Wildlife Refuges
PO Box 43050
Big Pine Key FL 33043
305-872-0774
www.fws.gov/refuges

Ft. Clinch State Park
2601 Atlantic Avenue
Fernandina Beach FL 32034
904-227-7274
904-277-7225 (fax)
www.floridastateparks.org

Ft. Cooper State Park
3100 South Old Floral City Road
Inverness FL 32650
352-726-0315
www.floridastateparks.org

Gasparilla Island State Park
PO Box 1150
Boca Grande FL 32921
941-964-0375
941-964-1154 (fax)
www.floridastateparks.org

Gold Head Branch State Park
6239 SR-21
Keystone Heights FL 32656
352-473-4701
352-473-0827 (fax)
www.floridastateparks.org

Guana River State Park
2690 S Ponte Vedra Boulevard
Ponte Vedra Beach FL 32082
904-825-5071
www.floridastateparks.org

Gulf Islands National Seashore
1801 Gulf Breeze Parkway
Gulf Breeze FL 32561
850-934-2600
850-932-8654 (fax)

Hillsborough River State Park
15402 US 301 North
Thonotosassa FL 33592
813-987-6771
813-987-6773 (fax)
www.floridastateparks.org

Honeymoon Island State Park
Gulf Coast GeoPark
#1 Causeway Boulevard
Dunedin FL 34698
www.floridastateparks.org

Hontoon Island State Park
2309 River Ridge Road
Deland FL 32720
904-736-5309
www.floridastateparks.org

Ichetucknee Springs State Park
SR-2 Box 108
Ft. White FL 32038
904-497-2511
904-497-3095 (fax)
www.floridastateparks.org

Indian Key Historic State Park
PO Box 1052
Islamorada FL 33036
305-664-2540
www.floridastateparks.org

Jennings State Forest
1337 Long Horn Road
Middleburg FL 32068
904-291-5530
904-291-5537 (fax)
www.fl-dof.com/state_forests

John Pennekamp Coral Reef State Park
PO Box 487
Key Largo FL 33037
305-451-1202
305-451-1410 (fax)
www.floridastateparks.org

Jonathan Dickinson State Park
16540 Southeast Federal Highway
Hobe Sound FL 33455
561-542-2771
www.floridastateparks.org

Kissimmee Prairie State Preserve
33104 NW 192 Avenue
Okeechobee FL 34972
863-462-5360
863-462-5276 (fax)

Koreshan State Historic Site
PO Box 7
US-41 & Corkscrew Road
Estero FL 33928
239-992-4050

Lake Kissimmee State Park
14248 Camp Mack Road
Lake Wales FL 33853
863-696-1112
863-696-2656 (fax)
www.floridastateparks.org

Lake Manatee State Park
20007 SR-64
Bradenton FL 34202
941-741-3028
www.floridastateparks.org

Lake Talquin State Forest
865 Geddie Road
Tallahassee FL 32304
850-635-7801
850-922-2107 (fax)
www.fl-dof.com/state_forests

Lake Woodruff National Wildlife Refuge
PO Box 488
DeLeon Springs FL 32038
904-985-4673
www.fws.gov/refuges

Lee County Parks and Recreation
3410 Palm Beach
Ft. Myers FL 32916
239-338-3300
www.lee-county.com/parks&rec

Lignumvitae Key Botanical State Park
PO Box 1052
Islamorada FL 33036
305-664-2540
www.floridastateparks.org

Little-Big Econ State Forest
1350 Snowhill Road
Geneva FL 32732
407-971-3503
407-971-3504 (fax)
www.fl-dof.com/state_forests

Little Manatee River State Park
215 Lightfoot Road
Wimauma FL 33598
813-671-5005
813-671-5009 (fax)
www.floridastateparks.org

Long Key State Park
PO Box 776
Long Key FL 33001
305-664-4815
www.floridastateparks.org

Lovers Key State Park
8700 Estero Boulevard
Fort Myers Beach FL 33931
239-463-4588
239-463-8851 (fax)
www.floridastateparks.org

Lower Suwannee National Wildlife Refuge
16450 NW 31st Place
Chiefland FL 32626
352-493-0238
352-493-1935 (fax)
www.fws.gov/refuges

Loxahatchee National Wildlife Refuge
10216 Lee Road
Boynton Beach FL 33437
561-734-8303
561-369-7190 (fax)
www.fws.gov/refuges

Manatee County Blueways
Ecosystems Administrator
Manatee County
112 Manatee Avenue West
PO Box 1000
Bradenton FL 34206
941-745-3727
941-745-3790 (fax)
www.co.manatee.fl.us/service/
planning/planning.blue.html

Manatee Park
See Lee County Parks
239-694-4042

Manatee Springs State Park
11650 NW 115th Street
Chiefland FL 32626
352-493-6072
352-493-6089 (fax)
www.floridastateparks.org

Merritt Island National Wildlife Refuge
PO Box 6504
Titusville FL 32782
407-861-0662
407-861-1276 (fax)
www.fws.gov/refuges

Monroe County
2798 Overseas Highway Suite 410
Marathon FL 33050

Myakka River State Park
13207 SR-72
Sarasota FL 32421
941-361-6511
941-361-6501 (fax)
www.floridastateparks.org

Northwest Florida Water Management District
Rt 1 Box 3100
Havanna FL 32333
850-539-5999
850-539-4380 (fax)
www.nwfwmd.state.fl.us

Ocala National Forest
Lake George Ranger District
17147 East SR-40
Silver Springs FL 34488
352-625-2520
352-625-7556 (fax)
www.fs.fed.us

Ocala National Forest
Seminole Ranger District
40929 SR-19
Umatilla FL 32784
352-669-3153
352-669-2385 (fax)
www.fs.fed.us

Ochlockonee River State Park
PO Box 5
Sopchoppy FL 32358
850-962-2771
www.floridastateparks.org

Office of Greenways and Trails
Florida Department of Environmental Protection
3900 Commonwealth Boulevard,
MS-795
Tallahassee FL 32399-3000
877-822-5208
850-414-0177 (fax)

Okefenokee National Wildlife Refuge
Route 2 Box 388
Folkston GA 31537
912-496-3331
www.fws.gov/refuges

Oleta River State Park
3400 NE 163d Street
North Miami Beach FL 37160
305-919-1846
www.floridastateparks.org

O'Leno State Park
Rt 2 Box 307
High Springs FL 32643
904-454-1853
904-454-2565 (fax)
www.floridastateparks.org

Oscar Scherer State Park
1843 South Tamiami Trail
Osprey FL 34229
941-483-5956
941-480-3007 (fax)
www.floridastateparks.org

Osceola National Forest
PO Box 70
Olustee FL 32072
904-752-2577
904-752-7437 (fax)
www.fs.fed.us

Perdido Key State Park
(see Big Lagoon State Park)
www.floridastateparks.org

Rainbow Springs State Park
19158 SW 81st Place Road
Dunnellon FL 34432
352-489-8503
352-465-7855 (fax)
www.floridastateparks.org

Rock Springs Run State Reserve
1800 Wekiva Circle
Apopka FL 32712
407-884-2008

Rocky Bayou State Park
4281 Highway 20
Niceville FL 32578
850-833-9144
www.floridastateparks.org

Sarasota Bay National Estuary
Program
5333 North Tamiami Trail
Suite 104
Sarasota FL 34234
941-359-5841
sbnep@gte.net

Sebastian Inlet State Park
9700 South A1A
Melbourne Beach FL 32951
407-725-6828
www.floridastateparks.org

Silver River State Park
1425 NE 58th Avenue (SR-35)
Ocala FL 34470
352-236-1827
www.floridastateparks.org

South Florida Water Management
District
PO Box 24680
West Palm Beach FL 33416
561-686-8800
www.sfwmd.state.fl.us

Southwest Florida Water
Management District
2379 Broad Street
Brooksville FL 34609
352-796-7211
www.swfwmd.state.fl.us

Spirit of the Suwannee Music Park
3076 95th Drive
Live Oak FL 32060
904-364-1683
www.musicliveshere.com

St. George Island State Park
1900 East Gulf Beach Avenue
St. George Island FL 32338
850-927-2111
www.floridastateparks.org

St. Johns River Water Management
District
PO Box 1429
Palatka FL 32178
386-329-4500
http://sjr.state.fl.us

St. Joseph Bay Aquatic Preserve
350 Carroll Street
Eastpoint FL 32328
850-670-4783

St. Joseph Peninsula State Park
8899 Cape San Blas Road
Port St. Joe FL 32456
850-227-1327
www.floridastateparks.org

St. Marks National Wildlife Refuge
Box 68
St. Marks FL 32355
850-925-6121
850-925-6930 (fax)
www.fws.gov/refuges

St. Martins Marsh Aquatic Preserve
3266 North Sailboat Avenue
Crystal River FL 34428
352-563-0450

St. Marys River Management
Committee
904-488-7904

St. Vincents National Wildlife Refuge
PO Box 447
Apalachicola FL 32329
850-663-8808
850-653-9893 (fax)
www.fws.gov/refuges

Suwannee River State Park
Rt 8 Box 297
Live Oak FL 32060
904-362-2746
904-364-1614 (fax)
www.floridastateparks.org

Suwannee River Water Management
District
9225 CR-49
Live Oak FL 32060
904-362-1001
www.srwmd.state.fl.us

Tates Hell State Forest
1621 US-98 East
Carabelle FL 32174
850-697-3734
850-697-2892 (fax)
www.fl-dof.com/state_forests

Tomoka State Park
2099 North Beach Street
Ormond Beach FL 32174
904-676-4050
904-676-4060 (fax)
www.floridastateparks.org

Tosohatchee State Reserve
3365 Taylor Creek Road
Christmas FL 32708
407-568-5893
407-568-1704 (fax)

Torreya State Park
HC2 Box 70
Bristol FL 32321
850-643-2674
850-643-2987 (fax)
www.floridastateparks.org

Twin Rivers State Forest
7260 133d Street
Live Oak FL 32060
904-208-1460
904-208-1465 (fax)
www.fl-dof.com/state_forests

Waccasassa Bay State Preserve
PO Box 187
Cedar Key FL 32625
352-543-5567

Wakulla Springs State Park
550 Wakulla Park Drive
Wakulla Springs FL 32327
850-224-5950
850-561-7251 (fax)
www.floridastateparks.org

Wekiwa Springs State Park
1800 Wekiva Circle
Apopka FL 32712
407-884-2008
www.floridastateparks.org

Withlacoochee State Forest
15019 Broad Street
Brooksville FL 34601
352-754-6896
352-844-2356 (fax)
www.fl-dof.com/state_forests

APPENDIX C

Clubs and Organizations

American Littoral Society
Southeast Region
4154 Keats Drive
Sarasota FL 34241
www.sealitsoc.org

Apalachee Canoe and Kayak Club
PO Box 4027
Tallahassee FL 32315
www.clubkayak.com/ackw/

Florida Competition Paddling
Association
1725 George Ave NE
St. Petersburg FL 33703
www.fcpacanoe.org

Florida Paddling Trail Association
PO Box 540444
Lake Worth FL 33457
www.floridapaddlingtrailassociation.
com

Florida Professional Paddlesports
Association
PO Box 1764
Arcadia FL 34265
www.paddleflausa.com

Florida Sea Kayaking Association
626 - 45th Avenue South
St. Petersburg FL 33705
813-864-2651
www.clubkayak.com/fska/

Friends of the Sebastian River
PO Box 284
Roseland FL 32957

Mugwump Canoe Club
9025 Sunset Drive
Miami FL 33173

Palm Beach Pack & Paddle Club
PO Box 16041
West Palm Beach FL 33416
561-683-2851
www.kayakfloridakeys.com/PP/
ppclub.htm

Seminole Canoe & Kayaking
Association
4619 Ortega Farms Circle
Jacksonville FL 32210
904-287-2830

Tampa Bay Sea Kayakers
PO Box 280266
Tampa FL 33682
www.clubkayak.com/tbsk

West Florida Canoe Club
PO Box 17203
Pensacola FL 32522
850-587-2211
www.clubkayak.com/wfckc/